THE PEOPLE'S PORN

THE PEOPLE'S PORN

A History of Handmade Pornography in America

LISA Z. SIGEL

REAKTION BOOKS

Published by Reaktion Books Ltd
Unit 32, Waterside
44–48 Wharf Road
London N1 7UX, UK
www.reaktionbooks.co.uk

First published 2020
Copyright © Lisa Z. Sigel 2020

Printed and bound in India by Replika Press Pvt. Ltd

A catalogue record for this book is available from the British Library

ISBN 978 1 78914 226 6

Contents

Introduction:
Alternative Sources for
American Sexual History

U p and down the Eastern Seaboard, local historical societies
and museums house collections of scrimshaw alongside figure-
heads and silver trophy cups as relics of the region's maritime
history. Scrimshaw refers to the folk art in which sailors and whalers
created art out of the bones, teeth, or tusks of sea mammals. Whalers
had both sea ivory and long periods of idleness to document their lives
and preoccupations. They hand-carved, etched, inked, and polished their
ideas of the world onto bone. Old, rare, and beautiful, scrimshaw speaks
of long voyages when sails connected the world's oceans and whaling
provided oil for lamps.

For the scholar and philosopher Leon Rosenstein, "To live among the
handmade is to live among the human."[1] Rosenstein built upon his background as an antiquarian to develop a good working definition of antiques
in his much-acclaimed *Antiques: The History of an Idea* (1995). Meditating
on a bejeweled pendant from the Renaissance period, Rosenstein suggested
that such a definition needs to consider criteria beyond the age of an object.
(Dealers debate whether an object becomes antique at fifty or one hundred
years old.) Rosenstein argued that, more than age alone, antiques are also
rare and beautiful handcrafted objects with provenance and materiality.
They represent the consciousness of their makers and allow us to generate
an idea of a past world. This definition of antiques provides a foundation
for considering an array of artifacts, starting with scrimshaw.

Out of its thousands of examples of scrimshaw, the Mystic Seaport Museum in Connecticut has a few well-authenticated examples of nineteenth-century erotic scrimshaw. One particular example of a scrimshawed tooth seems to embody the essence of whaling culture: on one side, the artist has etched and inked a whaling ship surrounded by leaves, cannon, anchors, and flags in a geometric decorative pattern. The balance and symmetry of the layout, with a circle enclosing the ship—which itself is further sectioned by masts, rigging, and sails—attest to the artist's skills (illus. 1).[2] The year 1879 has been carved onto the tooth, dating the piece.

On the reverse side, the artist has created the image of a nude woman sitting on the head of a mythical sea monster while holding an anchor aloft (illus. 2). The delicate shading of the woman's body shows attention to light and shadow, while her figure demonstrates the artist's sense of proportion. The imagery reveals how a mythical sea monster scene could be rendered erotic by a skilled amateur. Artifacts like this allow us to envision how nineteenth-century whalers saw the sea, women, and the monsters that held them aloft.

While the erotic scrimshaw tooth would be considered an antique for its age alone, it also fits with Rosenstein's other criteria. It is housed at one of the most important museums of maritime culture, which provides an authentication and provenance that few artifacts of its kind can match. It is a rare and beautiful handmade object that lets us envision maritime culture as it existed in the Age of Sail. The carvings done on sea ivory have a materiality and presence that cannot be replicated. (New carvings on old ivory are not considered scrimshaw, as recent controversies have shown.[3]) The invocation of sea monsters, sailing ships, and a beautiful young woman with the wind in her hair and water at her feet speaks to the consciousness of the article's maker. By these criteria, erotic scrimshaw items certainly can be antique, and thus Rosenstein's definition can apply productively to erotic artifacts.

It might be easy to see erotic scrimshaw work as valuable antiques worthy of study and consideration, but let us consider another object (illus. 3).[4] Rather than being carved on sea ivory, this small object has

1 Scrimshaw tooth, 1879, item 2007.7 (front), Mystic Seaport Museum, Mystic, Connecticut.

2 Scrimshaw tooth, 1879, item 2007.7 (back), Mystic Seaport Museum.

been cut from a bar of Colgate soap and still carries the "Colgate Floating" logo on the bottom. It is carved into the form of a horse and a woman engaged in copulation. The woman lies on her back with her legs flaring out to the side, supporting herself with bent arms and legs as a rearing horse mounts her. The horse's hooves come perilously close to her face and he has to kneel to be able to enter her. Clearly the artist had not studied horse copulation (let alone human–horse copulation) but was trying to envision what it might look like, and, just as clearly, the artist's imagination had ventured into dangerous territory. The soap figurine came from an American prison in the 1960s and had been sent to the Kinsey Institute, formerly the Institute for Sex Research (ISR) in Indiana, shortly after the publication of Alfred Kinsey's famous volumes on male and female sexuality. Thus it has provenance and authentication. The condition of the more than fifty-year-old soap sculpture is fragile, and parts of it are broken. As an object that shows its age, materiality, and the consciousness of its creator, this figurine displays the qualities that Rosenstein attributes to antiques, though no one would see it as in the same league as a Renaissance pendant or a piece of erotic scrimshaw. Nonetheless, it displays the same rarity and materiality that renders those objects invaluable. And, like other handmade objects, it represents the consciousness of its maker and his milieu.

Whereas Rosenstein took a bejeweled Renaissance pendant as his example, and his ideas apply equally to nineteenth-century scrimshaw, this book takes a tour of all sorts of handmade and homemade American pornographic objects, not just beautiful folk objects housed in renowned museums. This book historicizes erotic scrimshaw, soap carvings, and other erotic articles because these handmade objects tell us something important about the past. Whether crafted by masters or hacks, whether made in male-dominated institutions or more integrated environments, these objects tell us about individuals' desires. They tell us about how people understood sexuality through what they could visualize. They tell us about the materials that people found around them and how people could refashion them. Ultimately, their continued material existence also reveals something about the cultural value of the objects that common people made.

The People's Porn argues that, even more than other types of antique objects, handmade and homemade pornog- raphy—whether scrimshaw or soap carving—allows us

3 Zoophilia with horse, Colgate Floating, Realia, [196?], ISR 731, Kinsey Institute, Bloomington, Indiana.

to understand the past from which it came. I make this claim knowing that it sounds hyperbolic and grandiose. Yet handmade and homemade pornographic objects reveal a history for periods when sexual artifacts were pilloried, ransacked, incinerated, and destroyed. In many cases handmade and homemade pornographic materials might be the single artifacts left by their makers. Brought together, they tell a story about American sexual history that would otherwise go untold. These objects are also deeply human, much like Rosenstein's antiques. But where Rosenstein sees artistry and beauty as a reflection of the object's humanity, handmade and homemade pornography allows us to see a humanity that is protean. Handmade pornography plays with beauty and ugliness because people find sexual meaning in both. As much as the world might like to limit sexuality to the realms of the uplifting and transcendent, this pornography reminds us that we are imperfect in both body and mind, subject to pain as well as pleasure, willing to laugh at ourselves and each other, and moved equally by the ridiculous, violent, and sublime. The consideration of homemade and handmade pornography matters because we should be considering the history of sexuality in all of its variations if we ever want to understand sexuality as it existed rather than as we might like it to have been. We need therefore to tackle the human in all its iterations and consider both ordinary and extreme sexual pleasures.

To explore this story, this book will confront categories into which sexual objects have been sorted. To some readers, just the term "pornography" implies a certain ugliness. Such readers might suggest that scrimshaw or even soap sculptures should be categorized as something other than pornography in order to recognize the individuality of the artists who made such objects. Those objections recognize that to label something as pornographic has real consequences. This has long been the case. Walter Kendrick was first to note that the term "pornography" does not name a thing in and of itself but instead implies an argument.[5] Thomas Waugh extended Kendrick's claims and noted that the distinctions drawn between erotica and pornography are almost always "based in class or gender bias, or else in the historical myopia of homophobia, cultural snobbery, political instrumentality, or personality (my erotica is your pornography)."[6] Thus the labeling of objects as either pornographic or erotic remains arbitrary. Historians have skirted this issue by recognizing the contingent nature of such definitions. Instead of seeking a universal definition, historians recognize that objects like an erotic novel or figurine might have been understood as pornographic in the past, even if we do not look at them that way now. *The People's Porn* tries to capture a sense of that contingency. It shows how some objects became art while others did not and explores how shifting definitions leave behind an impoverished vision of what pornography can mean.

If one could write a comprehensive history of American pornography, handmade and homemade pornography would form but a small and idiosyncratic subset of the larger body of materials. Commercial pornography would no doubt swamp handmade artifacts in number and would provide a narrative about growing commercialization, while homemade objects would salt the main fare with interesting counterexamples and intersections. However, the complete story of pornography in America cannot be told, because more than a century's worth of seizures of sexual artifacts and prosecutions of their purveyors prevent us from fully knowing the past. Few examples of pornography remain from the nineteenth century, thanks in no small part to the zealousness of anti-porn crusaders. Anthony Comstock and other anti-vice activists destroyed books, illustrations, photographs, pamphlets, rubber-goods, typefaces, printing plates, even business records.[7] Judges refused to allow any obscenities, including the titles of obscene works, to be read into the record. The policy of obliterating sources continued well into the twentieth century. During the 1990s, the FBI incinerated its extensive collection of seized obscene objects, including films, magazines, pictures, and more.[8] As print historian Elizabeth Haven Hawley states, "Writing a cohesive narrative with so much of the historical record unrecorded or destroyed seem[s] an impossible task."[9]

The history of American pornography in particular has been elided because of the deficit of materials. Scholars of other national traditions have material records—including catalogs, bibliographies, criminal court records, and archives of record—that allow them to reconstruct the trade in commercial pornography; scholars working on the German, British, or French historical traditions can examine the relationship between changes in obscenity codes and pornographic production. They can consider the relationship between the state and pornography and can detail the ways that pornography evolved over time. They can explore the ways that pornography changed in relation to an evolving context and the ways pornography expanded with a growing consumer marketplace. While scholars of American history know that American pornography existed and responded to some of the same structural shifts, the documentary record has been devastated. As Helen Lefkowitz Horowitz explains, the destruction of erotic materials has contributed to a "deficit or silence that has distorted our understanding of the past."[10] Though we have innumerable documents that attest to what anti-vice crusaders said, we cannot see what they railed against. We cannot fill in all of the contours of the history of sexuality without the materials that have been destroyed.

The destruction of sources further obscures the history of pornography, an area that was hidden to begin with. In general, the history of pornography has often been referred to as a "secret" history. People in the trade had every reason to hide their participation.[11] They published under false imprints, provided false publication dates, and created pseudonyms for authors and publishers. Fake names, dates, and places were joined by falsified histories to hide the trade from the authorities. Historians have begun to document the proliferation of pornographic forms and pull apart the layers of falsified information. To do so they have relied on fragments from the marketplace, like sales notices, as well as police reports and obscenity campaigns to document the range of materials. To a great extent their sources hinge upon the public realm of production and circulation. Alongside the history of professional production, however, runs an alternate history to be documented.

While it is important to understand the large-scale destruction of commercial pornography by anti-vice crusaders and the way it limits what we can know, historians nonetheless have overlooked the corpus of hand-made and homemade objects that those crusaders never found. These objects remain intact despite numerous social purity campaigns. Crusaders did not find them because these objects circumvented the market and stayed out of the public realm, the area most vulnerable to discovery. Because people made and used these materials in the home, they were shielded from public life and prying eyes. Commercial pornographic books, however, even those with small print runs, entered the public realm at the points of both production and circulation. Writers, publishers, printers, shop owners, peddlers, and consumers all came into contact with the printed book. Small print runs of even a few hundred copies would generate hundreds, if not thousands, of contacts. Each set of eyes made that object vulnerable to discovery and prosecution. Each discovery could leave a documentary trail. Homemade and handmade materials, in comparison, never had to leave the safety of the private realm and could remain in the control of the artists who made them. These objects had limited visibility, at least in their first iteration, and had far fewer opportunities to be seized and destroyed. Consequently, they remain intact, scattered here and there, overlooked and relatively unconsidered. Such amateur materials are nestled in the shadows of an already secret history.

Neither historians nor art historians have fully embraced these works. Instead, dedicated connoisseurs like Nancy Bruning Levine in *Hardcore Crafts* (1976), Milton Simpson in *Folk Erotica* (1995), and the authors in *Raw Erotica: Sex, Lust and Desire in Outsider Art* (2013) have documented their existence. But they have not contextualized or historicized the materials. Art historians have considered a few individual artists, like Henry Darger or Dwight Mackintosh, though with a focus on the history of aesthetics and changing definitions of art.[12] Historians might come across an object here and an artwork there, but, by themselves, these objects remain anomalous to most historians' areas of expertise. There are very few historians who work on pornography as more than a one-off attendant to a larger project on revolutionary politics or intellectual history, for example. The number of historians who work on pornography can comfortably be counted on one's fingers, and they have much to do in tracing publishers, crusaders, and writers without also tracking down every stray artifact. As a result, scholars of pornography have not made sense of these handmade objects as a group.

If the history of these sorts of materials has been overlooked as an area of study, the recent upsurge in amateur pornography has been well considered. Many scholars recognize the way that recent technologies have enabled the creation of a plethora of amateur pornography.[13] As Jonathan Coopersmith states, "it is advances in these communications technologies, coupled with the increasing social acceptance of sexually-oriented materials, that have drastically changed the environment and nature of pornography."[14] Scholars have noted that inexpensive video cameras and computers have allowed people to create, upload, and exchange masses of amateur pornography worldwide over the past few decades.[15] Amateur sequences dominated the video market in the 1980s and 1990s and the popularity of the genre was such that how-to guides in book and video form proliferated.[16] When digital media overtook videotape, the trope of the amateur retained popularity. Today, amateur pornography ranges from sexting photos, to hardcore sequences that rival gonzo features, to "Girls Gone Wild"-style clips consolidated into profitable commercial films. Despite a diversity of forms, scholars tend to see change as the result of technological determinism, suggesting that technology causes transformation; in the process, scholars emphasize the core qualities of newness and change. But these claims about newness and change are made without examining the long history of amateur materials. We cannot know what is new without a historical foundation. Photography has been around for more than 175 years. If one wants to make claims about the newness of amateur photographic pornography, one needs to know the history of photographic pornography as a whole—an area that has not been well documented. We need longitudinal data to make claims about newness and the changed landscape of pornography.

Before we make claims about the distinctions of amateur material, we need to think carefully about what amateur production brings and whether it brings something not seen in professional porn. Dan Savage, the prominent sex columnist, created the amateur pornographic film festival called HUMP! Begun in 2004, it has become a yearly event. According to Savage in an interview at the *Washington City Paper*, "'The mission of HUMP! isn't to right the wrongs of the porn industry . . . But it does show that the problem with porn isn't porn itself; the problem with porn is the porn that's being created.'"[17] The touring festival has featured films of lesbian sex, sexual cartoons, fairy fantasies, porn involving trans individuals, rope play, and so on. It shows a range of bodies and desires; it shows sex as funny, alarming, and erotic. However, it doesn't quite show a radically different version of pornography—perhaps because Savage's description of the clear division between commercial productions (those produced by the "porn industry") and amateur production blurs upon further reflection. During the HUMP! tour in 2015, for example, profits were split among filmmakers, and the festival traveled from city to city, playing to sold-out audiences who admired the slick and professional production values. The individuals filmed might not have been full-time porn actors, but what really makes someone a professional? For writers, if you have been paid for your work, you are a professional. For actors, I suspect the same holds true. If profits were split, then wouldn't those involved in the films' production—the filmmakers and actors—be professionals as well?

The division between amateur and professional remains nebulous and problematic; supposedly, amateur works are real, authentic, and personal while commercial pornography is understood to be somehow laminated and plasticized, but neither absolute really holds up to scrutiny. People use the distinction between amateur and professional to make room for the personal realm against the dizzying swirl of commercial culture. By focusing on the amateur, individuals begin to recapture the idea of the individual making and remaking culture, rather than merely consuming it. Moreover, the focus on the amateur raises the issue of scale; just as the zine artist makes individual issues and then gives them to friends, so too does the maker of amateur pornography produce a small number of objects.

The limitations of amateur production seem amplified when pictured against commercial production; compare for instance the individual zine with a commercial magazine, for which the presses clatter out thousands of copies per issue each month and then do it again, month after month, filling mailboxes, newsstands, and readers' minds with a set of ideas. The difference in scale between amateur works and commercial culture is illuminating, but differences tend to be overdrawn both in claims about the juggernaut of commercial culture and about the individuality of the amateur.

Though current discourse suggests that the "porn industry" is well funded, well organized, and highly proficient at meeting or making consumer demand, actual evidence to this effect remains weak in the present and almost entirely absent in historical terms.[18] Historically, pornographers remained marginal in production and distribution methods. They were thus far less professionalized and their work far more accidental, loosely organized, and shambolic than is generally assumed. Early pornographers emerged from a revolutionary tradition, publishing pornography as part of a larger corpus of revolutionary and philosophic texts. European states outlawed works of pornography in tandem with philosophic works under sedition laws.[19] In the eighteenth and nineteenth centuries books and pamphlets dominated the trade; publishers tended to produce small print runs and skirt the margins of poverty rather than amass great riches.[20] Even in the 1970s, a period that might be considered the heyday of American pornography, the success of a few magazines and well-known films should not be confused with the broader market.[21] Rather than spearheading production and distribution transformations, pornographers tended to eke out profits using antiquated methods.[22] For most of the history of the genre, pornography meant small business; even the Private Case of the British Library, one of the world's great collections of pornography, amassed over centuries, has fewer than 2,000 titles in its catalog.[23]

Nonetheless, the idea that the production of pornography is big business has become axiomatic. Yet profits attributed to the industry remain in dispute. To give one example, in 2004 the film scholar Linda Williams wrote that pornography brings in revenue of between $10 and $14 billion annually.[24] To substantiate this claim, Williams cites Frank Rich, the editorial columnist of the *New York Times*. Rich, in turn, cites *Variety* magazine and a "1998 study by Forrester Research in Cambridge, Mass."[25] The *Variety* article, in turn, credits *Adult Video News*, an adult industry trade publication.[26] What seemed like a straightforward statement loses some of its credibility with each citation. But the problem with these estimated figures is more serious than that. Dan Ackerman, writing for *Forbes* magazine in 2001, responded to those estimates shortly after they were published. According to Ackerman,

> The idea that pornography is a $10 billion business is often credited to a study by Forrester Research. This figure gets repeated over and over. The only problem is that there is no such study. In 1998, Forrester did publish a report on the online "adult content" industry, which it pegged at $750 million to $1 billion in annual revenue. The $10 billion aggregate figure was unsourced and mentioned in passing.[27]

In contrast to larger estimates, Ackerman's *Forbes* article estimates the market for adult video, pay-per-view, Internet, and magazines would be more in the range of $2.6 billion to $3.9 billion annually.[28] The article also puts the figures in perspective: "What pornography lacks in cultural resonance, it also lacks in financial clout. The industry is tiny next to broadcast television ($32.3 billion in 1999 revenue, according to Veronis Suhler), cable television ($45.5 billion), the newspaper business ($27.5 billion), Hollywood ($31 billion), even to professional and educational publishing ($14.8 billion)." Despite serious flaws, the $10–14 billion figure is continually repeated, making the big business of pornography seem self-evident.[29]

Claims about the financial success of the pornography business colors the language of anti-porn activism and popular scholarship. The writer Mary Eberstadt, a former research fellow of the Hoover Institution, has referred to the pornography industry as "Big Porn" in order to make the parallels with "Big Tobacco" explicit. She hopes that any supporters of the industry, and those academics who study it, will "live to see their efforts reviled by a future public," much like those lawyers who defended tobacco interests.[30] In her book *Pornified* (2005), Pamela Paul employs the same analogy between the tobacco industry and pornography and goes on to state that "pornography is, at its core, the commercialization of women."[31] In popular formulations such as these, the porn industry seems only slightly less insidious than drug cartels, and the industry's ability to program desires seems to realize the dystopian dreams of Aldous Huxley's *Brave New World*. When critics see pornography as highly industrialized, they are looking at its recent commercial permutations.[32] They focus on the mass-produced materials and make claims about pornography as plasticized and commodified as a result. Further, they treat commercial pornography as if it affects its users in some sort of straightforward way.[33] However, there are innumerable problems with this model, from its understanding of the trade to the ways it conflates production with demand.

There is some small hope of disentangling these matters for the present day. The sociologists Feona Attwood, Clarissa Smith, and Martin Barker, recognizing that supply, demand, and use are very different matters, conducted an online survey about how everyday people use pornography. Generating data about use in the present might allow the researchers to explore how people choose materials, how they make use of them, and how they understand them. In contrast, historians have not been able to differentiate demand from supply and have instead assumed that the pornography people bought was the pornography they wanted.[34] Without letters, memoirs, autobiographies, and other documents, how can historians detail reader demand in the past? Gaps in the archival record make it impossible for scholars to answer basic questions about the history of pornography users. Who read pornography? Were they male or female, rich or poor, black or white, old or young? How did they read? Did they read quickly or compulsively? Did they identify with the male characters, the female, or both? Did individuals choose pornographic materials to meet their fancy or did they make do with what they found? Did the motifs in what they found shape their desires, or did the motifs articulate desires that already existed? How did users understand the materials? Did they treat them as fictions or milk them for sexual know-how? The list of unanswered questions could continue.

To begin to untangle some of these questions and address the issue of demand, this book considers handmade and homemade pornography, an area that has been overshadowed by the examination of more recent amateur efforts and by the history of commercial productions. The methodological payoff of this move is profound because handmade objects allow us to consider the desires of their creators, rather than the marketplace. Because there is no intermediary between the creator and the object, amateur materials provide a more direct view of personal sexual desire. Such objects show what people wanted to see by providing a shortcut that avoided the commercial market and state control. The examination of these materials shows us the ways that people told stories about sexuality in their own idiom. To be clear, this approach will not show us what people saw in commercial objects or how they used them. Instead, it focuses on objects emerging from the creator's consciousness.

In order to tell stories about sex, people altered coins and metal objects; carved objects out of wood and bone; handwrote stories in cursive or block letters; typed original short stories and carbon-copied them; wrote and illustrated comic books; drew, illustrated, and painted pictures; traced and altered pre-existing photographs and illustrations; and altered dolls and other everyday objects. People produced a near-infinite array of pornographic objects, including poems and stories, sculptures and sex toys, metal disks and homemade comic books. A. C. Halavais suggests that more recent amateur materials might be called "small pornographies" to differentiate them from commercialized materials, while Blaise Cronin, Garry Milius, and Betsy Stirratt describe a selection of such handmade objects as "inventive, whimsical, improvised, homespun, lampooning, crass, ludic, and touching in more or less equal measure."[35] More than just providing a backstory to the emergent present of amateur productions, these pornographic objects can show us the range and diversity of desires in the past.

The materials for this study come from private collectors, from art and ephemera dealers, from archives, and from museums.[36] The range of objects that fall into the handmade and homemade category has meant that materials end up in all sorts of places and become categorized in different genres. Some objects go to local or specialty museums and archives such as the Nantucket Historical Society or the Milwaukee Museum of Art. Others go to national museums focused on specific types of artifacts, like the American Folk Art Museum or Mystic Seaport. Older sculptures, paintings, and objects have been parsed into the folk art category, while some more recent productions have been categorized as outsider art; paper materials go to archives, while erotic objects are categorized as realia—objects from everyday life—when placed in museums but most often end up in private collections. Some objects become known as "trench art" if they were produced after the First World War by military personnel, and others become "outsider art" if produced by prisoners or other institutionalized people. If it accomplishes nothing else, this book hopes to pull together a historical record of homemade and handmade erotic objects for consideration. In contemporary parlance, it hopes to create an archive out of discrete objects.

Handmade and homemade objects confound traditional methodologies. Even if archived, the materials considered in this book come with little in the way of provenance.[37] They lack information as to their specific origin, date, or author—the markers that historians use as clues to context and meaning.[38] These objects are also strangely singular. In some sense, each is an artistic object, a piece of individual craftsmanship based upon the skills of the individual who devised it. But some of these objects (such as the Colgate soap sculpture (illus. 3) discussed earlier) are singular pieces created by individuals with limited talents and skills. Thus the language of aesthetics and art history has limits in its application here. Statistical analysis seems just as problematic. Though pornographic objects might abound, the history of obscenity prosecutions and the subsequent destruction of materials disrupt any claims about quantity. It remains impossible to know how representative a given subset of pornographic objects might be because there is no way to know the full extent of once-available objects. This means that these objects are representative only of themselves, rather than of a wider body of materials in circulation. Even the consideration of texts in relation to context is stymied by the singularity of these documents. Thus a photograph of Marilyn Monroe altered to make her appear naked certainly illustrates that someone saw her as a sex object, but perhaps people created similar images of Mary Pickford but destroyed them. Further, the illustration shows us nothing about how the artist saw Monroe over time or whether the artist conceptualized other actors in the same way. As a result, we can make some historical observations but should remain wary of making claims to newness and be careful to avoid overgeneralization.

Though there are limits to what traditional research methodologies can reveal about homemade and handmade materials, this does not suggest that these materials can be ignored—to do so risks distorting our comprehension of the past. These objects exist and they should not be overlooked; instead, their wide dispersal and their ubiquity call for a mapping that recognizes singularity. These objects—in all their incoherent, libidinal, confusing strangeness—remain acts of individual testimony that can and should be entered into the historical record. By working from the object to the creator and from the creator to the culture, we can get an idea of American culture and experience over time.

This book explores amateur pornography's history in the United States from the 1830s until the 1970s. The account begins with some of the earlier pieces I have found, but even earlier handmade and homemade objects exist in individual collections, archives, and institutions, just waiting to be discovered.[39] The first chapter, "Carving Out a Vernacular Sexuality, 1830s–1930s," demonstrates the existence of a robust vernacular tradition that has been mostly overlooked. It considers the proliferation of handmade and homemade objects during the period hardest hit by Anthony Comstock and his successor at the New York Society for the

Suppression of Vice, John Saxton Sumner. The restoration of these objects
to the historical record changes what we can know about the history of
sexual culture. Helen Lefkowitz Horowitz, in her prize-winning book
Rereading Sex (2002), suggests that we look to the sex manual and mid-
wifery book *Aristotle's Masterpiece* as "the central document of vernacular
culture."[40] The volume, first translated and published in England in 1684,
had a long publication history before it began its circulation in early
America. Many versions had been published in the eighteenth century,
making it a favorite to pirate among printers in both England and the
American colonies. This booklet provided basic information about sexuality to the populace. However, the popularity of the volume should
not be equated with vernacularity. It was still the product of commercial
production and commercial processes, and if it informed the populace,
it did so under the rubric of neoclassical erudition. Instead of looking at
what people *bought* from printers, we should turn away from commercial
products and look at what people *made*—out of wood, metal, bone, and
paper. Chapter One of this book therefore explores local traditions that
existed alongside the products of commercial presses. It documents the
wide range of ideas about sexuality that existed, articulated using the
media at hand.

The second chapter, "Adapting Commercial Culture into Handmade
Objects, 1910s–1970s," considers how the deepening of commercial culture affected erotic desires. The proliferation of magazines, ephemera,
photographs, coloring books, and other forms of commercial culture
affected how people saw sexuality. This chapter investigates how people
interacted with commercial culture by exploring what compelled people
and what they did with their compulsions. The examination of Henry
Darger's oeuvre within the larger body of remade objects shows the ways
that people adapted commercial culture to speak to their own internal
visions about bodies, sex, and desire. As this chapter shows, rather than
wiping out the handmade tradition or even supplanting it, the rapid
growth of ephemeral and commercial culture enlivened the realm of the
homemade, whether pornographic or not.

If homemade and handmade pornography in general offers the opportunity to consider expressions of sexuality produced outside or alongside the commercial market, then homemade prison pornography takes the outsider position to an extreme, as shown in Chapter Three, "Men and Time: Prison Pornography, 1940s–1960s." Social scientists have long considered criminals as the ultimate outsiders and have looked for ways to consider their perceived atavistic desires. The documentation on prisoners has yielded dense troves of data on human physiological and psychological states, but little has been done with prison pornography.[41] Similarly, although the history of censorship in general has been well examined, censorship of pornography in prisons has not been well documented. (Though few realize it, even today prisoners in the U.S. have no fundamental rights to pornography or to masturbation.) Wardens and guards confiscated commercial pornography as well as the homemade erotic materials that prisoners made in the absence of commercial materials. For the most part, confiscated objects have been destroyed. For a brief window of time, from the 1940s to the 1960s, however, wardens shipped seized materials to the Kinsey Institute, creating a unique archive of objects. This collection allows us to consider prisoner sexuality in ways that are unmatched by other sorts of sources. The materials allow us to see how prisoners conceptualized and articulated desire, bodies, and pleasures, how they wrote and drew themselves and others, how they plotted and narrated stories, and how they responded to the surveillance that they knew was taking place. Prisoners created pornography that detailed what they missed and what they wanted, articulating desires that ranged from the banal to the violent, in some cases brutalizing and subjugating others through fantasy as a refraction of their own experiences. And, because members of the Kinsey Institute kept good records, the examination of prison pornography can be located within the processes of collection and scientific study. When the Kinsey Institute faced its own skirmish with the federal government between 1950 and 1957 for breaking obscenity provisions under the Tariff Act of 1930, the Kinsey's lawyers successfully argued that the study of prison pornography with the goal of understanding criminal sexuality should justify the transportation and collection of materials that would otherwise be illegal. Ironically, the more that science was able to scrutinize criminal sexuality, the greater freedom it won for itself.

The unique cache of prisoner pornography can be placed within an even larger collection of objects handmade between the 1940s and the 1970s. It appears that more people created and more people kept home-made and handmade pornographic objects during this period than in previous ones, despite whipsawing political approaches to obscenity and despite the expansion in commercial pornography. Chapter Four, "The Postwar World and the Making of a People's Pornography, 1940s–1970s," demonstrates the rapid expansion of handmade and homemade objects in wartime and postwar America. It shows what men and women made for themselves during a period of rapid growth in commercial pornography following shifts in obscenity codes that took place between the 1940s and the 1970s. The sorts of materials that people made show a continuity with folk traditions as well as the influence of commercial culture. Both influences offered ideas and themes to handmade and homemade pornography. As they had in previous decades, people carved, drew, painted, etched, handwrote, and collaged pornographic objects, though new materials like the mimeograph machine and new styles like the comic book affected homemade pornography in both form and content. Instead of satiating desires, the deepening of commercial pornography stimulated dialogue. The extension of commercial culture encouraged a broader set of people to tell their own sexual stories in their own idiom.

Chapter Five, "Marketing Authenticity, 1970s Onward," looks at the commodification of authenticity as "the real" became one of the most valuable markers of art and erotica. This concluding chapter explores two changes that happened concurrently. Together, these transformations affected the conceptual models for amateur pornography and art. First, the rapid development of new technologies (cameras, video, and digital technologies) standardized the category of amateur pornography into particular visual forms. Second, the legitimation of folk art, art brut, self-taught art, and outsider art shifted certain types of sexual objects so that they seemed real and authentic rather than prurient. "Marketing Authenticity" explores the ways that these two phenomena transformed amateur pornography into its current form and remade sexual imagery as art.

As this description shows, the book is arranged along a rough chronology, though one marked by overlaps and deviations. This organization follows the history of homemade and handmade pornography, which has no set tempo or singular path. Some objects appear and reappear in almost the same form over decades. Articulated movable figures from the 1850s were being recreated a hundred years later using only slightly different materials. There is no single cause of change or even clear-cut chronological demarcation. Because of these factors, this book will show broad change over decades using particular objects as illustrative, even while dozens or even hundreds of alternative objects go unexamined. The immensity of the subject makes a full illustration impossible. Handmade pornographic objects from prisons alone number in the thousands, and the full range of handmade objects appears limitless. As a result, this book cannot pretend to be definitive; instead, it looks to provide patterns and directions. It does so knowing full well that new evidence could, and should, change the picture that is painted here.

Despite the uncertainty that the source material engenders, there is a value to including these materials in the historical record. Not to do so means that our materials for documenting the history of sexuality in America will remain sparse and impoverished. The incorporation of these objects into the historical record lets us see sexuality as individuals in the past understood it. By looking at the objects people made, we are able to explore what people wanted to see. Amateur pornography, partially insulated from the market and the state, provides an unmediated view of personal sexual desire, complete with all its contradictions, variances, infelicities, and questionable tastes. It is anarchic, semi-literate, and unglamorous, but it is also profoundly human.

4 Carving from a Maine logging camp, *c.* late 19th or early 20th century. Private collection, Pennsylvania.

1

Carving Out a Vernacular Sexuality, 1830s–1930s

Awooden carving from a Maine logging camp features a naked woman nuzzling into a large, upward-pointing index finger attached to a hand (illus. 4).[1] The woman stands on a pile of books, raising herself up to better grasp the finger the way one might grasp a lover, pulling it between her legs and breasts. Pressed against the forefinger, the woman, in essence, fingers herself while proving that books are clearly good for getting a leg up on masturbation. The artist who carved the figure merged two jokes—one about women and one about books—that work as well visually as they do in words. That's not bad for a bit of sly humor from a backwoods logging camp. The piece, carved and painted in the late nineteenth or early twentieth century, treats digital stimulation with a mocking humor at odds with most published records on the practice; exposés, medical tracts, and pornographic novels published in the nineteenth century tend to treat sex with great seriousness.[2] In contrast, this object displays an emotional register ignored in more traditional sources for the history of sexuality. Homemade and handmade objects like this one carved in the backwoods of Maine let us begin to sketch out the corners of an American sexual history that have remained obscured. What handmade and homemade materials reveal is the continuous existence of a robust, noisy vernacular tradition that has been overlooked in favor of the more heavily documented tradition of commercial pornography.

American commercial pornography emerged from a European tradition. Literature created for scientific purposes, for sexual pleasure, and for the philosophic consideration of corruption, religion, and liberty merged seamlessly into each other in the eighteenth century.[3] In colonial America, people imported the popular medical volumes *Aristotle's Masterpiece* (1684) and *Onania; or, The Heinous Sin of Self-pollution and all its Frightful Consequences, in both Sexes Consider'd* (1710) from England. These tracts were then copied and reprinted by American printers. By the nineteenth century, imported and reprinted versions of European erotic novels like *The Lustful Turk* (1828) and *Memoirs of a Woman of Pleasure* (*Fanny Hill*; 1748) were circulating in Boston and New York.[4] In 1842 Congress passed the first law banning the importation of obscenity, inadvertently helping to establish a nascent obscene publishing industry.[5] By the mid-nineteenth century American publishers had developed their own erotic print culture. As Patricia Cline Cohen, Timothy Gilfoyle, and Helen Lefkowitz Horowitz have demonstrated in their book *The Flash Press* (2008), by the 1840s sporting or flash culture—an urban culture of rogues and swindlers, deceit and decadence—began to generate racy publications. The development of an ephemeral press devoted to sensation and sporting culture offered popular opportunities for titillation and allowed men from a variety of classes to commodify and exploit women.[6] The flash press built upon white ruffian superiority over women and other outsiders, according to Elizabeth Haven Hawley, and worked as a "mass" phenomenon.[7] The flash press remained suggestive rather than explicit, but pornographic books and prints continued to circulate in limited quantities among gentlemen in the know. These were accompanied by woodcut prints, lithographs, paintings, pamphlets, and other obscene articles sold by peddlers, hawkers, and bookstore owners. When obscenity prosecutions rose in the 1850s, a serious consequence of such trials was increased publicity for erotic wares. The Civil War extended the demand and opportunity for commercial sexual culture as men, separated from their families, became ready buyers of sexual materials.[8] Scholars agree that a more hardcore pornographic press had also developed by the Civil War.[9]

American pornography was well established by the end of the nineteenth century, but pornographic productions would still be measured in print runs of three digits and remained marginal compared with other sorts of commercial culture like ladies' magazines, boys' papers, and postcard views of exotic locales.

The account of early American pornography can be deepened by incorporating the variety of pornographic artifacts that people made for themselves. To the patterns of early importations and an emergent print culture, homemade and handmade pornography adds coins, carvings, scrimshaw, and pamphlets—artifacts ubiquitous in early American history, though not often considered pornographic. The consideration of these materials moves the locus of the pornographic imagination from its European roots and emerging cosmopolitan centers toward a vernacular tradition that arose from the "making classes" rather than the "buying classes." Though wealthy city-dwellers might have had greater access to books, newspapers, prostitutes, and other purchasable pleasures, homemade and handmade pornography hints at the viability of local articulations and regional variations in sexual culture.

The introduction to this book began with a piece of scrimshaw from the Mystic Seaport Museum, one of the most important institutions devoted to the preservation and study of American maritime culture, and discussed an etched marine mammal tooth featuring a nude woman sitting on the head of a sea monster. The piece shows very fine craftsmanship and an easy eroticism. Emblematic of nineteenth-century whaling culture, scrimshaw artifacts remain hard to place geographically while at the same time speaking clearly to a maritime tradition. Generally considered a folk art, scrimshaw differs from other folk traditions in that it was not associated with peasant culture or the reproduction of standard motifs. Instead, scrimshaw built upon international, rather than regional, traditions, and its artists searched out novelty and innovation. Though practiced by sailors worldwide, the majority of scrimshaw work resides in institutions along the American Eastern Seaboard, making scrimshaw seem like the prototypical American folk custom.[10] Most of the institutions dedicated to

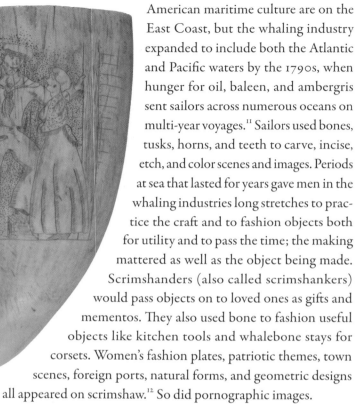

5 Scrimshaw tooth, [19??], ISR 630R A75.1 (front), Kinsey Institute.

American maritime culture are on the East Coast, but the whaling industry expanded to include both the Atlantic and Pacific waters by the 1790s, when hunger for oil, baleen, and ambergris sent sailors across numerous oceans on multi-year voyages.[11] Sailors used bones, tusks, horns, and teeth to carve, incise, etch, and color scenes and images. Periods at sea that lasted for years gave men in the whaling industries long stretches to practice the craft and to fashion objects both for utility and to pass the time; the making mattered as well as the object being made. Scrimshanders (also called scrimshankers) would pass objects on to loved ones as gifts and mementos. They also used bone to fashion useful objects like kitchen tools and whalebone stays for corsets. Women's fashion plates, patriotic themes, town scenes, foreign ports, natural forms, and geometric designs all appeared on scrimshaw.[12] So did pornographic images.

One scrimshawed tooth features two separate illustrations. On one side, a jaunty sailor in dress whites and a neckerchief talks to a woman who leans against a shingled building (illus. 5). This first scene looks like any other etching of a couple's wooing. On the reverse of the tooth, however, a man mounts a woman in bed. She lies on her back while he half-kneels on top of her (illus. 6). The position allows the viewer to see his swollen testicles and his penis as it enters her. An oil lamp rests on the bedside table, while an embroidery of "Home Sweet Home" decorates the walls. A fine wooden bed, a bolster pillow, beadboard, and trim complete the homey scene.[13] The image is a version of New England transformed from prim courtship to amatory celebration. It also provides an alternate inflection for the embroidered commonplace: the carefully wrought representation of an embroidered panel suggests a different reading of the sweetness of home, from home as a place to home as a sexual act.

Another scrimshaw object, created from a walrus tusk, illustrates a series of sexual scenes, separated by decorative motifs of acorns and leaves that wind their way around the images.[14] One scene documents a woman squatting over a chamber pot. The artist has carved her squarely facing the viewer so that her face, breasts, and vulva are rendered in symmetry. A single drop of urine falls from her body into the pot below. In her hand, she holds an erect penis—visible by the red-tinted head—which she aims toward her vaginal opening. Her hair spills around her shoulders and her bare breasts are rendered in a naive style in simple blackened lines. Her image is both scatological and erotic, a combination that commonly appeared in published pornography of the nineteenth century. On the same tusk, in another scene, a couple copulates. The man and woman face each other and their arms and legs form a tangle. On the tusk's reverse, a man with an erect penis sits in a chair as he reaches for a woman with exposed labia and bared breasts. The coloration of the tip of his penis matches the reddened lips of her labia. Period touches include muttonchop sleeves on the woman's gown, dancing slippers, and fancy garters. Another scene on the same tusk features a very well-dressed woman, drawing up her voluminous gown to touch herself. The fan she holds in her other hand, the delicate necklace around her neck, and her artfully done hair make this look like a fashion plate except for the single touch of red given to her labia, which draws the viewer's attention to the erotic impact of the

6 Scrimshaw tooth, [19??], ISR 630R A75.1 (back), Kinsey Institute.

scene. In this and other scenes on this artifact, the fascination with female anatomy is augmented by a fascination with feminine adornment. Though the artist etched male and female bodies, ideas of femininity as begowned and accessorized remained focal. Women in all their finery remained the erotic focus of the artist, whose skills, though naive, were nonetheless strong enough to transmit his sexual desires for women in all their fripperies.

As well as etching images, sailors carved objects out of whalebone and sea ivory. One artist carved a beautiful little ring in which a nude figure bends backwards to form a circle (illus. 7, 8). The care given to the figure can be seen in the etching and coloration of the individual pubic hairs, the placement of the belly button, the carving of the knees, and the expressiveness of the face. Despite this level of detail, the figure remains biologically indeterminate. The breasts look feminine, but the bald head does not. The genitals suggest a swollen labia with enlarged clitoris but might have been intended as a scrotum and penis. The artist's skill in carving and ornamentation suggests that this indeterminacy might have been intentional rather than accidental; perhaps the scrimshander liked the sexually ambiguous body. The delicacy of the ring and its sizing—at seven-eighths of an inch in diameter—suggest that the ring was made to be worn. With just a turn of the ring, a wearer could hide or reveal the sexual parts of the body, allowing it to be worn in public while keeping its eroticism a secret.

7, 8 Erotic ring, scrimshaw, New England, 1840s. Collection of Justin Enger.

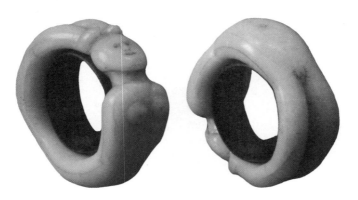

Erotic carvings graced other everyday objects. One small carving, described by Milton Simpson as possibly functioning as a toothpick, shows a woman pulling up her clothes to reveal her sexual organs.[15] Her generous breasts spill over the neck of her gown and her waist seems corseted in its circumference. Large eyes, a small smile, and pulled-back hair provide a youthful appearance, but the close alignment of her features gives them a cat-like cast and suggests the artist's inexperience as a sculptor. The limits to the artist's skills show in the paw-like hands that hold up the folds of her gown. Despite the simplicity of the hands, the artist carefully carved line after line of the figure's pubic hair, and from out of the nest of hair comes a distended labia with a carefully carved slit. The 2½-inch (6 cm) carving, which dates to about 1850, could have easily fitted into a pocket.

Other examples were purely decorative. One scrimshaw artifact produced between 1835 and 1845 belongs to a group of items made by the whaleman-artist known as the Banknote Engraver, a name coined by scrimshaw expert Norman Flayderman in 1971 to acknowledge the fine filigree work that borders the artist's pieces.[16] The scrimshawed tooth in question features three women in vaguely neoclassical gowns on one side and an almost naked woman on the reverse (illus. 9). The artistic talent of the Banknote Engraver can be seen in the delicate shading of the women's bodies and in his ability to replicate the weight and sheen of different fabrics. One of the women, for example, is dressed in a diaphanous gown. Translucent rather than transparent, it catches in folds around her waist and shapes her breasts while highlighting their weight. The women have delicately rendered hands and carefully drawn headdresses that give them a martial quality. The nude on the reverse gains a roundness from the shading on the underside of her arms, the line of her abdomen, and a curve that runs from below her breasts to around her hips. The artist had a great deal of skill to be able to render the softness and curves of a woman's body in this way.

A further example of erotic scrimshaw has been made from a sperm whale tooth (illus. 10). The scrimshaw's etching reveals a man and woman engaged in coitus. The mustached man, in a striped suit and high-collared coat, opens his pants to pull out his erect penis. The woman, neatly coiffed, dressed, and then ornamented with a cross, pulls up her gown and wraps one leg around his body for balance as he enters her body. The scrimshaw's appeal comes from its frank depiction of sexuality set against the markers of respectability, rather than artistry in the craft.

Scrimshaw artifacts show the range of scrimshanders' abilities. They also show the breadth of objects that articulated desires, from utilitarian toothpicks to ornamental etched teeth. They display inspiration ranging from the mythological realm, to neoclassicism, to the vulgar. Their production from the eighteenth century until the late nineteenth century as whaling peaked and then receded as an occupation shows the durability of scrimshaw as an art. Though there is no single place of creation (since sailors made such objects during voyages), these objects nonetheless displace the location of pornographic production from urban to oceanic. Rather than thinking about the production and circulation of pornography in larger and more libertine centers, the existence of scrimshaw objects puts pornography on the edges of settlements and in largely male locations. These objects show that whalers and sailors saw sexuality as worth articulating in the materials around them. Instead of speaking to elites as collections of published materials do, these objects came from among the working classes and only became collectable objects among the elite in the twentieth century.[17]

If scrimshaw's materiality emerged from a particular culture of production, coins gesture to a culture of circulation. According to Andrew Burnett, former

9 Scrimshaw tooth, Three women, n.d., "Mary + Ella" and "Anna + Mary," item 1997.76.11, Mystic Seaport Museum.

deputy director of the British Museum, London, coins remain one of the most important sources for historians because of their durability, quantity, spread, dateability, and designs.[18] Numismatics, or the study of coins, has proved valuable to the mapping of political sovereignty since the publication of Guillaume Budé's *De asse et partibus eius* in 1514 demonstrated the value of coins for historical research. According to William Monter, "coins offer an unusually clear and precise form of evidence about claims to sovereignty, since minting them was an essential and deeply cherished monopoly of legitimate rulers."[19] In the American context, part of establishing sovereignty after the Revolution was the development of a new coinage based upon new symbols. Robert Garson argues that a distinctly American currency allowed the population to reorient itself to a new national authority. "The pictorial images and the promises of negotiability conveyed on coins, banknotes and other financial instruments were repetitively encountered on a daily basis. They were visual reminders of the connection between finance, stability and national authority."[20]

10 Scrimshaw tooth, 1872–98, item 1987.88: Sperm whale tooth featuring a man and woman fully clothed, engaged in sex, Mystic Seaport Museum.

William Hunting Howell suggests that "more than stamped pieces of copper," pennies in early America "pointedly link the virtues of replication (and the replication of virtue) with decimal math and the mass production of specie."[21] According to Howell, the establishment of a base-ten currency encouraged commerce even while allowing common citizens armed only with basic math skills to understand the financial decisions of state. A decimal coinage guaranteed financial stability in making contracts and political stability in affairs of state.

For Benjamin Franklin, coins could help make a national character: "by seeing it every time one receives a Piece of Money, might make an Impression upon the Mind, especially of young Persons, and tend to regulate the Conduct."[22] The question of who or what would be stamped onto coins entered into national debate. Congress decided against gracing the coins with presidents in favor of impressions of liberty. With the establishment of Liberty coins, Americans received a mechanized lesson on national virtue with each economic transaction.

One set of coins that might also be used to explore the connection between symbols and politics is a collection of Liberty head pennies produced between 1812 and 1849 (illus. 11).[23] These coins feature the female embodiment of liberty on one side, surrounded by a spray of thirteen stars, one for each of the original states. On the reverse, a banner proclaiming "United States of America" encloses a garland and the simple inscription "ONE CENT." The Liberty pennies in the Kinsey Institute collection have been meticulously transformed, however, as the 'E' in "CENT" has been carefully filed and reworked into a 'U' so that the caption reads "ONE CUNT." These coins lack context and provenance, having arrived in the collection by donation generations after their original production. They have been separated from any details that would document their circulation. The questions of who handled these coins, when and where they were reworked, and how someone arrived at the idea cannot be answered without documentation. These coins thus cannot be used to follow the circulation patterns of pornographic artifacts in American culture.

What can be said of the coins, however, is that someone cared enough about articulating the word "cunt" to sacrifice effort, ingenuity, and hard currency to the recreation of these pennies. It is easy to imagine the creative moment in which someone—a blacksmith or jewelry maker, or a group of journeymen at a foundry—might have seen the linguistic possibilities that the coins presented. It is also easy to see the coins as an expression of desperation; who but the deeply lonely or the most committed to shocking would bother to invest their time, energy, and capital in such productions?

The re-forging of "CENT" to "CUNT" in the coins suggests the profound desire to see the word written and expressed in public. Given the dates of the coins in the collection, either one person found this articulation so compelling that he or she remade Liberty coins over 37 years,

11 A collection of four of the thirteen u.s. coins dating from 1812 to 1849 that have been altered to read "ONE CUNT" instead of "ONE CENT," Altered Currency, Novelties, Kinsey Institute.

or, more likely, several people across the early republic saw the same opportunity to make "CENT" into "CUNT," showing a shared way of seeing the world and a shared desire to break down linguistic restrictions against profanity and vulgarisms. A "ONE CUNT" coin, then, would remake national virtue into national vice as vulgar desire, a parody of liberty, and sophomoric hijinks replaced high-minded values. The debasement of specie in this arrangement debased the state. In the remade copper coins, Lady Liberty becomes a rather tawdry Venus, transformed by hand into a pocket-size joke.

The coins might have been erotic to those who reworked them or they might merely have provided some satisfaction to the producer in their power to shock. Nonetheless, the effort that went into their transformation suggests the extent of people's desire for an explicit articulation of sexuality. "ONE CUNT" coins suggest a degree of desire for straight talk and debased naming that signals base sexual urges.

Although the simplicity of these coins might suggest "simpler" sexual times when even dirty words had power to excite, when viewed in the context of other debased coins, "ONE CUNT" coins gesture less to simplicity than to widespread metalworking abilities. Two more pennies from the Kinsey Institute can act as examples of how people altered coins in ways more extensive than profaning words.[24] The Flying Eagle cent (produced between 1856 and 1858) allowed one individual a basic template for the creation of a winged phallus. The winged phallus motif reveals that its maker had a classicist background that went beyond a cursory education into more esoteric works of the classical world.[25] The winged phallus, though standard in Greco-Roman pottery, had been cordoned off into the realm of the obscene by the nineteenth century.[26] The transformation of eagle to phallus in this mid-nineteenth-century coin shows an attention to the similarity of the two forms, an ability to visualize the phallus beneath the shape of the eagle in flight, and metalworking skills beyond those entailed by simple letter changes. Another one cent coin, this time from 1930, was transformed through paint as well as metalwork. This example still has its banner of "IN GOD WE TRUST," but in the center of the coin someone has created a female vulva with carefully etched pubic hair. The vaginal opening has been enameled in red. Thus the slogan of religious unity links the enameled vulva with base currency, giving the slogan its own irreligious slant. These examples suggest that currency provided individuals with a canvas for revealing the obscene hidden in everyday objects.

The linking of sexuality and money has been documented by any number of scholars who consider the issues of prostitution and sexual commerce, but the etymological links between money and sexuality go even deeper than is generally assumed. As Will Fisher aptly demonstrates in his article "Queer Money," the term "queer" applied equally to counterfeit coins and sodomitical sexual practices from the end of the seventeenth century into the nineteenth century. In early modern texts, false coins and false coitus overlapped. Working from numismatic terminology, Fisher suggests that a piece referred to both a coin (a piece of eight) or a person (a piece of flesh). Both copper coins and sexual desires could be rendered queer, particularly since copper was Venus's metal—a base metal that contributed to the term "venery."[27] Copper pennies demonstrate that currency might be debased in more than one way.

While modifying pennies entailed a minimal financial sacrifice, the use of a silver Liberty trade dollar shows a serious commitment to erotic reworkings. A dollar minted in 1877 featured Liberty seated on a rock while holding aloft the torch of liberty. The same coin in its altered state shows Lady Liberty on a chamber pot (illus. 12).[28] An additional figure has joined her, and he reaches toward her breast. In place of the liberty torch, she holds his erect penis. Thus Lady Liberty masturbates a man while shitting on the pot. In this coin, any high-minded sentiments of state are deflated with ribald and scatological associations.

Other national currencies were similarly debased. A 1756 écu with the profile of Louis xv has almost been worn smooth over the years. The reverse side features the shield of France, the crown, and two crossed olive branches. On the obverse, five nude figures are etched onto the metal within the outline of the king's profile.[29] A seated man or boy masturbates. He is flanked by two naked women, while at his feet another couple copulate. This image can easily be read as a critique of the monarchy and a misuse of the throne and would join the flood of pornographic materials that used sexuality as a political weapon in Ancien Régime France. However, a French five-franc piece produced generations later similarly debased the symbols of the state. This coin, issued by the Third Republic in 1875, festooned on the reverse with a garland, has been altered.[30] On the obverse, under the banner reading "Liberté / Egalité / Fraternité," Liberty and Equality flank Hercules, a figure used as a symbol of the monarchy before the revolution, and then used by revolutionaries to symbolize the new republic. As Lynn Hunt demonstrates, Hercules was not a popular figure of the people, but a figure reimagined from the classical age. According to Hunt, Hercules was an "artist-intellectual-politician's image of the people for the people's edification. Hercules, like the goddess of Liberty who preceded him,

12 American silver dollar, inscribed 420 grains, 900 fine, trade dollar, 1877, Altered Currency, Novelties, Kinsey Institute.

was a classical figure, whose meaning was most available to the educated."[31]
While Hercules stood triumphant on the coins of the Third Republic,
on this altered coin he stands resplendent, masturbated by the twin
symbols of republicanism, Liberty and Equality, who flank him. As Liberty
and Equality join hands over his now erect penis, the bare-chested
Hercules becomes a reconfigured hero, less a classical hero and more of
a subversive hero, reproduced for erotic purposes.

Both devalued as specie and sullied as ideas, these altered coins
provided new renditions of national currency. The existence of altered
coins shows that individuals were willing to sacrifice time and assets to
remake these materials. They also demonstrate that people made obscene
goods from materials at hand. Coins—though hard to come by—con-
stantly circulated, making them tempting templates for alteration. Beneath
a surface of slogans and sanctity, people saw other possibilities, and they
used their skills to bring those hidden vulgarisms to light. Though the
alteration of coinage might seem to fit into the category of oddities and
souvenirs, these coins have lasted for centuries and traveled far and wide,
testifying to the enduring visions of their makers. Thus these little coins
might be the single markers of people's ideas of a corrupted and counterfeit sense of sexuality that could not be met by other means and which
had to be rendered by hand and at home as a result. Their centuries-long
circulation shows the ways their debased visions of state ideals and
symbols endured.

Wood carvings were even more common than scrimshaw or coins.
They ranged from curiosities to everyday objects, from the suggestive to
the erotic. Carved wooden objects from the late nineteenth-century and
early twentieth-century United States come from as far north as Maine
and as far south as Georgia. They spread from New Jersey to Minnesota.
(No doubt they spread even further west and southwest, but those objects
have not yet made their way into archives of sexuality.) Carved folk erotica built upon older craft traditions and reworked contemporary themes
for sexual appeal; they functioned as useful objects and strange curios,
focused on both male and female forms. Though some categories (like

the "man in the barrel") became standard and thus show a transmission of ideas across time and place, others remained singular and spoke only to the individual's conception of desirability.

Canes became a ubiquitous medium for folk carving in the nineteenth century. Though out of fashion now, they were part of standard men's dress for the time. As Edwards Park wrote in his inventory of canes and cane owners in American culture for the *Smithsonian* magazine, canes were "the perfect accessory for a man."[32] Out of the thousands of folk carved canes, a few erotic ones can stand as examples. A hand-carved cane from the 1880s features a woman doing a headstand (illus. 13). She rests her head on the shaft of the cane and tips her bent legs into the air so that they form the handle of the cane. The cane's maker skillfully replicated the way that gravity works on her exposed breasts and how her posture would create folds in her stomach and hip. The cane has been delicately painted, though much of the color has worn away over the years. Her position exposes her naked buttocks and vulva; the cane's user would have his hand nestled against her naked slit.[33]

Another carved cane, from a decade later, features a penis as the handle. The 5¼-inch (13 cm) penis-shaped handle has just the smallest bulge at the base that hints at tightened testicles.[34] Anyone using the cane would have to tightly grip the shaft of the penis, right beneath the carved head, while the palm of the hand and thumb would press into the base and touch the testicles. This average-sized penis carving would fit comfortably in an average-sized hand. Would grasping the cane be autoerotic, homoerotic, libertine, deviant? Who knows how users felt when grasping the penis cane, but the effect of the act of creation remains embedded in the artifact. For an object created at the height of anti-masturbation medical tracts, the creation of such a graspable object seems subversive.

A final example comes from Davenport, Iowa (illus. 14). The late nineteenth-century cane takes inspiration from the story of Adam and Eve. The handle features Eve clutching the Tree of Knowledge, her legs wrapping tightly around a single branch, while the snake beckons. Adam appears in relief along the bottom of the cane. The delicacy of the work shows the skill of the artist. Though biblical in nature, anyone using the cane would be grasping Eve's semi-naked body, rendering the experience as erotic as religious. One would feel Eve's delicately carved ribs and small breasts against the palm of the hand. Men's accessories like canes provided a canvas for eroticism that could easily go overlooked.

Carved wooden objects could also include any number of figures whose sole purpose seems to be surprised delight. A single figurine called "September Morning" (illus. 15) illustrates both the woodworker's skills and ideas of beauty. The artist carved the figure of a fan dancer from multiple pieces of wood and then assembled the arm with a dowel attachment so that the arm holding the fan could move. This figurine from the early twentieth century shows that the idea of an erotic fan dance had spread into the upper Midwest well before Sally Rand performed her famous act at the 1933 World's Fair in Chicago. Careful workmanship has created a short mop of hair, individual teeth, and smile lines at the eyes and mouth. The figure looks cheerful rather than overtly sexual, though a clear eroticism shows in the carving of the labia.

Some artifacts hid sexuality beneath a respectable veneer so that ideas of sexuality popped out for the audience in a rush of surprise. A small handmade box has a hand-painted hen attached to the lid (illus. 16). When the lid is pulled back along the tracks, a handmade cock springs out of the box on a wire and mounts the hen. The box has been painted and ornamented with endpaper so

14 Adam and Eve cane, carved wood, Davenport, Iowa, *c*. late 19th century. Collection of Louis Picek.

the box seems like a cherished object that might hold a treasured piece of jewelry. The box's appearance makes the rooster's leap all the more abrupt and startling.[35] Similarly, a carving in sea ivory or bone looks like a compass at first glance. The cover closes off any hints of impropriety into a smooth, round box (illus. 17). When opened, the needle, floating on a pin, seems to point true north. On closer inspection, however, the needle is a red-tipped penis, while true north is a swollen labia complete with individually etched public hairs (illus. 18). The compass thus shows how an erect penis can always find its way.

Some surprise objects reveal a sexuality that had become formulaic. One classic of the genre is the "man in a barrel." At first glance, all one sees is a man's head sticking out of a barrel, but when the barrel is lifted, the man's erect penis pops up. A version at the Kinsey Institute features a man in a barrel created from three separate pieces of wood; the small artifact has been carved, joined, painted, and then colored with marker pen.[36] Once conceptualized, the man in the barrel became a standard motif. It was repeated endlessly, sometimes with great delicacy and hidden mechanics and at others with ham-fisted spring-loading. This tiny example (illus. 19), less than 2 inches (5 cm) tall, could travel anywhere, waiting to spring on the unwary.

15 September Morning, carved wood, Minnesota, early 20th century. Collection of Louis Picek.

16 Cock and Hen (novelty movable figures), [19??], ISR 759, Kinsey Institute.

The fascination with men's bodies showed itself in any number of figures, many with pop-up penises. A handmade Abraham Lincoln figure demonstrates the artist's investment in the masculine form (illus. 21). This Abe has been rendered distinctively enough to be instantly recognizable. Dressed in formal wear, including top hat, white dress shirt, and black suit, he has been made to thunder from the mount. Abe points the index finger of one hand and raises a fist with the other in a gesture of masculine authority. Articulated joints at the elbow, shoulder, knees, and hips let him gesture and move. Finally, when a panel is removed, the president reveals a healthy movable erection. This figure from the 1880s shows the way that some folk artists saw eroticism in a historical figure of masculine authority.

17 Compass lid, carved from bone or ivory (closed cover), acquired in Maine, *c.* 1900. Collection of Mark Rotenberg.

Other figures demonstrate less attention paid to how the body is put together. Some barely suggest features at all, let alone the striking ones that mark an individual. But even without giving attention to the rendering of the face, these folk objects still focus on masculinity and the male sexual body. In essence they define the male form by the erection of the genitals. One primitive figure shows little individuality in the face or form (illus. 20). The man's cylindrical body lacks arms. The simplicity of the torso is offset by a pair of legs complete with bent knees and heeled

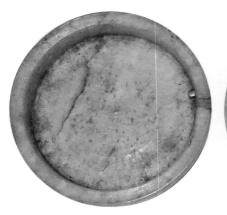

18 Compass interior, carved from bone or ivory, acquired in Maine, *c.* 1900. Collection of Mark Rotenberg.

19 Man in a barrel,
novelty figure, n.d.
Author's collection.

20 Male figure, carved and painted wood, late 19th or early 20th century. Collection of Jim Linderman.

21 Articulated Lincoln figure, polychromed wood, 1880s. Collection of Kirk Landauer.

22 Articulated male figure with movable tongue, late 19th or early 20th century. Collection of Jim Linderman.

shoes, and a large movable penis. Another primitive figure (illus. 22) has been carefully pinned together. His arms and penis move and even his tongue waggles. The features have been penciled in, showing a hawk nose and mustache. The artist has also drawn in a fine buttoned suit with a fancy dress shirt and an ornamental lapel.

An earlier carving (illus. 23) features a male figure in uniform. Made from a single block of wood, painted and then draped with a leather loincloth, the male figure seems balanced and solid. The artist's attention to detail shows in the care given to the eyes and mouth and the slight suggestion of cauliflower ears that make the figure seem like a bruiser. The broad shoulders and wide stance only add to that idea. The figure has been given a uniform, with black cuffs on the sleeves of his green jacket that match the solid black cap. Though fully dressed, the figure is rendered erotic through the delicately carved erect nipples and the semi-erect penis and testicles,

23 Loincloth Larry, c. 1920. Collection of Justin Enger.

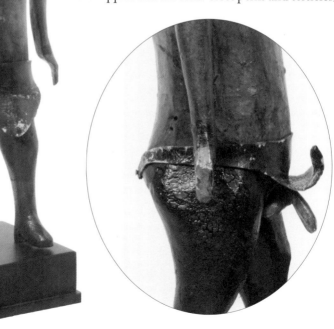

covered by the leather loincloth. Respectable at first glance, "Loincloth Larry" shows that there's an erotic and desirous body hidden beneath the uniform.

Though wood was a favored medium because of its ubiquity, people also made use of other materials.[37] A good set of tin snips let people craft erotic objects from thin sheets of metal.

Artifacts could even more easily be cut from leather. In one such example, two animals copulate. The squat bodies and long ears suggest that these might be donkeys (illus. 24). The item came from a Georgia estate and has been dated to the 1930s. The female donkey and base are cut from a single piece of leather, while the male donkey is composed of separate pieces held together by pins. The articulated joints let the male donkey move at the hips, shoulder, penis, and ankles, to rock back and forth to simulate sex.

Another leather object, from New Jersey, features two figures joined at the arms and ankles (illus. 25). Five pins hold the figures together as they move side to side, straightening and bending. Though one figure has a penis and the other does not, both figures are bald and feature the same rounded bodies, rectangular legs, and squared-off feet. The penis alone sexes the figures. While it is possible that the artist wanted to represent two men having sex as a way to envision queer sexual relations, it is equally possible that the artist rendered the body female by the lack of a penis alone. Whether intentional or not, the visual equality between figures stands out. The two, whatever the sex, are the same with the exception of the penis that bridges the gap between them.

Other articulated figures confirm the pleasures that the makers must have had in the creation of movement to simulate sex. One object from the 1920s or '30s, rendered in metal and wood, is controlled by a single lever (illus. 26). The many hinges at the ankles, hips, shoulders, and hands let both figures move in tandem. The female figure, sexed by a hair bun and breasts, is meant to move along with the male. With each shot of the "gun," the couple rock forward. Another "gun" has been carefully painted, though time has chipped much of the paint and broken off a

24 Donkeys, made from leather, from an estate in Georgia, c. 1930. Collection of Mark Rotenberg.

25 Articulated figures, from an estate in New Jersey, c. 1920. Collection of Mark Rotenberg.

26 Articulated figures, c. 1920–30. Collection of Mark Rotenberg.

27 Articulated
figures, *c.* 1920s.
Author's collection.

foot (illus. 27). The care given to creating such toys suggests the joint
pleasures experienced in crafting these objects and envisioning the sex act.

This accounting of small objects would be incomplete without men-
tion of the popular motif of the dead man in a coffin. Complementing the
popularity of memento mori in nineteenth-century society, pornographic
coffin figurines featured corpses with erections that popped out when
the coffin lid was moved (illus. 28).[38] Often rough-hewn and unpainted,
most coffins contained poorly wrought figures. Faces might be featureless,
bodies would be mere cylinders, but the makers graced the bodies with
genitals. At a time when people washed their own dead, wrapped the
dead in shrouds, and even built their coffins, coffin figures kept the dead
with the living, gracing solemnity with burlesque humor.[39]

The form adapted itself to endless variations. One maker gestured
to then recent Egyptological finds by carving the name "King Tut" onto
the lid. Inside, the coffin figure displayed a mummy with an erection
mounted on a dial (illus. 29). While figures painted in blackface suggest

racial mockery, others in whiteface provide evidence that such figures crossed race lines (illus. 30, 31).

The popularity of the coffin figure even lent itself to a coffin couple. In one example, the pair, clearly made by the same folk artist, seem well matched. The male figure carries a classic pop-up penis. The female figure sports clearly defined breasts, and what appears to be a smaller pop-up clitoris completes the female form. Adorable rounded kneecaps grace both male and female forms, demonstrating the artist's skill.[40]

One artist used the coffin figure for a self-portrait (illus. 32), raising questions about how the artist understood themselves in relation to the objects. The carefully made coffin has been stained in a dark, somber tone, leaving the paler wood figure in contrast. The coffin figure lies on a bed of cotton wool. As the coffin opens, the penis, surrounded by a swirl of white pubic hair, pops up. The figure's smile and posture—with his arms

28 Coffin figure, n.d. Collection of Mark Rotenberg.

29 King Tut coffin figure, from an estate in Virginia, c. 1930. Collection of Mark Rotenberg.

crossed—suggest jauntiness rather than solemnity. His red cap matches the red tip of his penis. The label "Not Dead Yet Darling" suggests the man speaking directly to a lover. Instead of mockery of the dead, this figure gestures to the pleasures of sex in old age. These nineteenth- and twentieth-century hand-carved figures combine sex and death in ways meant to surprise.

As this review has shown, folk objects spoke of the sexuality embedded in everyday life. They illustrated a sly and surprising sexuality in which sexual gestures stood right behind propriety and where erections popped up in staid places. They imagined nudity beneath any number of clothing items. They looked to women as glorified in fripperies and as nude and dripping. They saw men's anatomy as sexual, women's anatomy as sexual, even animal anatomy as sexual. They illustrated nudity, self-fondling, and

30 Coffin figure, from an estate in South Carolina, n.d. Collection of Mark Rotenberg.

31 Coffin figure painted white with matchstick penis, n.d. Collection of Mark Rotenberg.

32 "Not Dead Yet Darling," from an estate in North Carolina, *c*. 1930. Collection of Mark Rotenberg.

penetration. They placed desire in the kitchen, in the barnyard, and in the graveyard. They made home into a sexual embrace.

While vernacular objects might be accused of adopting a leering attitude toward sexuality, they do not look like the slick leer of the rich man used to commodified sex. Instead the objects appear amateurish and are defined by their primitivism; problems with angularity and proportion suggest a grasping toward the embodiment of ideas rather than a sense of control over the medium and representation. Paw-like renderings attest to an attempt to envision a woman's small hand. Eyes drawn onto carved figures hint at an inability to render depth and shadow. Handmade and homemade objects speak to an individual's ability to gesture toward desire, rather than the connoisseur's ability to pick from a range of desires or to purchase objects to suit one's taste. At the same time that individuals carved folk objects from wood and bone, snuff boxes whose lids contained miniature paintings of erotic scenes and fore-edged paintings where erotic scenes lay hidden beneath the gilded surface circulated among the rich.[41] In contrast, handmade and homemade objects were made not for sale to the fancy, at least not in the nineteenth and early twentieth centuries. Instead, they spoke to less cosmopolitan desires and they contained less sophisticated cosmologies.

In communities where neighbors made one another's coffins, an erotic memento mori might lighten the seriousness of death. Barnyard scenes like the cock mounting the hen or the two copulating donkeys stand as a reminder of the porous divide between animals and humans and between public and private. Handmade and homemade objects represented male sexuality as well as female sexuality in complicated ways that counter any ideas that pornography commodified women's sexuality alone. These objects offer representations of male and female, both clothed and unclothed, erotic and awkward. They suggest the contours of male sexuality: physically, as in the carving of the phallic cane, and metaphorically, as in carvings of male desire like the scrimshaw of coitus as "Home Sweet Home." These objects show that for men, female bodies had a complicated erotic allure, and that behaviors not typically associated with sexual responses—such as urinating over a chamber pot—could evoke desire.

Material artifacts like coffin figures, erotic scrimshaw, and reworked coins testify to the durability of the raw materials and the willingness of people to invest time, assets, and skills for the pleasure of executing an idea. In contrast, paper goods took less skill and fewer assets, particularly as paper grew less expensive over the course of the nineteenth century with the transition to wood pulp paper, as literacy rates rose, and as more people had access to paper goods for inspiration and modeling. However, erotic pamphlets remain ephemeral, and few early examples have been archived. The rarity of these objects makes each one particularly valuable.

Homemade pornographic pamphlets fall somewhere between pamphlets and zines. The overlaps between sexuality and pamphlets was well established by the eighteenth century, when the term "pamphlet" implied obscene and libelous materials made about the monarchy or State. Pamphlets allowed individuals and agitators to intercede into the political world and to popularize their ideas of reform and revolution. Pamphlets and pamphleteering had a central place both in the American Revolution and the Glorious Revolution of 1688 that preceded it.[42] Though the political importance of the pamphlet continued well into the nineteenth century, the magazine—the pamphlet's more commercial cousin—with its new emphasis on fashion, fiction, and family life, began to dominate. Growing literacy rates, cheap paper stock, specialized content, and advantageous postal rates meant that magazines reached mass audiences in the late nineteenth and early twentieth centuries. In the 1930s zines emerged as a way to differentiate one's writings from commercial media even while patterned after it. First organized as fan fiction and then developing as a countercultural response to industrial society, zines allowed individuals to write, narrate, draw, and craft their own stories.

Obscene homemade and handmade pamphlets might be thought of as early zines. Stephen Duncombe has described zines as "scruffy, homemade little pamphlets. Little publications filled with rantings of high weirdness and exploding with chaotic design."[43] And like zines, these materials were made meaningful through their hand-production, their materiality, and their individuality, which countered industrialized consumer culture. As Alison Piepmeier states, amateurishness defined these objects, with their makers lavishing care as part of the pleasure. Unlike books, pamphlets, and magazines, which demand professionalism in writing, printing, binding, and transportation, these objects register a "care that is invested in the material."[44] Like zines, obscene pamphlets resisted industrialization and allowed individuals who otherwise might have no voice to register their stories in intimate ways. Both in content and in form, pornographic pamphlets, like zines, celebrate the singular.

One pamphlet, "A Pretty Girl's Companion and Guide to Loves [*sic*] Sweetest Delights" (illus. 33), exemplifies the ways that pamphlets allowed for individual free expression.[45] In this homemade object, the

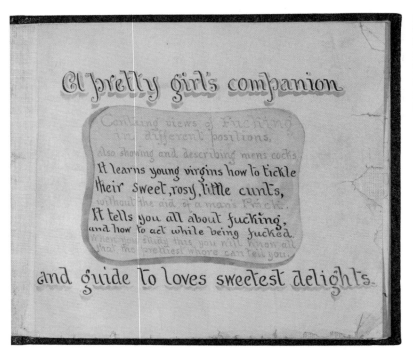

33 "A Pretty Girl's
Companion and
Guide to Loves
[*sic*] Sweetest
Delights," cover,
n.d. [1900–1910?],
manuscript, Kinsey
Institute.

author resisted sexual propriety and instead developed a sexual idiom to describe every interaction. The pamphlet demonstrates how the author saw his world as rife with an erotic subtext deserving of detailed explication. "A Pretty Girl's Companion" appears to have been written at the end of the nineteenth century. Though the pamphlet was neither published nor dated, its illustrations featured the waistcoats, striped stockings, spectacles, and facial hair popular at that time. Further, an embedded reference to Kahn's Museum, at the corner of Broadway and Waverly Place, dates it to after 1874.[46]

The pamphlet offers every evidence of careful and loving creation. The writer ruled the paper by hand. The writer then wrote, inked, and colored each of the 28 pages. The back-slanted block letters on the cover suggest that the script might not have been second nature to the writer; instead, the lettering shows the author's desire to embellish his creation. Each illustration was penciled, inked, and then colored. The writer of the pamphlet gave a great deal of thought to how to illustrate the booklet: drawings illustrate sexual activities by showing all the actors and actions simultaneously. The approach created problems with perspective, scale, and chronology. In one example, titled "Sucking his sweetheart's cunt" (illus. 34), the writer has tried to illustrate cunnilingus, but the attempt to capture the act in its entirety has distorted the visualization of a "man and girl" (to use the writer's terminology).[47] The illustrator drew the girl on her stomach with her rump in the air while the man reclines beside her. The man looks over his shoulder to consider her labia. The awkwardness of the pose is compounded by problems in scale. Her behind stands as high as his head, her torso appears twice as long as his, and his legs seems dwarfishly short and fat. The coloration of the flesh tones is a sickly pinkish-brown.

All of these attributes together suggest a self-taught artist rather than any formal training. Nonetheless, as an illustration of cunnilingus, the image emphasizes what the author thought mattered: the woman's

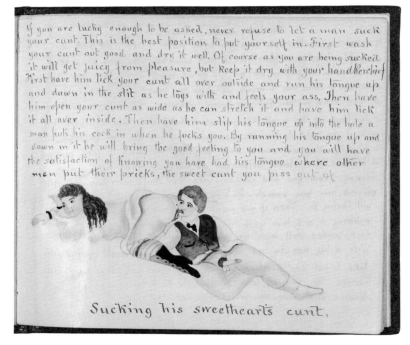

34 "A Pretty Girl's Companion and Guide to Loves [*sic*] Sweetest Delights," p. 13, entitled "Sucking his sweetheart's cunt," Kinsey Institute.

labia, the tongue that connected with it, the woman's dangling breasts, and the man's erect penis. Head and labia are on the same plane and the sexual organs are fully exposed to view. The distortions in anatomy and perspective illustrate the writer's ideas about sex, rather than obscuring them. The mechanics of the booklet thus suggest that this work came from a dedicated amateur who spent hours contemplating and then executing the panels.

The pamphlet details a cookbook of sexual desires that indicates an expansive sense of sexuality, including how to "back-skuttle" in a rush, "fucking a boy in the ass-hole" (illus. 35) "jerking off," cunnilingus, bestiality, the "safe" periods for intercourse (recommending this to be fifteen days after a girl's "flowers"), how to make a candle into a dildo, the history of the author's penis, various angle drawings of the penis, information of how to make a penis hard, and descriptions of various venereal diseases of the penis. The pamphlet resolutely sexualizes the world; homemade gravy becomes an aid to training a lap dog, and a pretty girl's brother becomes the inevitable object of male advances. The range of sexual pleasures undercuts any ideas of a pinched or sanctimonious sense of sexual opportunities. The writer details how he fellated men as a youth and the ways that he enjoys giving oral pleasure to both men and women. Sexuality pervades his life and colors everything in the pamphlet. Everyone—male, female, canine—becomes a possible sexual partner.

Supposedly written as an educational guidebook for girls, the pamphlet loses track of its purpose and descends into an "everyman's guide" to forbidden knowledge. It begins with a clear imaginary reader, the young girl of its title. The implied reader receives direct advice from the writer. By giving directions, the writer explains how "you," meaning the "young girl," can maximize pleasure: "you throw your legs over his shoulders . . . you can reach down."[48] By the fourth page, however, the pamphlet loses track of who the reader is supposed to be, and the latter shifts from a young girl to an implied male reader.

The pamphlet gives advice on how to seduce boys: "show any boy a few pictures and as you feel his cock you get him so hot he will suck

35 "A Pretty Girl's Companion and Guide to Loves [*sic*] Sweetest Delights," p. 4, entitled "Fucking a boy in the ass-hole," Kinsey Institute.

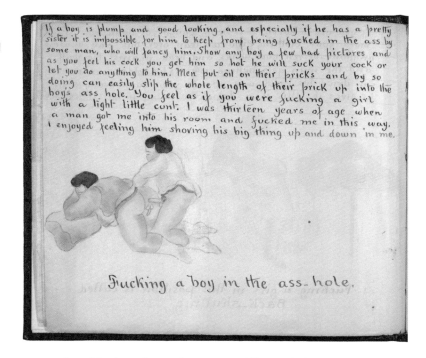

If a boy is plump and good looking, and especially if he has a pretty sister it is impossible for him to keep from being fucked in the ass by some man, who will fancy him. Show any boy a few bad pictures and as you feel his cock you get him so hot he will suck your cock or let you do anything to him. Men put oil on their pricks and by so doing can easily slip the whole length of their prick up into the boys ass hole. You feel as if you were fucking a girl with a light little cunt. I was thirteen years of age when a man got me into his room and fucked me in this way. I enjoyed feeling him shoving his big thing up and down in me.

Fucking a boy in the ass-hole.

your cock and let him do anything to you."[49] The shift in implied reader suggests how the author sees himself. In some places he wants to use his supposed experience and knowledge as a platform for teaching girls how to see, understand, and treat men; in these moments, he puts himself in the position of sexual tutor engaged in a mutually beneficial relationship in which he exchanges wise counsel for the pleasures of sexual pedagogy. In other places, he is a man among men, exchanging knowledge and information about various sorts of acts and positions and he writes as an authority on matters of sexual health, illness, pleasure, and opportunity. Indeed, the author might never have cut a dildo from a candle and almost certainly didn't experience the pleasures of having both a "cock" and "cunt," which he describes in the first person. Nonetheless, the writing of this pamphlet demonstrates how much he wanted to imagine lecturing those around him, both male and female, on the truth of sexual opportunities. The writer positions himself as the sage who provides free access to sexual knowledge.

While this pamphlet shows a certain familiarity with the world of commercialized sexuality, it seems as if the writer developed much of his material from his own imaginings. From the amateurish quality of the drawings to his directions for making dildos from candles (whereas published materials hailed leather and rubber goods as the materials of choice),[50] this pamphlet illustrated this particular writer's conception and vision of sexuality. An amateur effort, the pamphlet demonstrated a vernacular, rather than a commercial, vision of sex. The desire for sexual variation (oral sex, anal sex, vaginal sex), an expansive sexual culture (men, women, dogs), and the circulation of information (how-tos, information about disease and conception) illustrates the man's vision of a sexual good life. This pamphlet demonstrates the writer's breadth of desires, rather than just wanting straight sex. The writer, who clearly lacked the technical skills to create professional-standard art or literature, created his own pornography and used it to articulate his own sexual stories. The author throws himself into the breach by articulating what he saw as missing from a sexually fulfilling life; a longing for articulation colors every page of the pamphlet. In the absence of commercial pornography and information, the writer willed this pamphlet into existence. Even more, however, the pamphlet reads like the articulation of a vernacular sexual tradition that envisioned a vibrant sexual world antagonistic to propriety and at war with all tenets of social control. It waged a one-man war against a society that emphasized self-control and moderation.

This single pamphlet joins thousands of later hand-typed and handwritten pamphlets, suggesting that the pleasure of making DIY pornography became popular among many. The BEM collection, named after the initials of the anonymous donor, was donated to the Kinsey Institute when it was still called the Institute for Sex Research (ISR) during the 1960s.[51] This particular collection specializes in handmade pamphlets of American and British origin, although some documents were typed on New Zealand military and intelligence stationery. The diversity of the materials' origins shows the wide circulation of documents across borders and boundaries, while the thousand such pamphlets the collection comprises suggests that the desire to author materials about sexuality was widespread. Further, the existence of the BEM as a single large collection implies that the acquisition and curation of materials had its own appeal.

Handwritten and hand-typed, the materials in the BEM collection run from the single page of much edited poetry in which the author worked out the meaning and rhythm of erotic verse, to carbon-copied stories dozens of pages long that might have been produced on commission (illus. 36). The collection has been divided by bindings and themes into series like the Black Binding Series, the Red Binding Series, the Beige Humiliation Series, and the Wallpaper Series. As with the broader corpus of British pornography, a large proportion of the pamphlets focus on torture and humiliation. Some of these materials suggest that homemade and handmade objects augmented mechanically produced ones rather than replaced them. One file of miscellaneous bawdy poetry, for example, includes a typed version of "'The Enchantment' by Lord Byron" on three A4 carbon-copied pages, held together by a straight pin, as well as a two-page excerpt of Robert Burns's "The Merry Muses of Caledonia, 1768."[52] These documents attest less to a gap in published works and more to the technological limitations of replication. Before the age of xeroxing and scanning, rarity demanded the hand-typing of such books. The line between production and duplication in those cases was narrow indeed.

Other writers produced stories typed onto carbon paper that ran to dozens or even hundreds of pages.[53] Stories included plots driven by the desire to sexually humiliate and dominate women, bestiality, rape and torture, and even sexual murder.[54] The relative slickness of these productions showed itself in the very fine typing skills and the ability of the writer to sustain a single plot over an extended piece. An examination of pamphlets, like coins, shows the ways that people saw sexuality around them.[55] They transformed scraps of paper into complete sexual stories and envisioned a world replete with opportunities for sexual stimulation. Few were immune from sexualization in these stories; the sexual gaze was turned on country girls, honeymooners, international drug dealers, secretaries, bosses, executives, old men, young men, servants, the rich,

So Susan's scene achieved results
Finding her birch quelled all revolts
~~For Pops John upon their knees~~
With birch et as sceptre, lolled at ease
As ~~White~~ Pop & John ~~wept~~ squirmed ~~one~~ on their knees
So ~~was~~ quickly now they're reunited
With Mother really quite excited
~~Then every~~ To ~~be~~ each Sunday after church
Pops & John meet Susan's birch
And if Pop nags ~~and~~ stamps & rants
There's no excuse, down come their pants
Should brother John speak out of turn
~~And~~ She'll Susan's birch his butt will burn
For all bored on he flung out the door
And none can think how they before
Could bicker squabble or be bored
While Within a young sister so assured
For secretly Pa's rather proud
~~That~~ Scarlet weals his butt's endured
And Brother John's ~~stand~~ quite at ease
To be by Susan's ~~That~~ he should ~~he by~~ birch enlaced
~~For~~ female Susan's birch
~~When by her birth~~
Mama's amused if ~~her~~ they moan
As if to use her to sleep will ~~pursue~~ mind falls
While Susan's ~~tanned~~ ~~glad~~ ~~tormented~~ fills
Who no take ~~both~~ pleasure when she will
~~Will~~ subtler ~~joy~~ ~~joy~~ her ~~self~~ then fills
That she fly within but less pleasure
With really ~~glad~~ entrancing thrills
~~Whatever~~ And not exciting ~~inspiration~~
~~of each~~ ~~forthcoming~~ ~~Flagellation~~ ~~anticipation~~
At contemplating Flagellation
Of each forthcoming

And in the week she pleased laughs
to see
If either should be late for tea

While Susan smiles ~~in~~ as mind fills
With pleasantly ~~really~~ thrills
Delighted that the anticipation
~~& joyly~~ they in anticipation
~~of each~~ forthcoming Flagellation

? Of planning in contemplation
the next ~~package~~ their flagellation

36 Miscellaneous
Poetry Series,
n.d., BEM Erotic
Manuscript
Collection, Kinsey
Institute.

and the poor. Further, sexual desire meant more than a simple desire for coitus. Rather, these pamphlets detailed the gamut of sexual desires, from sexual tomfoolery to mutual pleasure to sexual coercion and violence. The vernacular tradition acknowledged a wide range of impulses and an even wider range of sexual acts.

Whereas etching and stamping coins entailed metalworking skills and equipment, the creation of pornographic pamphlets demanded little more than a fervent imagination. A few sheets of paper and a couple of crayons were all it took to create a homemade, hand-illustrated pamphlet. The typewriter (and carbon paper that accompanied it) made the production of pamphlets faster still as the expansion of office skills eased people's ability to detail their desires. While some writers referred to published pornography and racy literature, others showed little awareness of mechanically produced materials. Paper goods offer an even wider idea of vernacular sexual culture because of the very limited set of skills necessary to make them.

The continued production of pamphlets and other forms of handmade and homemade objects well into the twentieth century suggests a longing that ran outside and alongside the growth of the commercial "porn industry." Even during the years that saw the expansion of commercial products, first with pulp magazines and then with blue movies, people created their own pornographic materials. Rather than merely consuming culture, some people responded to the growth of consumer culture by creating their own, building an assemblage out of the various mediums and idioms and creating their own narratives of sexuality. Individuals illustrated, ornamented, stitched, and glued together materials; they combined colloquial expressions and local knowledge about bodies, fertility, pleasures, and disease with existing frameworks like "how-to stories" or "office romances." Homemade and handmade pamphlets and other pornographic objects let people pitch their voices into the din. The hand work in the hand-typed, hand-lettered, and hand-drawn pamphlets shows the care given to both the physical form of the object and the ideas that the form embodied. Whether callow or skilled, individuals gave care to storytelling. Person after person wrote, illustrated, and explained that their ideas mattered and that they were agents of their own desires. In their insistence on individuality and the irreducibility of desires, hand-made and homemade objects evinced a radical nonconformity. That radicalism might look inchoate compared with the formal radicalism of Enlightenment pornographers and their contributions to anti-clerical and anti-monarchical agitation, but handmade and homemade pornography existed as a sort of democratic sexual expression that refused quiescence. Rather than relying upon commercial interests to generate sexual narratives or fitting in their own desires to preexisting stories, individuals plotted out their own tales of sexual desire.

When joined with other pornographic artifacts like scrimshaw, carvings, and coins, pornographic pamphlets suggest that the impulse toward making pornography embraced whatever medium was available. Each etched and stamped coin, each illustration, each handwritten story, each hand-lettered and hand-drawn pamphlet demonstrate individuals investing themselves into the articulation of sexual energy. People who would never have had the chance to create high art or publish fine litera-ture created their own pornography and used it to articulate their own sexuality. What these documents suggest, besides people's ingenuity, is the void that people filled through these articulations. Commercial cul-ture did not satisfy people's needs, and people fulfilled their own needs in surprisingly painstaking ways.

The consideration of early American homemade and handmade materials allows us to expand our understanding of sexuality, particularly the vernacular sexual tradition. Whereas Helen Lefkowitz Horowitz sees the early American sexual vernacular expressed in *Aristotle's Masterpiece,* that volume was but one of the European publications imported to the United States.[56] While the ideas of humoral medicine in that volume might have seeped into the local idiom, the materials considered in this chapter offer more compelling examples of sexual vernacular expression. This vernacular culture, though it ran alongside manufactured materials, did not rely on networks of circulation, or on the availability of texts to communicate. Instead, the materials that people produced speak to their own individuated sense of sexuality and means of expression.

The addition of homemade and handmade objects to the historical record allows us to understand the history of pornography more completely by expanding the range of artifacts to consider. Their inclusion challenges the dominant narrative about the growth of an industrialized and commercialized sexuality. Alongside the growth of the commercial market ran a tradition of homemade artifacts. Commercialization neither won nor lost; in fact, it was not a marketplace battle at all. As the exploration of handmade objects dislocates the narrative of consumerist sexuality, so too it relocates the site of sexual articulation. From where did pornography emerge? Commercial pornography emerged from commercial centers like London, Paris, Amsterdam, New York, and Boston; noncommercial pornography seems to have been more rural in origin or, in the case of scrimshaw objects, emerges from the high seas. Pornography from logging camps, from whaling vessels, and from rural communities shifts the site of erotic longings from the parlor to the barnyard and the kitchen. If commercial pornography spoke of cosmopolitan pleasures, vernacular pornography spoke of other sorts of sexual pleasures—a good joke, an easy feel, an erotic sight, or a quick poke. These objects show that people saw the world around them as highly sexualized and conceived of a sexuality both rampant and creative. These materials also indicate the worldviews of their creators, showing how they thought about the world of sex: people wrote about fucking boys and sucking off men as one of any number of available pleasures. They drew female bodies as lush and distorted and men's bodies as awkward and erect. They saw gazing at a woman's form as pleasurable; they saw rape and coercion as pleasurable; they saw a woman on a chamber pot as pleasurable; they saw crudely made memento mori as pleasurable; they saw biblical passages as pleasurable; and they saw finely carved artifacts as pleasurable.

If handmade and homemade pornography documents what people wanted to imagine, then nineteenth-century people wanted to think about a sexuality firmly embedded in daily life. Rather than looking for sex with partner after partner in the dizzying progression that often appeared in commercially produced pornography of the nineteenth century, these objects looked carefully at individual sexual acts and sexual actors in everyday places. In that, these objects tell us something important about sexuality in nineteenth-century America that might otherwise be too easy to overlook. Nineteenth-century homemade and handmade materials offer very pointed examples of sexualities unrestrained and slyly laughing at the slickness and cosmopolitanism available in other venues.

2

Adapting Commercial Culture into Handmade Objects, 1910s–1970s

On the Alta-Glamour website, an online store selling historic erotica and pornography, the proprietor, Ivan Stormgart, has documented someone's strange obsessions. Stormgart has created a gallery called "Sex Doll Polaroids."[1] This gallery features scans of a few dozen faded Polaroid photographs with altered dolls posed in sexual simulations (illus. 37, 38). GI Joes, Kens, Barbies, Skippers, and other plastic figures made for child's play have been given tiny penises, pubic hair, and erect nipples. The figures have been arranged to simulate oral sex, anal sex, penile–vaginal sex and so on and then photographed in tableaux. Stormgart bought the Polaroids, scanned them, and then resold the original collection. When looking at the images online, viewers see a digital replication of the Polaroid replication of the plasticized replication of flesh. In the place of bodies or sex acts, the website provides an after-image of sexual deviancy left on the server of an online retailer. What could be more transitory? And how did we get here from the materiality of scrimshaw, pamphlets, coins, and the like?

The French theorist Jean Baudrillard would have considered the online gallery a simulacrum.[2] A simulacrum is a copy with no original. As modern economies move into the phase of late capitalism, according to Baudrillard, representations no longer point to reality at all; instead, they gesture toward copies, or copies of copies. This occurs as part of a movement toward consumer saturation where hyperreality offers more pleasures than the banal truth of the world. People pick and choose the significations that they enjoy like reflections in a carnival of mirrors. Instead of committing to strategic rebellion or revolutionary change, people are swayed through an ecstatic communication with simulacra.

This chapter excavates the emerging simulacra of sex and locates a critical period in its development in the middle decades of the twentieth century, when the proliferation of ephemera and consumer culture allowed them to become the raw matter for new sexual ideas. By the early twentieth century what used to be rare had become plentiful enough to transform people's obsessions. Using altered magazines and newspapers and then turning toward the artwork of Henry Darger as a case study, this chapter shows how people used consumer products to create their own handmade and homemade sexual artifacts. By considering how people reworked magazines, newspapers, photographs, and other ephemera, this chapter suggests that consumer culture generated sexual fantasies and then became the raw matter for the expression of those fantasies, allowing for uncomfortable assertions of selfhood in a

37 "Sex Doll Polaroids," 1970s, image 1. Collection of Brian Emrich.

38 "Sex Doll Polaroids," 1970s, image 2. Collection of Brian Emrich.

culture that made no room for such desires. People took ideas—including those that supposedly remained outside the realm of the erotic—and recast them, allowing the expression of desires that could not be articulated in other ways. This simulacra of sex let people shadow-box with an ecstasy that might otherwise elude them. A simulacrum might be a poor substitute for deep social change or other forms of transformation according to Baudrillard and other philosophers, but for many who made pornography by hand at home, a poor substitute might well be better than nothing at all.

Between 1870 and 1900, as the population of the u.s. doubled, the number of daily newspapers quadrupled and the number of copies sold increased sixfold.[3] The number of magazines also rose geometrically, helped by the passage of cheap postage rates for shipping.[4] Wood pulp paper, experimented with in the 1860s and widely adopted in the 1880s, and linotype printing, first devised in the 1880s and rapidly adopted in the same decade, made any number of cultural changes possible, from the growth of newspaper circulation, to the advent of cheap books, the proliferation of magazines, and even the outpouring of children's fiction.[5] The adoption of photoengraving, though developed in the 1860s, was not adopted by newspapers until 1897, at which point photography became incorporated into mass media. Although the number of newspapers peaked between 1900 and 1914, advertising revenues, numbers of readers, and the number of towns that could support a newspaper continued to climb between 1910 and 1930.[6] By then, new media technologies allowed American cities and towns to become awash in print. Newspapers ranged from regional weeklies to national dailies, from local to foreign-language papers; books were divided into highbrow, middlebrow, and lowbrow categories and within that into fine editions and paperbacks, subdivided again by age, gender, and genre; finally, magazines were lumped into "pulps" and "slicks." Pulps were 7 by 10 inches (18 × 25 cm), with untrimmed edges, covers printed with coal-dye images and a rough surface on a lower-grade paper. Slicks were printed on higher-grade paper with a shinier finish that better facilitated the printing of images. R. D. Mullein states that general magazines or slicks were priced at about 35 cents a copy and had about 175,000 subscribers.[7] Pulps crowded newsstands during their heyday in the 1920s, '30s, and '40s.[8]

In this rising floodplain of print culture, commercial pornography formed but a small tributary. Photographs produced as pornography were created, reproduced, circulated, and sold as a separate genre of materials.

Likewise, pornographic magazines, Tijuana bibles or handmade comic books, novels, "readers" (short books that excerpted longer novels), and films had developed but existed in relatively small numbers. Vendors used mail order to ship materials to customers nationally and internationally; books and ephemera were printed in the U.S. and smuggled in from abroad. Bookstores sold erotic and pornographic materials from storefronts in New York and other major cities.[9] While commercial forms of pornography began to proliferate, the expense and awkwardness of obtaining materials limited the effect of pornography, at least as compared to the saturation of other forms of visual media.

More common forms of print culture fed the minds of the masses, filling them with advertisements, fashions, adverts for films, stories, and tales of romance, adventure, and intrigue. These materials structured characters, narratives, plots, sensibilities, and desires for people to use and reuse as part of how they scripted themselves. The industrialization of consumer culture also allowed new behaviors to emerge, like compulsive hoarding. In older models of hoarding, the miser hoarded wealth.[10] In newer versions, hoarders accumulated material culture, which seemed to have no limits in the scale of its production. In 1947 the deaths of Homer and Langley Collyer helped birth a new pathology. Rumors about the brothers before their deaths emphasized the untold riches stored in their Harlem mansion, but when the police investigated after Homer's collapse, they found rubbish. It took days for them to find Homer's brother, Langley, who had been crushed by piles of refuse just a few feet away. The excavation of the mansion after their death transformed the fabled riches into canyons of trash as the police found over 100 tons of materials in the mansion, which was eventually razed because it had become structurally unsound. The idea of hoarding old newspapers, posters, and other ephemeral objects was predicated upon the endless production of objects. Consumer culture seemed to bring with it its own obsessions.

The vast flood of material culture also allowed for the articulation of sexual narratives. As more ephemera and material culture circulated, people came into contact with more objects that sparked desires. People responded to print culture by reusing ideas that they encountered in print as the basis for their own stories of self. They also altered images to express a sexuality that they saw hidden in material culture. In other words, people made their own sexual stories out of commercial foundations.

The ways in which people altered the images that circulated demonstrates how that visual culture worked as fodder for sexual fantasies. The widespread circulation of photographs and magazine images allowed these images to reach the populace in mass numbers and create coherent and recognizable ideas of sexuality. To consider the impact of consumer culture on sex, this chapter makes use of altered photographs, magazines, and newspaper articles, salvaged materials, and erotic art based on such objects from the 1920s through the 1970s. Though newspapers, magazines, wrapping paper, coloring books, photographs, and so on proliferated, only a few archives and museums have saved the remnants of them. Some archives and libraries collect ephemera, and virtually no major institutions search out "defaced" materials. However, when Alfred Kinsey's fame skyrocketed with the publication of *Sexual Behavior in the Human Male* (1948) and its companion volume *Sexual Behavior in the Human Female* (1953), law enforcement agencies shipped objects to the Institute for Sex Research that would have otherwise been destroyed. As a result, the Kinsey Institute has boxes of "altered photographs," erotic versions of the eyeglasses and mustaches drawn on the pixilated newspaper photographs left in coffee shops and airports. Other small collections of altered ephemera pass through the hands of dealers and collectors like Ivan Stormgart and Jim Linderman. Finally, museums like Intuit: The Center for Intuitive and Outsider Art, Chicago, and the Museum of Sex, New York City, which is dedicated to serious exhibits on the subject of sexuality, have created exhibitions that acknowledge such artifacts.

Many of the images in the Kinsey Institute's Altered Photographs Collection come from gossip columns and human interest stories about stars and starlets that were printed in newspapers and magazines. Hollywood cultivated starlets as sexy, and people completed the sexualization through alterations: Hollywood dressed, individuals undressed.[11] Alterations of these images include the addition of genitalia and pubic hair to clothed figures, the switching of heads of well-known figures onto naked bodies, and the redrawing of bodies in erotic ways.[12] It comes as no surprise that the best-known Hollywood celebrities become eroticized in these alterations: Janet Leigh, Liz Taylor, Betty Grable, and Jane Russell appear in magazine photo shoots, retouched so that they appear naked. A much reprinted image of Betty Grable lifting a leg to take off a shoe allowed illustrators to draw Grable's pubic region beneath her skirts. A photograph of Virginia Mayo posed before a diving board becomes a canvas for envisioning her naked, though whoever altered the illustration had limited talents. The crude alterations tore the edges of the paper along her right hand. Though the person making the alterations took care to match the lines of the shoulder and leg, Mayo's real proportions and the drawn ones do not agree, drawing attention to the curve of the waistline and angle of the pelvis. Marilyn Monroe has been visually undressed in one image, and Janet Leigh limbering up at the barre has been rendered obscene. The June 25, 1951 cover of *Life* magazine, featuring Janet Leigh, was altered so that the image rendered the actress topless (illus. 39). The cover has been torn two-thirds down, just above the line of her strapless dress. The retoucher has erased the line of frilly and lace-covered fabric that formed the bodice of her dress and has penciled in the lines of her breasts. As a result, the actress stands nude except for a line of pearls and a hand to her breastbone.

Less well-known celebrities also receive erotic retouching. Ice Capades figure skater Donna Atwood's leap into the air has been modified so that her leap exposes her vulva and pubic hair to close inspection. In another version, Atwood is rendered nude except for her skates. The illustrator seems to have been incapable of visualizing how she leapt into the air and how her body contorted to allow for such acrobatic feats. The nude rendering of her right thigh, her pelvis, and breasts distorts her body. Clearly, this attempt to strip the body could not envision the lines that lay beneath the clothes. These retouched photographs and magazine prints demonstrate that individuals tried to imagine bodies beneath clothes, bodies in motion, and bodies performing before the camera.

LIFE

ANET LEIGH
A MARRIAGE
CAREER

Retouched and altered photographs and illustrations required few technical skills. Retouchers mostly erased the ink off the images and then drew over the area. The results were mixed. Most often, the process left the surface of the paper roughened and scarred, and any image drawn over the altered patch would not match the texture of the initial print. However, illustrators did more than add simple line drawings to signify sexual organs. Illustrators took time to carefully shade nipples and try to simulate individual pubic hairs. Retouchers tended to keep the pubic hair sparse and short, making the full shape of the vulva more visible. They tried to render transparent the sexual codes that Hollywood simultaneously revealed and concealed.

The idea that clothes conceal a hidden sexuality allowed one illustrator to queer illustrations in evocative ways. In a series of altered images, the artist rendered individuals naked, aroused, and resplendent. In one newspaper photograph, two boxers, Tony Zale and Rocky Graziano, roughhouse over the middleweight crown. According to the caption of the original newspaper article that ran alongside the image supplied by International Photo, "ROCKY'S GOT IT, Tony wants it! Here's a little pre-fight horseplay between Tony Zale (left), who'd like nothing better than to lift that middleweight crown, and Rocky Graziano, who has definite ideas about holding onto it in their Newark battle."[13] The boxers battled in 1946, 1947, and 1948 for the middleweight title and the final fight in Newark allowed Zale to recapture the crown.[14] In the redrawn version both men have capes and are festooned with pearl garlands that wind around their bodies and around their flaccid organs. The images are delicately tinted in pencil. The new meaning for the caption "Rocky's got it, Tony wants it" highlights a homoerotic subtext to male sports. The act of remaking the newspaper illustration, highlighting the genitals and intertwining garlands around the two boxers' bodies, transformed a run-of-the-mill photographic illustration into erotic art. This artist had no small degree of talent, and used it to detail a hidden erotic world.

The same artist used a "Norman Rockwell"-style magazine illustration to uncover a hidden sexuality in the articulation of Americana. This

39 Janet Leigh,
Altered Photographs,
Kinsey Institute.

By Anita
Rowe
Block

NYC. 48. W.TMS

40 "Norman
Rockwell"-style
magazine
illustration
(original),
n.d. Altered
Photographs,
Kinsey Institute.

full-page illustration (illus. 40) features an adolescent boy in a crook
of a tree, gesturing to an adolescent girl who sits in the grass a few feet
below. The redrawn version (illus. 41) shears off the girl's hair and
minimizes her curves so that she becomes an adolescent boy, complete
with an erect penis and exposed and vulnerable ears. The boy in the tree
is also rendered nude with an erect penis. It is simultaneously the same
picture and one completely altered, inserting queer desire into the

41 "Norman
Rockwell"-style
magazine illustration
(altered), n.d.
Altered Photographs,
Kinsey Institute.

homiest of images of small-town life, complete with picket fence and charming doggy companion.

Through the artist's alterations, bathing suit advertisements, sporting events, and marriage banns all became fodder for seeing the world poised, naked, masculine, desirous, and desirable. Naturally, the publicity still of Marilyn Monroe in her white dress from *The Seven Year Itch*, which has become the iconic image of her smoldering sexuality, received a remake.[15]

An alteration of that image in the Kinsey collection allows viewers to look under her dress and inside her panties. However, the Kinsey version gives Marilyn male genitals.[16] This altered Marilyn suggests that the illustrator saw the world as both profoundly erotic and phallic. The alterations also reveal that the illustrator saw the world in ways that commercially manufactured pornography did not. Through alteration, this illustrator used the popular press to express queer desires and transformed heterosexual images into those of hidden homosexual longing.

Whether individuals changed the biological sex in images or not, these altered images show people's attempts to visualize beneath the surface of the image to see the sexual bodies that lay beneath. One retoucher took a pin-up from an unnamed magazine and used a marker pen to highlight the model's lips, nipples, and pubic area (illus. 42). Such images demonstrate the ways that people saw sexuality lurking in their everyday ephemera—in the newspaper photographs and magazine articles that abounded. People read sexual cues in prints featuring movie stars or honeymooners. They connected the dots between the erotic and ubiquitous and sought to strip away the mantle of privacy and make sexuality fully visible. Though many of these reworked images had little artistry, their value comes not from skills as much as from the fact that they reveal the hidden ways people viewed their world.

One set of alterations shows the underlying tensions embedded in the growing body of representations. As Joanne Meyerowitz argues, the proliferation of sexualized representations of women was one of the "most significant developments" in the history of sexuality.[17] Images of scantily clad and semi-nude women proliferated in both slick men's magazines and the more pulpy cheesecakes—cheap productions that featured little more than photolithographs of woman. By one count, more than fifty slick men's magazines and another fifty-plus cheesecakes circulated in the late 1950s, not counting small pocket-size magazines

42 Pin-up (altered image), n.d. Courtesy of Jim Linderman.

43 Altered image, *Frolic: The Magazine of Entertainment*, XI/1 (October 1961), pp. 34–5. Courtesy of Jim Linderman.

or joke books that focused on sex.[18] The rate of production was so overwhelming that the Kinsey Institute collected only a single volume per year of each magazine, and even then could not keep up with the flood.

As women's bodies became ubiquitous in mass culture, according to Meyerowitz, commercial pornography began to experiment with sadism, masochism, and fetishism.[19] Though fetish literature had circulated earlier, throwing doubt onto the causal relationship between commercial pornography's turn toward kink posited by Meyerowitz, a BDSM (bondage, discipline, sadism, and masochism) aesthetic began to consolidate in the 1940s and '50s, best known through the illustrations in *Bizarre* magazine.[20] The visualization of BDSM made itself felt even in girlie magazines like *Frolic* that fitted into the cheesecake category and featured naked and semi-naked women. One individual took select images from an issue of the magazine and altered them. Though the pulp featured dozens of women suitable for repurposing, only a select few were remade by this artist. The first image seems merely to highlight the hidden sexuality of the models by coloring and then tasseling the bathing suit. However, subsequent remade images draw the models as bound, shackled, gagged, and chained (illus. 43, 44). The retoucher had clearly flipped through the magazine, picking out the specific women he wanted to enslave. One double-sided display called "A Brace of Bombshells" features four photo insets (illus. 45). Three women remain untouched, while one woman has had her image altered. For this retoucher, some women apparently must have called for modification, while others did not. This version of *Frolic* shows an underlying overlap between pin-up poses and bondage poses; women often posed with

44 Altered images,
Frolic, p. 18. Courtesy
Jim Linderman.

their arms crossed in front of them, on their hands and knees, with their necks elongated. With just a marker pen, the retoucher could add chains, shackles, manacles, and collars (illus. 46), transforming a widely available cheesecake magazine into the much harder to find BDSM publication.

Another set of such alterations to a 1954 issue of the magazine *Physique Pictorial* demonstrates the overlap between bodybuilding magazines and queer desires that has been well documented by Thomas Waugh. Waugh suggests that consuming images was one of the most important political activities for gay men in the 1950s.[21] Bodybuilder, physique, and nudist magazines provided a treasure trove of ideas and images and provided an "alibi" for looking at the physical form of other men. According to Waugh, more than a hundred physique magazines circulated during the 1950s and

'60s in America and Europe, mostly by mail order, allowing the formation of a furtive, perhaps even unconscious community.

Physique Pictorial premiered in 1951. Bob Mizer had been selling photographic images of men in erotic but legal poses since 1945 and even served a half-year prison sentence as a result.[22] He began to bundle these images into a magazine, which generated a subscription list within a year. Called "thinly veiled pornography" by a newspaper columnist, who attacked queer images despite the legal circulation of heterosexual pornographic magazines like *Playboy*, the outcry against the publication in Los Angeles led to the arrest and trial of Mizer in May 1954. While Mizer won his appeal in 1955, he subsequently stifled his visual exploration of male sexuality in an attempt to stay out of jail, as Whitney Strub explains, though the magazine became more overtly homophile after the prosecution.[23]

45 Altered image, *Frolic*, pp. 36–7. Courtesy of Jim Linderman.

An altered version of *Physique Pictorial* from fall 1954, published right in the middle of his obscenity trial, demonstrates how people saw the earlier pictorials from the magazine.[24] The original spread of images

from the magazine featured men in a variety of poses that highlighted youth, nudity, and physical display. These images showed men posed as ancient Greek statuary, boxers, nudists, and bodybuilders and provided alibis for gazing at the male form. Despite their supposed presentation in the name of art, health, or violent sports, readers saw the erotic implications of the male body and filled in the missing details to make the models into desiring subjects. The altered images show man after man stripped of clothes and sporting erections.

The cover of the magazine featured a male model, Gene Meyer, dressed in a bathing suit and standing in the sun against a rocky outcrop (illus. 47).[25] His bathing suit and raised leg obscure his genitals. Meyer looks outwards and smiles to something beyond the frame. The amateur retoucher has inexpertly erased his bathing suit and has then drawn in an impressive erection that stands above the model's bent leg. His erect penis has been highlighted to create the impression that sunlight is glistening off his oiled skin, in keeping with the original's nudist flavor.

46 Altered image, *Frolic*, p. 45. Courtesy of Jim Linderman.

Now, Kathy Lodge seems like a pretty square title, doesn't it? She says her pals call her "Sweetie," but she doesn't say whether or not she approves of the handle.

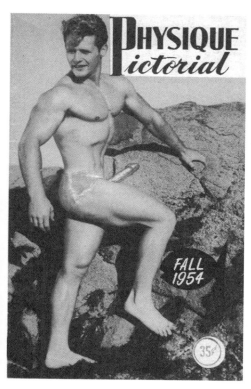

47 Altered image, *Physique Pictorial*, IV/3 (Fall 1954), cover. Courtesy of Alta-Glamour.

The redrawn erection points towards the model's hand in a geometric suggestion of desire. Transformed by the inclusion of an erect penis, Meyer's glance into the distance seems to invite the reader to join him.

Another set of images features a pair of men posing as Greek statues (illus. 48). In the original illustrations, the two men's genitals are hidden in a pouched G-string. The first man, Paul Lloyd, is seated on a draped dais while the second man, Peter Gordon, standing behind, bends his leg and holds his arms up with a slight arch to his back. The men look in slightly different directions and have no physical contact with each other. The altered illustration strips the "statuary" of its artistic roots by eschewing the G-strings and the matte finishes to the models' bodies and instead giving the men glistening erections. By drawing in erections, the retoucher created a relationship between the men; the two penises lean against Paul Lloyd's arm, and the angle of their organs cross even though their gazes do not.

In a second image, two models pose together without touching. The first man, Dale Curry, stands on the statuary base on a single leg while his three other bent limbs hint at motion. The second man, Louis Rightmire, kneels at the base and looks upward. Diffuse lighting and a plain backdrop put the focus in the picture on the arrangement of the two men and their dramatic postures. The retoucher gave both men impressive erections. The retouched figures change the meaning of the image; the kneeling Rightmire seems to gaze directly at the erection above him. Instead of worshiping at the base of masculine beauty, he seems to kneel staring at an erect penis, giving the image a drastically different inflection.

Another image features Jack Thomas and Jack LaLanne posing together in the sun. The photograph borrows from the German naturist magazine tradition, which celebrated health and fitness through displays of beauty and strength. Thousands of nudists in Germany believed that nude bathing and sun worship would wash away the stains of industrial capitalism, and individuals across Europe and America saw Germany as the center of the movement.[26] The photograph of Thomas and LaLanne in *Physique Pictorial* connects with the German visual tradition through the creation of a mirrored symmetry. The two men join hands and lean away from each other, flexing the muscles in their torsos and arms and creating a mirror image of each other. Bathed in sun and air, posed before nature, the two men are matched reflections of health. The retoucher transformed the implication of the image by refocusing attention not on symmetry or strength but on desire. He erased their G-strings and added

48 Altered images, *Physique Pictorial*. Courtesy of Alta-Glamour.

erect penises to their poses. With the addition of a matched set of erect penises, their clasped hands seem more erotically charged.

One by one, image after image, the magazine has been transformed. The retoucher drew an erotic subtext from the magazine and explicated it. Before retouching, the erotics of *Physique Pictorial* could be sublimated into the alibis of culture, health, fitness, and aggressive masculinity. Before the retouching, the images could speak to any number of readers who might know or might not know Bob Mizer, his obscenity trials, and the production context of the images. With retouching, the images evince a more singular way of seeing the world, one that names desire and defines it as explicitly sexual. The act of retouching turns the models into desiring subjects who, through their erections, are actively engaged in a sexual exchange.

In reinventing the meanings of the magazine, the retoucher articulated a homoerotic element in the photo spreads. In doing so he ignored other aspects of the magazine, including its fixation on youth. The magazine followed up the cover illustration of Gene Meyer with a series of earlier photographs that featured him at the ages of twelve, fourteen, sixteen, and eighteen respectively and advertised additional photos of the young Meyer, including a set of miniatures for 60 cents. The model Forrester Millard, aged sixteen, struck a ballet pose, while Frank Veitenheimer, aged fourteen, sold photographs of himself to pay for college, according to advertisements. The retoucher ignored the obvious fixation on youth and did nothing to highlight it in his erotic rearticulation. While texts supplied meanings, individuals remade them to fit their own desires.

Both in "one-offs" and in larger series, people demonstrated their erotic understanding of commercial culture. In many cases, people drew what commercial culture already pointed toward, highlighting the aspects they enjoyed and ignoring aspects that they either didn't see or didn't like. However, our understanding of the relationships between makers and materials remains limited given the anonymity of the artists and the separation of the materials from their context. In order to read such materials in the context of the larger culture, it helps to move the

consideration of individual cases of altered ephemera toward individuals
with a more developed source base and biography. The work and life of
Henry Darger, an outsider artist, can help illuminate the reuse of ephemera in articulating an obsessional fantasy world generated by materials.

Henry Darger (1892–1973), unknown as an artist during his lifetime,
became the hero of outsider art after the discovery of his oeuvre: tens
of thousands of pages of stories, illustrations, and works on paper. He
hoarded his art, keeping it all in his small Chicago apartment, where his
landlord discovered it sometime between Darger's transfer to a nursing
home and his death.[27] In the decades following this discovery, his work has
generated serious attention by critics and a cult following by the public.
The American Folk Art Museum, New York, transformed its reputation
through the acquisition of his artwork,[28] and the exhibition "The Art of
Henry Darger: The Unreality of Being" set the institution's attendance
records.[29] His works have been collected by the Museum of Modern Art,
the Art Institute of Chicago, the Smithsonian Institution, the Collection
de l'Art Brut in Lausanne, and others.

Darger used piles of discarded print media as the basis for his
illustrations. According to his landlord's widow, Darger "would walk
around the neighborhood picking through garbage—string, magazines,
newspapers, books, anything."[30] His personal library contained books by
Charles Dickens, the Oz series, articles on the Civil War, copies of *Life*, the
Saturday Evening Post, *National Geographic*, *Parents* magazine, and the
Ladies' Home Journal, as well as children's coloring books and ephemera.[31]
He made use of these materials for images and ideas. Without a world
of mass media to scavenge for ideas and images, he and others like him
could not have created their artwork.

Darger was an artist who bridged the gap between book arts and
visual art. Darger's stories include "The Story of the Vivian Girls, in
What is Known as the Realms of the Unreal, of the Glandeco-Angelinian
War Storm, Caused by the Child Slave Rebellion," a handwritten and
then typed 15,000-page manuscript; *Crazy House*, which continued the
story for another 10,000 pages; and *History of My Life*, a 4,000-page

autobiography and weather journal. He also created illustrations for his books, which ranged from small, simple pencil sketches to double-sided painted pages that ran to 10 feet (3 m) across. His most famous volume, known as the *Realms of the Unreal*, combined writing and illustration to tell the story of the Vivian Girls, who fight a war against child slavery. He used newspapers, comic books, coloring books, and magazines that he transformed through cropping, tracing, projection, painting, enlargement, coloring, and collage. Darger took the raw matter of cheap print and remade stock motifs to fit his internal landscape. *Realms of the Unreal* was filled with children captured by adult men who enslaved them and sometimes hanged them or eviscerated them in anger. The Vivian Girls, beautiful princesses, lead an army against these child enslavers. In *Realms of the Unreal*, girl children are often naked and drawn with male genitals.

The unsettling combination of girlish figures and flaccid male genitals, of child nudity and adult violence, has received a number of explanations. According to Mary Trent's trenchant summary of the historiography, Michael Bonesteel suggests that perhaps Darger remained unaware of female anatomy, that perhaps he wanted to give his child heroines male status, or that he gave them male genitals as a way of identifying with girl victims; Leisa Rundquist sees a Catholic iconographic element to Darger's art; John MacGregor reads Darger's art as a result of childhood trauma and as a displacement of his own vulnerability onto children, while Trent herself sees the motif of child sexuality as emerging from the historic figure of the Romantic child who called up adult desire so that it could be punished in the larger culture.[32] These scholars see a disturbing eroticism in Darger's work, but one that makes his art visually and narratively compelling. Galleries have also seen the disturbing aspects of Darger's storytelling as central to its energy. The Kevin Kavanagh Gallery in Dublin featured Darger's illustrations in a show on the subject of narrative and suggested that "The desire for narrative, and the resolution it can bring, is often a hangover from childhood. But while the works in this group show . . . are concerned with storytelling, they offer no comfort blanket."[33]

Darger was born in 1892 in Chicago to a German-born father. His mother, Rosa Fullman Darger, came from Wisconsin. Darger grew up as part of the urban poor at the turn of the century and suffered the sort of treatment that rallied progressives to the call of reform. His mother died of childbed fever when he was four, and his newborn sister was adopted out of his family before Darger met her. Darger lived alone with his father, an impoverished tailor who suffered from ill health. Darger went to a local Catholic school but had a hard time fitting into the classroom or playground. He was smart enough to skip two grades but suffered from social problems with teachers and students. It is unclear whether he bullied or was bullied by other children, or both, but Jim Elledge's biography suggests that his early relations with other children had a lasting effect.[34] He reputedly fought with other children, throwing sand in the eyes of one girl and trying to slash another girl with a knife.[35] Another student who tried to befriend him appeared later in his fiction as an arch-villain, General John Manley.

When his father could no longer care for him because of ill health and destitution, Darger was institutionalized, first at the Mission of Our Lady of Mercy, a Catholic charity, and then at the Illinois Asylum for Feeble-Minded Children, a children's institution attached to an adult, all-male prison. In 1907 Darger's father died in a Catholic nursing home for the poor, leaving him an orphan. After a series of escapes, he made his way back to Chicago, where he began working as a janitor in Catholic services, a job that left him emotionally isolated. He was conscripted into the army during the First World War but was found unfit for service and sent home. His draft registration card described him as having "poor eyesight and mentality not normal."[36] In Chicago he returned to working at St. Joseph's Hospital, living in a single room at the Workingmen's House, a housing facility for St. Joseph's employees. When he quit his job, Darger was forced from his home and moved into a boarding house, where he made friends with the landlord and landlady, Emil and Minnie Anschutz. They sold the building in 1931 and Darger moved into another boarding house. When Nathan Lerner bought that boarding house in 1955, Darger came with it.

Darger had a single good friend as an adult, William (spelled by Darger as Whilliam) Schloeder, and the two men shared an imaginative world devoted to child-saving, including a secret organization that they named the Gemini (for "twins"). The two men made up rites and paraphernalia for the Gemini based upon Catholic religious services. Henry and William also enjoyed the pleasures of city living, taking trips to the amusement park. They also tried to adopt a child through Catholic organizations but were denied. In the 1930s Schloeder moved to Texas with his family, leaving Darger even more isolated. Darger wrote to Whillie, but Whillie's sister had to respond for him since he did not write in English.[37] After three years in Texas, Whillie died of Asian flu. Darger wrote, "since that happened, I am all alone."[38]

Darger's poverty, isolation, and ill health affected his daily life. He suffered from leg pain that his work as a janitor, bandage roller, and dishwasher made worse. He grew angry at nurses at work who bossed him around, but he had no recourse but further labors, even when he complained about the conditions and long hours. He accumulated little money, finding himself impoverished and alone in his old age. He lived on the second floor of an apartment building in the Lincoln Park neighborhood before that area's gentrification and revival. Though he went to Mass daily, he remained at odds with the Church on matters of doctrine and practice. Eventually, when he could no longer take care of himself, his landlord, Nathan Lerner, helped him move to the same institution where his father had died. When Lerner and David Bergland, a fellow tenant, sought to clear his two-room apartment after his death, they found it filled with trash and ephemera.[39] The rooms had a pathway to the table, but were otherwise knee-deep in trash. Bundles of magazines and newspapers rose along the walls. Collections of Pepto-Bismol bottles, rubber bands, and balls of twine covered the surfaces. Beneath the hoard were Henry's books, journals, ledgers, and illustrations.[40]

Darger began the chronicle of the *Realms of the Unreal* in the 1910s, and then added to the account for an additional sixty years.[41] In *Realms of the Unreal*, Darger created an alternate universe with continents, oceans, weather patterns, nations, leaders, armies, flags, villains, animals, mythic creatures, heroines, and heroes, including alter egos for himself and the people he met. The central story of *Realms of the Unreal* concerns the Satan-worshiping nation of Glandelinia, which has allowed child slavery in the area of Calverinia. The nations of Abbieannia and Angelinia fight Glandelinia to end this slavery. Darger built his idea of the war and its participants from his readings about the Civil War. As he detailed his imaginary world over six decades, the real world experienced the First World War, the Second World War, the onset of the Cold War, the Korean War, and the Vietnam War. The imaginary and the real touched tangentially as Darger incorporated images of actual wars, cut from magazines and newspapers, onto the battlefield of his imagination.[42] The language of contemporary war was also incorporated into his account as he remade the brutal world of the Second World War concentration and extermination camps into imaginary lands filled with sweet-faced child slaves.[43]

The arc of the war against Glandelinia is recounted in its entirety in the first few pages of *Realms of the Unreal*. After explaining the trajectory of the war, the remaining thousands of pages fill in the details of battles, backstories, weather, intrigues, and other smaller parts of the larger war. The structure of the story, with the full narrative arc self-consciously explained at the beginning of the book, suggests that Darger's impetus for storytelling came not from narrative development or narrative closure, but from backfilling the parts of the grand battle. Knowing how it ended allowed Darger to detail the construction of imaginary events.

Darger wrote and illustrated apparently for the pleasure of creation alone, rather than as part of some system of communication. There is no evidence that he tried to show his art or stories to others during his lifetime. Instead, he kept his ever-increasing number of artifacts in the same room for decades, making his space tighter over time. Rather than the process of communication expanding his world by connecting him with others, his art diminished his space and took the place of emotional or intellectual exchange.

Darger's illustrations sometimes feature adult men, often uniformed, among the repurposed angel-faced girls cut and traced from paper-doll collections, coloring books, advertisements, and newspaper stories.[44] The contrast between the naked children and dressed men emphasizes the erotics of nudity (illus. 49). Nostalgia clings to the form of the girls, transmitted in their bobbed hair, bobbysocks, and simple Mary Jane shoes, and in their persons, with dimpled knees and cherubic arms. Darger removed clothes from the figures, making the paper-doll girls into nude figures to be dressed or undressed as the imaginary scenes demanded.

Though boys and men appeared in some scenes, the vast majority of the subjects were girls. The dressing and undressing of the girls had extraordinary significance for Darger; he saw their nudity as an aspect

49 Henry Darger, "At Jennie Richee are rescued by Evans and his soldiers," n.d.

of slavery in some places and as a step toward magical transformation in others. Darger explained the slaves' nudity: "we may say as a rule the girls all wore short bobbed hair and the boys' hair was clipped short. Not one little girl was seen to wear her hair long, in braids, pigtails, or curls. The majority of the children were compelled to go half-naked and those who were dressed were made to wear rags, and were made to go barefoot in the summer and winter, as they were never allowed to wear shoes."[45]

In one image (illus. 50), girls have been stripped and tied down while the men remain clothed and free. At the center of the page, two men dressed in buff and blue, their rifles beside them, tie a naked young girl to a stone. The partial figure of a soldier in Civil War uniform at the side of the page continues the scene beyond the edges of the frame. Who knows how many more soldiers tie girls to tombstones around them? The girls' male genitals face square to the viewer. The horror of the scene emerges slowly. What at first glance seems like an array of girls set into an idyllic landscape of palm trees, rolling hills, and puffy clouds consolidates into one of girls stripped, tied down, and enslaved by the armed and still uniformed men. The girls lie open, immobile, and vulnerable. They seem paused in an unfolding scene of violence.

The hair and figures of the girls grew increasingly outdated as Darger grew older, the ephemeral foundations of his art becoming more ante-dated. When his room was cleared in the 1970s he still had newspaper articles, coloring books, and paper-doll cutouts from the 1930s and earlier.[46] Darger left his works undated, but even without a date the uni-forms, often modeled after Civil War uniforms, situate the illustrations outside the contemporary realm, while the girls' fashions date them to somewhere between 1930 and fairyland. The interspersing of flowers and mushrooms as large as the children themselves and the idyllic green and blue backdrops, with birds, frogs, and butterflies, connects the children to a mythical landscape. Birds nest in trees and groves of trees shelter cool streams. Palm trees line lagoons. Simple houses dot the countryside, and fields and pastures, brimming with flowers, grasses, and animals, stretch into the distance.

And in these scenes are endless numbers of children. Children remain central to Darger's illustrations, whether romping in idyllic circumstances or tortured and enslaved. Darger self-consciously addressed his conflicted relationship to children in his autobiography: "You remember I wrote that I hated baby kids. So indeed I did. Yet what a change came in me, though, when I grew somewhat older. Then, babies were more to me than anything, more than the world. I would fondle them and love them. At that time, just any bigger boy or even grown up, who dared to molest or harm them in any way, was my enemy."[47] The idea of children loved and children hated allowed Darger to fixate on their physical beings. In the following passage, Darger details the ways that children are being tortured:

> children, all slaves, being tortured by flogging, suspensions, pouring boiling tar or water over their heads, suffocation, strangulation, amputation of their fingers, burning with hot irons, temporarily crucifying them, and, even for wicked purposes, making the children go through the very horror of the Passion Plays, but in reality, and almost killing the innocent ones with this blasphemous practice.[48]

The description of the many sorts of child torture focuses on ways to cause them pain. It is not merely a recognition of the pain of children; it is a lovingly detailed list of how pain can be caused. List-making allowed for the simultaneity of all sorts of child torture. The grammatical construction does not allow the reader to identify who is doing the torturing at the same time as it distances the reader from identifying with the children. There is no "I" in the passage; there are only children being tortured at a remove.

Darger would replicate the image of the child countless times in a single image, removing the individuality of figures in a mass of multiples. The multiplication of figures depended in part on the number of copies he first scavenged and then traced. After the Second World War, he began to make duplicates using photography and enlargement. When placed on the same page, the multiplied images of children transformed into a near-infinite number. Even the heroines of the war, the Vivian Girls,

50 Henry Darger, "Untitled (Many Girls Tied to Slabs of Stone)," n.d. Gift of the artist's estate in honor of Klaus Biesenbach, Museum of Modern Art.

remained multiples rather than individuals with discrete sensibilities and countenances. As described by one character in his book,

> They had soft fine golden hair which could curl up beautifully, or which they could wear in any fashion they chose; they had big blue eyes and long eyelashes, and the most darling little faces … They felt that everyone was their friend, and when anyone spoke to them, they would give the stranger one serious sweet look with their blue eyes, and then follow it with a lovely and most friendly kind of smile.[49]

Affections, reactions, sensibilities, all of which usually mark the individual, become multiplied into the mark of a mass character in this model. The Vivian sisters share a look, a hair style, a character.

Behind this multiplication of child visages remained a singularity often noted by critics. In 1911 Elsie Paroubek, a small girl, went missing in Chicago. Her disappearance caused a media outcry; after a hunt for the missing girl, the police found her body and concluded she had been murdered. Darger had cut out a photograph of Elsie Paroubek, but then lost the clipping from the newspaper. He suggested Elsie was really Annie Aronburg, a character in his writings, and that the disappearance of the print was tied to an even greater mystery. He considered the disappearance of this image as the "Aronburg Mystery" and in his introduction to the *Realms of the Unreal* he suggests that it was somehow tied to the Glandeco-Angelinian War. As he explains, "The Aronburg Mystery as well as the murder of the Aronburg child, had threatened the doom of the three Christian states, for the whole length of the great Glandeco-Angelinian war, and it was predicted that solving the Aronburg Mystery and revenge on her assassins was the only hope for any chance of the Christian nations winning the war."[50] The loss of the newspaper reprint of the photograph of Paroubek became written into the imaginary world, generating an uprising against child slavery and torture in Darger's account. The simulation generates its own imaginative battles.

The illustrations Darger created, though preoccupied with issues of slavery and the American Civil War, are remarkably devoid of the consideration of race in ways that bear thinking about. Darger illustrated a white world, one filled with white, and often blond, girls. The girls, whether dressed in folk costumes, shift dresses, or simple baby-doll dresses, have but the barest wash of color, except when they are choked, when Darger carefully discolored their tongues. The colors in their hair complement their clothes, if they wear clothes, and set off the whiteness of their skin. The men, too, are white, even the evil Glandelinians. His paper-white conceptualization of race was an ideation of desire rather than a reflection of the world around him. Doris Wilkinson has shown the sorts of racialized artifacts that were created and advertised during the period of Darger's productions. Though many of the toys, dolls, and surrounding advertisements were deeply racist, they provided a font of commercial materials that Darger might have pulled from. Generating an all-white world was an act of imagination rather than just a reflection of the material culture of the world around him.[51]

Darger lived in a Chicago that grew increasingly racially and ethnically diverse. Darger lived through some of the most racially turbulent times in Chicago history. The Chicago Race Riot of 1919 that left 537 people injured and 38 dead would have been impossible to overlook for someone so committed to collecting materials from the ephemeral press.[52] Though Darger remained shielded in some ways by his immersion in Catholic institutions and parish life, he was well aware of the ethnic diversity of Chicago. His landlady, Kiyoko Lerner, born in Tokyo, noted that the neighborhood was dotted with Italian and Mexican grocery stores.[53] Darger lived in a multi-ethnic community and this sensibility affected his vision of himself. Though of German descent, he said that the name Darger derived from Dargarius, which he identified as a Brazilian name.[54] He also changed his name on his army draft registration to "Henry Jose Dageris."[55] His fictive ethnic identity suggests that he saw himself as non-white in a Chicago that calibrated ethnicity with care.[56] In many ways, his ethnic identification as non-white suggests that he saw himself as part of the ethnically diverse community in which he lived. Rather than seeing beyond ethnicity or race, these issues preoccupied him. He carefully chronicled the ethnic world around him, noting the ethnicity of people as a meaningful way of organizing the world.[57] His descriptions of children in the neighborhood, for example, centered on their particular ethnic groups—"most kids were of Irish descent"—and he saw himself as ethnic too, writing: "I was of German descent, and I do not know why my father did not learn me the language."[58] However, his imaginary world became white in a way that his real world, even the reflection of himself in the world, did not. His creation of an all-white imaginary world that contrasted with the world around him, even contrasting with his own fictive ethnic makeup, shows how compelling he found the idealization of white childhood.

The insistence on whiteness becomes more pointed given that he made *Realms of the Unreal* into a battle over slavery. His slavery is of a particular time and place; he took the sensationalist literature about slavery of the American South and elaborated upon it. This slavery interlocked abuse and race. Darger acknowledged the source of his ideas even while he avoided the problems of a race-based slavery by whitening the cruelties of slave life. His possessions included *Uncle Tom's Cabin*, and he wrote characters from the novel into his own creation, as Klaus Biesenbach notes.[59] Thus the slavery in his art is another form of simulacra. He created a slave system from fictionalized accounts of historic slavery.

Darger's focus on tortured white children caught in the violence of slavery reflects a fixation on the spectacle of pain both in his art and in the broader culture. In one image, "At Norma Catherine" (illus. 51), even as a cyclone helps the girls escape, they are strangled, choked, and tossed around by the men, whose faces have been rendered as death masks. The girls' nakedness attests to their status as slaves. Their knock-knees and pouty bellies underline their youth and contrast with the hulking forms of the uniformed and armed men. The horror of the scene comes from the naked, vulnerable children caught in the death grips of their slavers.

Karen Halttunen notes that the genre of humanitarian literature that emerged in the late eighteenth and early nineteenth centuries focused on the spectacle of pain and encouraged the consideration of suffering to arouse a moral conscience. Sensational accounts focused on the cruelties of slavery, murder, and violence and demanded an imaginary reflection on the suffering of others. The impact of sensationalism grew ever more pronounced in nineteenth-century fiction as publications encouraged readers to act as witnesses against cruelty through their own reactions. Pornography at the time also grew enamored with violence and asked readers to witness pain as spectacle. The two forms of fictional identification overlapped. According to Halttunen, humanitarian literature's "treatment of scenarios of suffering, if not narrowly pornographic in

51 Henry Darger, "At Norma Catherine," 1940–50. Collection of the American Folk Art Museum.

nature, assumed that the spectacle of pain was a source of illicit excitement, prurience, and obscenity—the power to evoke revulsion and disgust."[60] Humanitarian literature eroticized pain just as pornographic literature eroticized the lash. Historically, the most popular sensationalist account of pain was *Uncle Tom's Cabin* (1852). In his *Psychopathia Sexualis* (1886), Richard von Krafft-Ebing noted that one of his patients' first feelings of sexual excitement came from reading that novel; "In reading *Uncle Tom's Cabin* (which I read at about the beginning of puberty) I had erections."[61] Sigmund Freud noted the same connection between reading the novel and arousal in his essay "A Child Is Being Beaten" (1919).[62] *Uncle Tom's Cabin* aroused pity and desire simultaneously. As Halttunen concludes, "The humanitarian sensibility fostered an imaginative cultural underground of the illicit and forbidden, accessible through the expanding cultural practice of solitary reading, at the center of which was a flogging scene."[63] Darger spent years engaged in the solitary practice of thinking about the torture of children. Even after he finished writing *Realms of the Unreal*, he kept creating illustrations for the book, new visualizations of the grand battle between pleasure and pain. The compulsion to generate visual imagery continued well after Darger achieved narrative exhaustion.

The erotics of slavery had been a popular motif in the nineteenth century and took a new racial turn at the end of the century. Writers and publishers of pornographic literature between the 1860s and 1890s explored the sexual impact of slavery in a variety of permutations, such as serialized fiction published in *The Pearl*, "The Secret History of Linda Brent, A Curious History of Slave Life," published in the pornographic magazine *The Cremorne*—both British publications that circulated throughout the Anglo-American world—and *The Memoirs of Madge Bufford; or, A Modern Fanny Hill*, a pornographic novel that might have been American, though it was published in Europe.[64] By the 1890s, slave pornography, which had begun to be played out as a cultural and commercial category, began to be revitalized through the incorporation of the white female slave, a rhetorical construction popularized among anti-prostitution activists. As Colette Colligan shows, fantasies around the flogged victim, "preserving elements from flagellation literature and slave narratives, now shifted their focus from the flogged black woman to the white woman."[65] The white slave woman literalized abuse found in older sensationalist fiction. In *The Memoirs of Dolly Morton*, for example, a novel set in the Antebellum South though published in France in 1899, a lynch mob strips and flogs Dolly for running an underground railroad. Novels like these played with the erotics of slavery by moving them outside of a historically specific racial system.

While the pornography of white slavery sold the ideas to a small commercial audience, the idea of white slavery had a much broader impact because of the ubiquity of the terms and the variety of media that used it. The language of "white slavery" gained international prominence when applied to prostitution to heighten tensions around race and sex for polemical purposes. The issue of the coerced sexual trafficking of white women took on various racial hues; in England, "white slavery" referred to British women trafficked to Continental European countries through Belgium; in New York it referred to white women trafficked in Chinatown,[66] or women engaging in interracial sex with African Americans.[67] The outcry against white slavery kept the issue culturally alive. In the U.S., Chicago and New York competed as the locus for "white slave panic."[68] According to Cecily Devereux, "Between 1885 and the 1920s, the United States produced what may be the biggest archive anywhere of white slave material, including, along with a proliferation of newspaper reports, tracts, pamphlets, and books comparable to those which were also being generated in Britain and throughout the Empire, a number of white slave films."[69] Concerns about the white slave condensed anxieties about race and gender and then advertised those anxieties in lurid terms. A series of diplomatic conferences held in the 1900s and 1910s to address prostitution and immorality made the links between sex/race anxieties and writing explicit. In 1912 the name of the international diplomatic venture had become the International Conference on Obscene Publications and the White Slave Trade.[70] Writing and sex came together from the world of ephemera and then was projected back onto the same platform. Thus the idea of "white slavery" as an erotic and troubling idea permeated the popular press just as Darger came of age. His fixation on the idea that white girls were captured for slavery reflected a rhetoric that had permeated the mass media, emphasizing race and making girls seem vulnerable to sexual slavery and abuse. Darger understood that vulnerability for women to some degree. He wrote in volume five of *Realms of the Unreal* that "girls were often bought from thieves and kidnappers at the age of four or five years, and after ten or fifteen years of service at hard toil, were either sold to factories of ill fame or forced into scout service against their will, and if surviving, to grown age, forced to marry persons who pay for the ill-gotten wives."[71] The idea of ill fame or forced marriage implies that the rhetoric of white slavery had permeated Darger's consciousness. However, he avoided illustrating adult women. While he knows that a particular form of sex slavery awaits his characters, the absence of grown women in his imaginary world leaves only young girls as counterparts to adult men.

Darger's focus on children reflected a broader cultural fixation.[72] Margot Hillel argues that the legacy of late nineteenth-century children's books created a dual idea of childhood as at once innocent and seductive: according to her, by the twentieth century, children's books allowed for a "contradictory construction of childhood in which the very innocence of children was open to sexual interpretation and in which innocence and an apparent experience were intertwined. The seductive attraction of Shirley Temple and others like her was echoed in a range of picture books."[73] Ellen Key and Marie Franzos declared the twentieth century as "The Century of the Child," and the period between the 1890s and 1930s saw the creation of children's rooms at libraries and children's books as a part of most major publishing houses.[74] The same industrial dynamism that affected other sorts of media affected the production of children's products. Children's literature, games, and toys became notable commercial products producing goods both for and about children: "The value of American toys and games rose from 8.29 million dollars in 1899 to 70.17 million in 1919 and to 103.65 million in 1929."[75]

As well as being the consumers of such materials, children were also consumed. A pornography focused on childhood became its own genre in the late nineteenth century, one that continued to circulate in the twentieth century.[76] Pornographic novels featuring childhood sexuality included *The Autobiography of a Flea* (first published in 1887 in London and reprinted in 1890, 1915, 1926, and 1930), *Sweet Seventeen* (1910, and still for sale in 1930), and *Flossie, a Venus of Fifteen* (first published in 1897 and then frequently reprinted). These books circulated for American and European consumers and they encouraged readers to see children as desiring subjects. These stories often displaced tensions from such socially problematic desires by bathing them in the glow of nostalgia and remembered pleasures. Their continuous republication only deepened that ruse.

Darger's fixation on children used both the expanding range of products geared toward children and the representations of childhood in the mass media. He repurposed materials targeted for children like coloring books to create his art, but he also used popular representations of children from other sorts of media. Children appeared in advertisements, news stories, and public interest accounts. Darger merely extended the pre-existing erotic tension in those mediums. As Hillel shows, "the very innocence of the child, often emphasized in illustration by large eyes, a finger in her mouth or against her lips, and with rather skimpy clothing, may also be interpreted as a kind of 'come-hither' sexual look, inviting the gaze of the viewer."[77] In Darger's case, he took that latent eroticism and exacerbated it. He removed the skimpy clothes, he contrasted the child's naked body with the adult male's clothed body, and he emphasized the mouths of young girls by coloring their open lips, mirroring the lipsticked mouth of an adult woman. These reworkings of girls allowed him to heighten the sexual impact of torture scenes.

The suggestiveness Darger saw in children showed itself even in his portrayals of battle scenes and child strangulation. In a double-sided illustration, "At Sunbeam Creek," backed by "At Wickey Sansia," Darger documents both (illus. 52, 53). At first glance, "At Sunbeam Creek" doesn't seem like a battle scene at all. The creek meanders through the bucolic landscape of fields and forests with charming yellow cottages set into the hills. In the foreground, fully dressed girls smile and wave as if they are gesturing to more of their number beyond the boundaries of the frame. Three adult men dressed in uniform interrupt the scene. Two point their bayoneted rifles at the girls, while the third slashes at a running girl with a sword. The expressions on the girls' faces seem blank, as if the attack had happened too fast for fear to register. The illustration seems as if it has been captured in the middle of the event, unclear in which direction it might unfold. The backed illustration provides a counterpart. "At Wickey Sansia" moves indoors, where the children have been stripped of their clothes. These girls seem younger, their expressions empty. Clustered together are half a dozen cherubic blondes. They dig with little beach shovels and do chores. Surrounding them is a massacre; problems in its proportion, placement, and perspective make it seem like it could be a mural painted on the walls. If so, the mural commemorates girls being strangled. The coloration of the girls' open mouths gives their pale forms a touch of color. One figure is clearly a young girl; Darger gave a slight distension to her belly and the short hair of a cherub. Two hands grasp her around the neck, though the arms are so disproportionately large that they begin beyond the top edge of the paper. The rounded eyes that show the whole pupil let Darger represent the girl's desperate danger. A fully dressed man strangles another girl, her arms rising up futilely as he stands relaxed. Two

52 Henry Darger, "At Sunbeam Creek," 1950–60. Collection of Robert A. Roth.

53 Henry Darger, "At Wickey Sansia," 1950–60. Collection of Robert A. Roth.

other men battle with girls. One man grabs and strikes a girl with a mace. He holds her effortlessly with a single arm that curls around her, spanning her chest. Men strangling naked girls demands some sort of narrative closure about the scene and the relationship between play and death, girls and men, bucolic scenes and torture rooms, but this remains unrealized.

Darger's process of reworking popular cultural images allowed him to strip female figures of their clothes like they were paper dolls. He carefully traced girls' figures and then worked from the tracings to find the lines of the body. In one large collage, more than five dozen girls have been rendered nude through the process of tracing and altering their forms.[78] Darger has roughed in belly buttons and nipples as well as the smallest suggestion of the pubic area. Girls stand in two rough lines at foreground and middle-ground, gesturing, talking, playing, reaching up. The collage has no central figure to grab the viewer's attention and no bold shock of color to command focus. Instead, the effect becomes an endless wallpaper of nude girls, suggestive in and of itself.

Darger saw sexuality through the language of violence. In an interview Kiyoko Lerner told a story about Darger that suggested he understood sexual interactions at some level. Though old, disheveled, and malodorous, Darger stated that he had been "raped by a beautiful 17-year-old Italian girl in the vestibule of the building." Kiyoko Lerner understood this statement as attesting to Darger's ability to live in the world of his imagination.[79] Whatever happened, and she thought something had happened because of the disappearance of Darger's wallet, this episode shows that he grasped a vocabulary of sexual force.

Darger wrote himself into the story. He was at once the storyteller and the subject. The character of Henry Darger multiplied in *Realms of the Unreal*. He was Captain Henry Darger of the National Guard, who was systematically promoted to General. There is a war correspondent called Henry Darger and a spy master, Hendro Darger. In volume one, Darger describes one of his alter egos as "a stern looking man, with a thick brown beard, brownish complexion, Herculean build and tall enough to embrace 6 feet. He had the fierce visage full of determination, his hair was light brown, his eyes light blue, and if people happened to see him looking at them, they would have felt like rushing away to safety at once."[80] The fictional Darger—the Darger he wanted to embody in his child-saving efforts—contrasted with his real person. At 5 feet 8 inches (173 cm) tall, 125 pounds (57 kg) and sallow complected, the real Darger had far less physical authority than his fiction of himself.[81] There are also other Dargers, including Judas Darger and Henry Joseph Darger, both of whom fight for the child-slaving Glandelinians.[82] Darger positioned himself throughout the storytelling as both child-saving hero and child-wrecking brute. He acts on all sides of the conflict.

Even in his fiction Darger shows himself as confused and conflicted, rather than creating a world that simply allowed for his own authority and success. He writes himself into the story as an unreliable narrator who cannot be trusted to react to children with kindness. Nor can his characters understand the mysteries around him. Instead, Darger the character has the same problems with his temper that Darger the writer noted about himself and suffers from an intellectual or spiritual incapability. In one section, war correspondent Henry Darger communicates with the ghost of Annie Aronburg, perhaps the embodiment of the murdered child Elsie Paroubek. The child has been demanding that Darger "withdraw the curse on the Christians" for the loss of the picture, something that Darger denies doing. Darger the character grows angry at the child and offended at the implication that somehow he is at fault by cursing Christians or acting in league with the Glandelinians. He wants to seize the child and shake her in anger, but she mysteriously disappears. Upon reappearing, the murdered child says,

> As you were the one who had secured my picture, and many others that had once belonged to me. I had trusted that, as you alone had the situation of both sides in your power, I decided to appeal to you to avenge my assassination or the poor Vivian Girls will have to die for me to save their nations and their father's armies from complete ruin and defeat at the hands of their Glandelinian enemies.[83]

This passage captures the way that Darger's prose expressed a dream state of shifting meanings and identities.

The character Darger explains himself as angered by the child and then confused by the charge placed upon him. In other parts of the work, Darger as character cannot work out the implications of the plot that the writer seems to be creating. Despite the importance of finding the lost picture and removing the curse, Darger cannot solve the Aronburg mystery. Even his alter egos General Darger and Gemini Darger cannot hold on to the picture of the murdered girl and cannot unravel the mystery. The meaning of the missing portrait eludes all versions of Darger as character and Darger as writer. He cannot imagine a world where any version of himself could solve the matter.

The splitting of Darger into multiple and even antagonistic versions of himself shows the ways in which representation cannot be reduced to a simple one-to-one correspondence. Theorists of pornography have discussed the ways that there is no guarantee how a reader fits him- or herself into the characters in a novel or image. A man reading pornography will not necessarily see himself as the male character having sex with a female character, but might mentally position himself as the woman, as a voyeur watching the action, or even as the writer creating scenes for the woman and the man. In the splitting of Dargers, Darger showed an intrinsic understanding of the instability of representation. He is simultaneously child-murdering villain, child-saving hero, and frustrated observer. Intrinsically, as character, he enjoys the savagery even while, as another character, he participates in hunting down such savagery. As a character he is both actor and observer, while by extension, as a writer he takes the splitting even further.

At the same time, Darger shows himself as seeing a world that is beyond what he is able to logically arrange and explicate. In the inability to solve the Aronburg Mystery that haunted him, Darger hints at his own acceptance of a world he cannot control or even understand. Darger did not remake the world through fantasy into a tidy package subject to his control. Instead, he represented a world of desires that aroused and disgusted him and one whose logic eluded him. He could not understand how it fitted together, and he could not even stand above the materials to see them in their entirety.

His world of desires showed itself in multiplication and excess. He envisions "millions of children alone . . . the poor children had lain bound and bleeding in Glandelinian child-slave prisons of horror."[84] Just as he generated compelling images through the multiplication of forms in illustrations, so too did he multiply images, stories, and books in the physical space of his apartment. The overflow of materials simultaneously limited his physical space and expanded his fantastical space. This relationship between limitation and excess seems to speak to the impact of overflowing consumer production in general.

Darger's works demonstrate the heady and obsessive power of ephemera—the persuasive pull that the ephemeral world could have on the mind. It was not just that Darger found elements of the ephemeral world engaging. His response over multiple decades, over hundreds of illustrations, and over thousands of pages shows how the world of consumer culture could become an obsession of its own. The novels, newspapers, magazines, comic books, and coloring books that he collected became the foundation for his fantasies. He collected, traced, enlarged, reproduced, altered, and stripped images from the ephemeral press. He then took ideas and images and magnified, filtered, and transformed them so that they spoke to cultural undercurrents about white slavery, race, childhood, and violence. On one hand, the transformation of ephemera seems like a very small change—just a change in the raw materials for making fantasies. Is using a magazine for the raw matter much different from using a piece of wood as a material for carving? On the other hand, the manipulation of ephemera to make fantasies shows that even the most intimate level of self has become constructed through consumer culture. There is no place that consumer culture has not touched, and even the construction of the imaginary sexual self has been remade with consumer cultural forms.

Darger's alternate universe emerged from the engagement with aspects of consumer culture and the fantastical rearrangement of those elements of fictional texts and ephemeral production that compelled him. But the process did not allow closure. Although his artistic processes became more sophisticated and he developed new techniques for creating art, he did not resolve the tensions relating to the erotic component of childhood. Instead, the consideration of children and men, torture and idyllic pleasures became an expanding complex that he continued to generate. It became something he couldn't think beyond.

But to expect an individual like Darger—impoverished, ill-educated, and sent to a home for the feeble-minded—to move past his fixations does not recognize the opportunities for the ordinary in society. Baudrillard states that society's fixation with simulacra lands people in a funhouse of mirrors where they are mesmerized by the proliferation of the fantastic rather than productively organizing for real change. Baudrillard's analysis speaks to a profound shift in society's relationship to consumer culture. As people grew obsessed with consumer culture, they uncovered its under-lying sexual currents and articulated those that interested them in their pornographic recreations. Baudrillard's comments suggest a problematic disengagement with the world, a way of choosing to lose oneself in the fantastic instead of choosing to fight for change. However, fantasizing about the realms of the unreal may be a retreat, but retreating can also imply creativity.

The modern world can be a cruel place, as Darger's life experiences illustrate. The desire to retreat into fantasy, where good and evil can be named, where beauty can be astonishing, and where battles might be heroic is a reasonable response to cruelty and alienation. For ordinary people to create their own fantasies out of the remnants of consumer culture might be a small act, but it is not trivial; it is still an act of personal assertion set against a biopolitics that would prefer people to be pliable consumers. For queer individuals, just staring at a man's physical form in *Physique Pictorial* was a radical act; it was all the more so to actively reimagine the desire embodied in the alibied image. To draw an erection was to name a desire that was more comfortable if it remained nebulous. For individuals like Darger who had some sort of erotic fixation that involved children, there was little room to express such convolutions of desire. Although there was a geometric rise in the number of consumer artifacts to whet desires and then meet them, the creative impulse remained powerful and individuals continuously reclaimed it. Perhaps this impulse evidences Baudrillard's point about simulacra most powerfully: even embedded in a funhouse of mirrors, people creatively expressed their desires, whether or not they reflected the normative demands of sexuality. To speak against restriction meant taking consumer culture and remodeling it for the self, rather than taking the self and remodeling it for consumer culture. In this, remade objects, though not revolutionary, still constituted a form of radical expression.

3

Men and Time: Prison Pornography, 1940s–1960s

Even today, prisoners in the United States have no fundamental rights to the possession of reading materials.[1] Citing safety concerns, federal and state prisons restrict access to publications considered incendiary, threatening, or disruptive. Many prisons have decided that pornography fits into the latter category. Separated from sexual partners and then kept from commercial fantasy material, prisoners have tended to hand-make a great deal of erotic and pornographic art. The single greatest archive of homemade prison pornography is at the Kinsey Institute, formerly the Institute for Sex Research (ISR). Containing thousands of pieces of art and manuscript literature, the prison collection documents a wide range of desires and ways of thinking about sexuality.

This chapter will explore the Institute for Sex Research's prison pornography collection. The cache, seized between the early 1940s and the late 1960s, documents how imprisoned men conceptualized and expressed ideas about sexuality. The collection was gathered systematically during a period of cooperation between a number of prison administrators and the ISR, perhaps the only systematic attempt to gather such materials in history. Not curated for artistry or differentiated by taste, this collection documents prison sexuality so that members of the ISR could use the materials to understand prisoners, their psychological makeup, and the accommodations they made to living under prison restrictions.

Members of the Institute argued that they needed to study prisoner sexuality in order to understand the criminal mind. Not only did they collect materials seized through guard shakedowns, but the Kinsey team incited the production of homemade pornography and then collected the pornography that resulted, as this chapter will show. By considering prison art and the context of its creation and collection, this chapter will explore the many ironies embedded in the mutual constitution of pornographic and scientific knowledge that happened as part of the proliferation of sexual discourse in mid-twentieth-century America.

In preparation for his first book on sexuality, *Sexual Behavior in the Human Male* (1948), Alfred Kinsey, an entomologist turned sex researcher, interviewed people from as wide a spectrum as possible. He began by surveying students in his classes at Indiana University, but he quickly realized that he needed to balance his sample of college-educated respondents with a pool of working-class men. Where might an erudite and rather isolated biologist gain access to men that could counterbalance the surveys participated in by the young, white, middle-class set of college students who took his classes? Kinsey turned to prisons.[2]

As early as 1940, Kinsey began to interview prisoners in Indiana.[3] To get permission to interview inmates, he established relationships with a number of prison officials, including wardens and staff psychologists. The process of gaining contacts and enlarging his pool of potential interviewees continued after the publication of his volume on male sexual behavior. As he expanded the geographic scope of his interviews, Kinsey found the California prison system particularly responsive to his overtures. When Kinsey began his investigations at San Quentin in 1948, he interviewed fourteen inmates, including a prize fighter, an influential Mexican American, and an important African American—people whom he saw as "prison leaders"—in order to influence the larger prison population into giving their sexual histories.[4] Six of the fourteen prison leaders had already read the recently published *Sexual Behavior in the Human Male*. According to Wardell Pomeroy, a colleague at the ISR and

Kinsey's co-author, the response was so positive that 95 percent of the prison population would have given their histories if time had allowed.[5] Instead of interviewing everyone, the team concentrated on getting the case histories of men imprisoned for sex crimes.

Kinsey and his team sought these case histories at a propitious moment. During the late 1940s and early 1950s, concerns over sex crimes generated a broad interest in sex research and sex reform. Citizens, legislators, and prison officials all wanted to understand how to generate change in sexual culture. According to an in-house history written in 1954 about the Emotional Security Program, a program instituted in the California prison system for "sexual psychopaths" to effect rehabilitation,

> In November 1949, with the consternation of the public at the increase in sex crimes in California, a special subcommittee of the Assembly Judiciary Committee was appointed to investigate these sex crimes. And in December the Governor called a state-wide citizens' conference along with a special session of the Legislature to consider the problem. Out of this activity came the conclusion that dealing with the sex offender was a much deeper problem than just passing laws could handle—and that there was an urgent need for research in the entire field.[6]

Along with funding basic research, the state of California developed new programs to deal with sexuality and criminality. From an experimental program at Norwalk that placed prisoners in a non-punitive environment and emphasized group therapy, to a self-help group for sexuality at Chino modeled after Alcoholics Anonymous, attempts at reform rippled through the prison system.[7] The dual focus on research and reform legitimated collaboration with bona fide researchers at Langley Porter, California's first neuropsychiatric institute, founded in 1941, and the Institute for Sex Research. In this atmosphere, the Director of Corrections encouraged cooperation in ways that benefited Kinsey and his team. Wardens saw themselves as contributing to projects that would speak to the relationship between sex and criminality and that would yield valuable statistics on the issue of prisoner accommodation to an institutional culture. Prison officials supplied Kinsey and the ISR with access to inmates, privacy for interviews, confiscated materials, and documents about directives and policies of interest.

Although he began the process of interviewing prisoners before the publication of his first book on human sexuality, Kinsey developed further questions about men's sexuality in prisons. As he developed more insight into prison culture, Kinsey and his team realized that little had been done on the topic of male sexuality while in prison. He began to be less interested in questions of sexual deviance among prisoners and more interested in exploring how men accommodated themselves to prison culture. How would men respond to a sex-segregated environment? Would they masturbate more? Would they engage in same-sex relations? Would they fantasize? Would they turn to violence? Surprisingly little had been done to explore questions regarding sexual accommodation to prison life. This issue began to drive Kinsey's research into prison culture, and he envisioned the production of a statistical survey that would allow scholars and correctional officers to know how men dealt with prisoner sex segregation. However, he did more than just take histories from prisoners. His fascination with the diversity of human sexuality and his well-known commitment to very large sample sizes meant in practice that he collected virtually everything that he could get his hands on from the prisons he visited.

It is from this starting point that the Kinsey Institute began its collection on prisons. The prison collection began in 1940, and the ISR continued actively collecting into the late 1960s, though the collection is the strongest in the period from the 1950s to the early 1960s. It includes sexual histories, letters between prisoners, confiscated commercial pornography, questionnaires, and examples of prison writing and prison art. There are letters written between Kinsey and his staff and prison officials, and there are copies of working and professional papers on prison policies. The ISR collected materials from San Quentin, Alcatraz, Chino, Vacaville,

Soledad, and Lompoc Federal prisons in California; Huntsville in Texas; Leavenworth, Kansas; the Maryland State Department of Corrections Patuxent Institution in Jessup, Maryland; Terre Haute, Indiana; and Minnesota State Prison at Stillwater.

While this group of prisons is not representative of the range of prisons and correctional institutions that existed during those years nationally (a 1934 estimate suggested that there were more than 3,000 such institutions in the U.S. at that time),[8] it still provides a range of institutions from a variety of regions and states. San Quentin houses the oldest prison in California and is the site of California's death row. Terre Haute prison contains a medium- and high-security prison and is a site of federal executions, including the 2001 execution of Timothy McVeigh. Vacaville houses a medium-security prison. Leavenworth is a medium-security federal penitentiary, often confused with the sole maximum-security facility of the United States Military. Alcatraz, of course, was a military barracks turned maximum-security federal prison, now turned tourist site.[9] Chino, at that time, had a minimum-security prison that prepared prisoners for return to society.[10] Minnesota State Prison had a much smaller and an older population than the California prison system.[11]

Between the 1940s and the 1960s these locations held prisoners convicted of a wide array of crimes, from sex crimes to murder, burglary, and property crimes. Sex crimes were proportionately small, but state governments in the late 1940s and 1950s were growing increasingly concerned about them, particularly because the prison population had expanded overall. In the state of New York, there were 24,760 arrests for major crimes in 1949; 1,338 of those arrested were charged with rape and 708 were charged with other sexual offences.[12] Between 1944 and 1954 the California system had expanded almost threefold from 5,710 inmates to 15,376 inmates. The California system housed 15,532 prisoners on December 31, 1956.[13]

As the California system expanded, it developed new programs to deal with the influx of inmates. As part of a program to reduce overcrowding, a subset of prisoners who had been diagnosed as criminally insane or as sexual psychopaths were sent to Atascadero, a maximum-security hospital, for treatment.[14] Of the 599 men who were identified as needing hospitalization, 5 were alcoholics, 2 had committed arson, 41 attempted rape, 3 committed bestiality, 11 committed cunnilingus on a minor girl, 188 had engaged in exhibitionism, 1 had stolen a child, 7 had contributed to the delinquency of a minor, 20 had been convicted of fetishism, 140 had been labeled homosexuals, 118 had committed incest, 18 kidnapped others, 40 were convicted of being lewd and lascivious, 1 was convicted for sending lewd notes, 2 for sending lewd pictures, and 2 for making lewd phone calls.[15] The number of criminals imprisoned for robbery, forgery, and narcotics dwarfed the number of sex offenses in the state overall. However, the focus on sex crimes by California state authorities made the numbers of sex crimes seem larger than they were.[16] Kinsey and the members of the ISR were particularly interested in the work done at Atascadero and Norwalk with sex offenders and they collected materials that reflected their preoccupations.

Certain constraints limited the representativeness of the materials they collected. Kinsey and the ISR members collected materials only from male prisoners, rather than from both men and women.[17] Prison materials were confiscated and archived for just a few decades; therefore they speak more to synchronic rather than diachronic issues. Members of the ISR did not interview a representative subset of prisoners. (Indeed, the issue of statistical representativeness dogged Kinsey's work during his lifetime and after his death.) Prisoners whom Kinsey and his team interviewed were racially diverse, though, as historians point out, African Americans were and continue to be overrepresented among the prison population. Regionally, the set of prisons had a northern and western bias and might therefore miss the racial dynamics and meanings entrenched in southern prisons, which tended to disproportionally house more African Americans and used a particular gang-style of labor. Nonetheless, the confiscated prison pornography collection is unique, expansive, and underused.

Not only has the ISR prison collection been largely ignored, but the genre of prison art as a historical source has been overlooked. Even as a type of art, the genre has scarcely been examined. Phyllis Kornfeld's *Cellblock Visions: Prison Art in America* (1997) was the first full-length examination of prisoner art as a genre. Since then, scholars have examined prison art for correctional, therapeutic, and educational reasons.[18] These examinations look at currently operating prison art programs and place these materials in a rehabilitative context; that is, they explore how art can change prison life and ameliorate prisoners' problems. Prison-made folk art or hobby art has received little attention, according to Melissa Schrift, in part because criminologists have dominated the study of prisons and criminology, fields that have only emerged recently.[19] Prison erotica remains a subfield caught behind in an already lagging area.

Historians examine criminality, the carceral state, and prison policies, but they have largely ignored issues of sexuality and have certainly ignored the issue of prisoner sexual art. As Regina Kunzel states in *Criminal Intimacy* (2008), "While historians of sexuality have paid little attention to prisoners and prisons, historians of the prison have paid scant attention to sex and sexuality."[20] Her work charts the ways that the examination of sexuality in prisons queers the larger trajectory of American sexual history. Her book looks at "one of the most marginalized of American spaces—the prison—and its most stigmatized practice—same-sex sex."[21] The exploration of same-sex sexual practices has since received more examination than other sorts of sexuality in prison.[22] Although same-sex sex has been stigmatized in American society, scholars have documented the workings of same-sex desires and practices in prisons. In contrast, little attention has been given to other forms of sexuality, including masturbation and opposite-sex desires and practices.[23] Further, the consideration of the representations of sexual desire—one step removed from sexual practice—has been entirely ignored.

The refusal to engage with issues of sexuality has a long precedent. For decades scholars and activists have raised issues regarding sexuality in prisons and, for decades, nothing has been done about them. As early as 1934, the problem of sexuality in prisons was called to national attention by Joseph F. Fishman, a former federal prison inspector, a board member of the American Prison Association, and a Guggenheim fellow.[24] His volume *Sex in Prison* documented the lack of provision made for men's sexuality. He believed that "prison inmates spend several hours each day confined to their cells during which they can day-dream and indulge in sexual fantasies."[25] Without some sort of conjugal visit (his preferred solution for maintaining heterosexual familial relations), prisoners would be forced to bribe guards, to suppress, sublimate, or "gratify [sexual desire] by masturbation, homosexuality, bestiality, pederasty, or some other form of perversion."[26] Despite Fishman's rabble-rousing rhetoric, the issue of sex in prison received no attention and remained a critical issue, as a prison questionnaire from 1943 demonstrates. Administered to a decidedly small number of prisoners, guards, and administrative officers, this questionnaire pointed toward the centrality of sex to male prisoners. The majority of surveyed men believed that inmates would get along better if they had regular sexual outlets and that self-masturbation (rather than mutual masturbation between prisoners) would be the most appropriate sexual outlet.[27] Concerns focused on how excessive masturbation could lead to later impotence.[28] One guard who worked with prisoners preparing for their release noted that the prisoners themselves shared the concern. As he explained, "A number of men who have confided to me have said that during the first part of their incarceration they have masturbated more than at any other period of their lives. A number of these men have also said that after a while they have become emotionally flat and have expressed the fear that their institutional experience has rendered them impotent."[29] Concerns about masturbation affected both prisoners and prison officials. Though prisoners worried about the effects of masturbation on their bodies and minds, prison officials worried about the effects of masturbation on prison discipline, while others posited that masturbation in prison would lead to mutual masturbation and homosexuality even after release from incarceration.[30]

Broad changes in how American society viewed masturbation over the course of the twentieth century normalized the practice,[31] but in prisons masturbation and so-called "sexual incontinence" remained fraught.

Indeed, even today, the issue of masturbation remains problematic for prisoners. *Prison Sex Culture*, a sociological volume published in 2014, noted that masturbation was "normally forbidden during incarceration." Catherine Marcum, editor and author, notes that a 2001 study about masturbation in prisons, one of the few studies done on the topic, found that 99.3 percent of the men who were interviewed reported masturbating despite it being forbidden.[32] A *Slate* article from 2012 noted that prisoners still did not have any constitutional right to masturbate and that numerous states still had restrictions on the practice in correctional environments.[33]

Both the practice of masturbation and materials abetting it were forbidden during the 1940s, 1950s, and 1960s, the period under discussion. Prisoners had limited civil rights and the sorts of materials that they could own and view in prison were subject to the broad discretionary powers of prison administrators. According to the doctrine of *Ruffin v. Commonwealth* (1871), prisoners were civilly dead, effectively slaves without rights. As Kunzel states, "the disinclination on the part of the courts to intervene in prison matters left prisoners with virtually no recognized rights and with little recourse beyond appeals to prison administrators."[34] As a result, administrators could censor prison mail and other correspondence and could limit the reading materials of prisoners.[35] The ability to limit reading materials meant that prison administrators could decide what was appropriate or inappropriate. Only in 1964 did the Supreme Court recognize Muslim prisoners' rights to the Quran. In this context, prison officials seized illegal prisoner pornography with no reservations and even confiscated legal images that might be used for masturbation. Even today, prisoners have no fundamental legal rights to possess print materials, and prison administrations limit access to books, newspapers, and magazines.

Throughout the period under discussion in this chapter, prisoners had few rights to print culture and prison officials seized a wide range of objects because of their sexual content. Images seized by officials included commercial pornography and personal photos; they might be professionally photographed or produced by amateurs, in pristine shape or worn and falling to bits.[36] Confiscated goods show the popularity of photography, testifying to the medium's extraordinary evocative capacity and the ease of carrying photographs compared with other pornographic forms like comic books, magazines, novels, or art. The materials also show what American men during this period carried for sexual and sentimental purposes when arrested and incarcerated. For the most part, confiscated images reflected broader social preoccupations with idealized notions of prettiness and women playing for the male gaze; they showed attractive blondes performing stripteases or buxom nudes smiling for the camera. The photographs mostly illustrate the way that the nude or semi-nude woman stood in for sexuality. The confiscation of ethnographic and nudist prints showed that these materials either passed as masturbatory materials or that correctional officers understood them as such. Though less common, photographs of interracial sex scenes and cross-dressing also appeared in prisoners' possessions.

Most confiscated materials had been produced as commercial pornography. A set of playing cards confiscated in 1954 featured smiling nude models.[37] Some photographs tried to attain a degree of artistic expression; one artfully photographed image featured a woman holding a picture frame to "frame" her face and torso.[38] Some commercial photographs appeared time and again, achieving real popularity among the population of prisoners. Prison officials at San Quentin noted that "a large quantity of the above three prints was confiscated in 1953. These evidently escaped until 1954." The three images, in wallet-size format, featured the same woman doing a striptease. In one image, she faces the camera wearing a bra and underpants; in another she turns and removes her bra; and in the final shot she stands nude, her back to the camera as she turns her face toward it and smiles. A later set includes two additional "striptease" photos, with notes explaining that nineteen fully clothed reproductions and twenty-nine topless copies featuring the same model had been confiscated.[39]

Other confiscations show the range of materials that either prisoners or guards thought of as masturbatory. A San Quentin official confiscated a 1947 nudist magazine, published by Sunshine Book Company in Mays Landing, New Jersey, that extolled the virtues of the nudist lifestyle and featured stories and photographs of nudist camps,[40] and two ethnographic postcards. One featured a woman baring her breasts from a parted green robe while hoisting a water jug onto a shoulder. The other showed a bare-breasted woman lying on pillows against Oriental carpets.[41] Ethnographic images from a magazine were also confiscated, like a bare-breasted woman in a grass skirt both with and without a baby.[42] Likewise, two fully clothed glamor shots of Lena Horne were confiscated,[43] as was one perfectly chaste personal photograph of an African American woman in a white bathing suit, posed outside a home.[44] Folsom officials even confiscated a newspaper cutout of a yogi sitting cross-legged that featured the caption "Yogananda, Aged 16, The light was blinding."[45]

Some of the confiscated materials were more explicit or more overtly sexual. A much-worn image shows two women posed in a room: one woman sits in a chair and the other leans against her. The seated woman is naked except for garters and stockings, and her breasts are being touched by the other woman.[46] Another set of images, confiscated in 1958, featured a black woman fellating a white man and a woman mounting a man.[47] A photograph showed a cross-dressed man, his features obscured by a face mask, dressed in gloves, garter belt, stockings, and fluffy mule slippers.[48] We thus know that lesbian sex, interracial sex, and cross-dressing sex appeared in the repertoire of prisoners' desires.

A study of sex offenders produced by staff at the Institute for Sex Research in 1965, after Kinsey's death, stated that "It is common for men to keep, for varying periods of time, sexual pictures in their wallets, pornographic booklets and playing cards in their bureau drawers, and humorous pornographic drawings in their pockets."[49] The researchers understood pornography primarily as a way for men to bond, and they thought that "dirty pictures" functioned like "dirty jokes"—as a form of social lubricant. If that was the case, male society in and out of prison was well oiled. Out of their study of 2,721 white men, only 14 had never been exposed to pornography. That set included a control group of 477 non-incarcerated men, 888 men in prison for crimes other than sex offenses, and 1,356 men convicted of sex offenses.[50]

The commercial materials seized from prisoners provide a basis for comparison with the materials that prisoners made for themselves. The consideration of handmade prison pornography offers the opportunity to explore prisoners' own visions of sex and sexuality. In contrast to what they brought with them, prisoners made objects that illustrated far more complicated, confusing, and disturbing ideas about sexuality. The corpus of confiscated prison art lets historians see how prisoners understood and saw sex, how they conceptualized bodies and intercourse, how they wrote, colored, sketched, and articulated their desires, what they wanted from sex, who they wanted for sex, and how they thought about desire.

Handmade Prison Pornography

Prisoners brought different levels of skill and distinct visions of sexuality to their creations. They drew single images and wrote long complicated stories. They made pornographic carvings and wrote explicit valentines. They carved soap, wood, metal, and items of trash. They sculpted figures, both movable and stationary. They wrote novels, how-to tracts, comic books, poetry, and song lyrics. The subjects and themes of these materials varied as well. Some were violent while others were not; some were so incoherent and disorganized that it becomes impossible to tell whether they were violent or not.

Despite these differences, some commonalities emerge. In general, these objects were made using readily available materials. They were constructed with little artistic talent and they tended to emphasize raw sexual ideas, overtly rejecting sentimental depictions of sexuality. Not surprisingly, the most common subjects were naked women, masturbating men, and male–female sexual intercourse. Naked women were the hallmark of desire and appeared in a variety of visual forms. Images of men masturbating, though less common, also appeared standard—the erect and ejaculating penis spoke overtly to sexual arousal, but the flaccid penis also appeared. Men and women having sex completed the trifecta of standard images.

Though men, women, and intercourse are genre standards, the ways that prisoners conceptualized these topics demonstrates what they saw and what they privileged. Breasts tended to have a distinctly conical shape (perhaps mirroring the shape produced by 1950s and '60s bra technologies), and prisoners often used a bright Crayola red for the lips and labia of women, a strategy representative either of art supplies in prisons or the way prisoners saw the coloration of women's bodies. Any number of these images placed the vaginal opening of women directly in the middle of the abdomen, showing that the artists worked from memory (and perhaps tactile memory rather than visual memory) rather than from models.

The most popular category of images, the beautiful woman, was limited only by the artist's skills. One prisoner transformed his rough muslin sheet into a drawing of a woman using nothing but pencils and a black pen (illus. 54).[51] The hand-drawn image of a nude woman is roughly three-quarters life-size. The woman stands in partial profile with a bent arm holding a cloth that

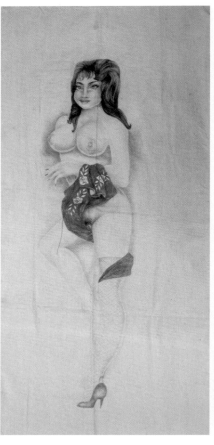

54 Woman drawn on sheet, Prison Art, [1965?], Realia, ISR 905, Kinsey Institute.

twines around her torso and standing leg. She has kicked off a red high-heeled shoe and bent her fishnet stocking-clad leg behind her as she looks back at the viewer. The woman has blue cat-shaped eyes, set off by blue eye shadow. The artist has used pen to deepen the color of her black hair. He has also shaded the figure's breasts and body and set off the tan of the body with pink nipples and a deep red cloth, covered with red roses, that twines around her body. The cloth has been pulled to the side to display her labia. To get color saturation from pencil onto cloth required skill and physical commitment. The red of the cloth and shoe and the pink of the nipples and lips are fully saturated, as are the blue eyes. Despite the roughness of the sheet, the picture is very finely wrought and carefully drawn. The woman has all the hallmarks of a stripper, from the fishnet stockings and red shoes to the hourglass figure that beckons from behind the carefully draped cloth.

One set of drawings, confiscated from a San Quentin prisoner in 1954, repeated the popular motif of women and martini glasses, which suggested a sort of decadence and luxury.[52] In a particular scene, a woman stands in a martini glass while an enormous tongue with carefully drawn taste buds licks her. In this image, the tongue almost touches the woman's nipple. She holds behind her back some sort of instrument, and she stands with a cherry or apple on her head. In another image by the same artist, an enormous tongue licks a martini glass and cherry while to the side a bearded lady in evening dress and pearls smokes a cigarette in a long cigarette holder.[53]

Red shoes marked another man's drawings as erotic. Confiscated in 1949 from a San Quentin prisoner, the series featured a variety of beautiful women. Each image shows a different woman, from a dark-haired and dark-skinned woman in a red dress, to a black woman in an opened pink robe, a white woman sprawled open-legged on a pink background, an auburn-haired woman raising a short white dress, an auburn-haired woman in matching white bra and panties trimmed with black edging, and a dark-haired woman posed spread-eagle. All the women wear the red shoes with a high heel and an ankle strap. These illustrations show the man's desire through the poses of women and the red shoes they wear.[54]

Prisoners also created illustrations of nude men in prison pornography. Although it is not clear whether these figures are supposed to be self-portraits or images of others, they gain their erotic edge from a focus on the male genitals and seem like a reflection of masturbatory pleasures. Rather than enjoyment of the male form or figure, these objects suggest an erotic pleasure reflected back at the viewer. One small clay figurine of a reclining man with his arms tucked behind his head proudly sports an enormous erection.[55] The bald gray figure is made of snakes and balls of clay that have been rolled and then attached with brown slip. The man

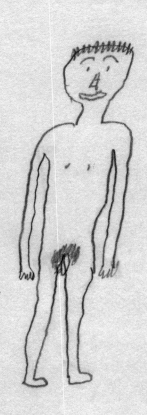

has two pinprick eyes, a carved semicircle of a smile and a red triangle of a nose. His erect penis equals the size of his torso. The head of the penis has been painted red and the testicles—which are fully as large as the figure's head—draw attention to the organ. Further, pubic hair made from artificial brush strands have been attached to the testicles. The figure looks pleased with his enormous erection, happy to let it dominate the scene. A childish rendering of a smile suggests that the figure reflects back at the viewer a happiness at masturbating, rather than inviting a sensual appreciation of the male form.

Another image of a nude man (illus. 55) was produced by a prisoner in the Maryland State Department of Corrections Patuxent Institution in Jessup. The simple drawing has all the hallmarks of a children's drawing. The line-drawn pencil-on-paper figure has a broad semicircular smile with a triangle nose, two dot eyes and raised semicircular eyebrows. The only shading comes from the pubic hair that frames the figure's flaccid genitals. Listing to the side, missing ears, and disproportionate, the figure, staring back at the viewer, radiates a kind of goofy happiness.

Even something as homey as hot cocoa could be repurposed for prison pornography of the masturbating male figure. A Nestlé's EverReady Sweet Milk Cocoa box, for example, has been cut in half to show a pipe-cleaner figure glued inside. The figure has a round flat face, tubular torso and limbs, and a carefully wrought penis that was made thicker than the torso by twisting in additional lengths of pipe-cleaner. The genitals are accented with a dark bead for the testicles. While the outside of the box proclaims that "The Sweet Milk Cocoa makes a 'cup of delicious nourishment' for the whole family," the figure inside the box masturbates when the thread that connects the arm holding the penis to the back of the box is pulled.[56]

The third popular theme, intercourse, remained the hardest to represent. Though commercial pornography established visual cues like the "money shot" as representative of intercourse, handmade pornography did not build off the same lexicon. Glaring anatomical errors show how these men saw bodies and what they thought important. One artist who drew

55 C.E.W., line drawing, 1960, Box 2, Series II, G.15, Folder 1, 001, North America: United States, 20th Century, Prison Art, Maryland State Department of Corrections Patuxent Institution, Jessup, Maryland, Kinsey Institute.

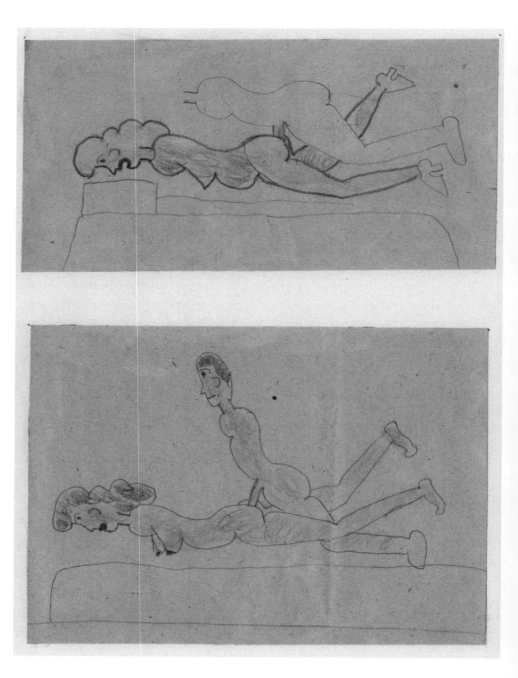

56 Crayon drawings, item 2011.50.1.120A xxxiv-4, North America: United States, 20th Century, Prison Art, San Quentin, California, Box 1, Kinsey Institute.

a variety of images made the same anatomical errors repeatedly, drawing bodies without arms, without feet, and without clearly male features (illus. 56). The San Quentin inmate made a 1950 crayon and pencil drawing of anal intercourse. Only the male's penis is completed and colored in crayon. The rest of the man's body remains a line drawing, and the male body lacks a head. In contrast, the woman has been fully penciled and colored: she has masses of yellow hair and a red-lined open mouth. The level of completion privileged the female body and the man's penis over the whole of the man's body. Perhaps the incomplete body allowed the artist/viewer to project his person into the drawing. Also clear from the image is the way that longing outstripped talent: the forms are armless either because arms would get in the way of picturing intercourse or because arms eluded the illustrator's capacities.[57]

57 Personified penis inserting itself in vagina, acquired 1961, North America: United States, 20th Century, Prison Art, Kinsey Institute.

The same inmate drew another armless couple engaging in anal intercourse. The male body levers over the female at an impossible angle given his lack of support. The carefully drawn penis enters into the woman so that the full length can be displayed. The woman has red-tipped nipples

and matching red lips. While the prisoner lacked artistic skill, he did have a very clear vision of the sexual elements that engaged him: lips, breasts, penises. A wooden toy featuring an armless man engaging in anal intercourse with an armless woman might have been modeled from this image.[58]

The same illustrator produced a larger and more detailed drawing that was also confiscated. This illustration shows a home complete with two couples engaging in intercourse. The illustration features a curtained window, a picture on the wall, and the lines of the roof. One couple is on a bed as the man penetrates the woman from behind. Both man and woman are again missing arms, and the woman is face-down in a pillow (looking rather smothered). The other couple have sex in a chair. The man has arms while the woman has very large nipples that embrace him like arms. Both of the women wear yellow stockings. The crayon coloring in red, yellow, blue, and orange provides a cheerful counterpoint to the drawing. The care given to coloring in the curtains, bedframe and stockings provide more polish, but even here skills could not do justice to ideas.[59] This inmate's drawings show what a basic box of crayons can produce in a pinch, like a portrait of a happy home complete with furniture, curtains, and two copulating couples.

The visualization of sexuality in all of these drawings emphasized penetrative intercourse. To achieve this, the prisoner drew and painted bodies levered apart rather than close together and positioned those bodies in ways that allowed for visible penetration. He also drew the barely inserted penis against the vaginal or anal opening so that viewers could see and measure the length of the penis. The artist thus froze intercourse to a pre-insertion moment in order to open sex to an external gaze.

Other artists also saw penetration as the critical moment to envision. One inmate made the penis into a small independent creature complete with its own arms and legs (illus. 57). Sprays of liquid that emanate from the insertion point make the process seem onerous, though the squiggly pubic hairs give the scrotum a relaxed air. The small penis seems overwhelmed by the woman's proportions. Vaginal penetration, in this artist's rendering, is both comical and vaguely horrifying, as if the penis might be swallowed whole and disappear. Instead, the penile figure shoves his top half in, emerges, and then bends over to vomit in the two remaining drawings. He remains whole but vanquished in this rendition of intercourse.

Another example that combines humor and horror overlays a man and woman's faces with their genitals (illus. 58). The man's love for his bearded woman plays itself out both with the hearts that leap toward the woman and the drops of semen that fall from his penis-nose. Although the labial slit of the woman's mouth makes her look horrified, the hearts in her eyes counter the effect. Clearly, according to this inmate's pen, men and women were made to fit together, though the image highlighted the oddity of genitalia.

58 "A well adjusted couple," item 2010.4.498, North America: United States, 20th Century, Prison Art, Baltimore, Maryland, Kinsey Institute.

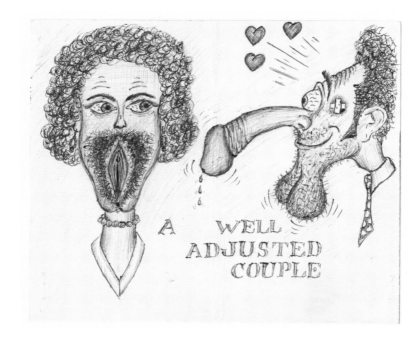

The shift from a single illustration to multiple cells or pages let creators focus on penetrative sex through a narrative arc. A 1963 story entitled "Miss Jones and Bill," confiscated at Leavenworth prison, develops a boss and secretary fantasy in which Bill calls Miss Jones into the office.[60] They immediately begin to have sex. At the beginning of the pamphlet (illus. 59), the secretary, Miss Jones, is fully drawn and shaded with a see-through sleeveless blouse and see-through skirt. In contrast, Bill, the boss, is drawn as merely an outline. As the story develops, Bill becomes embodied, first in outline (though his legs end abruptly at the bottom of his trousers). He then gains feet, and finally substance through pencil coloration. He wavers in and out of embodiment in subsequent panels depending on the intensity of the sexual activity (illus. 60). In a panel showing vaginal penetration, he has a completed body and carefully wrought and colored penis complete with drops of ejaculate. In other scenes, the figures are more cursory. The dialogue throughout the pamphlet remains wooden and the

Oh. sir you got My shirt pulled up oh", oh. sir I don't Think This is right. But i Like iT, oh Bill

Yes Baby we can get real Closer that right Now and I got My hand on your Nice Ass, And Now I want To feel your pussy. Of course you like iT But These Pants Are in the way. I Think we Better do somthing about Them punctuation and spelling suggest a limited literacy. In one scene (illus. 61), after repeating that it hurts, Miss Jones says "please pleas, oh, oh, that feel bill now it don't hurt so much now; I like it; oh Bill fuck me in the ass again it was good." The artist had a hard time drawing proportions and could not render the basic lines of the hands and feet, and sometimes left them blank. In comparison, the penis, the line of the buttocks, and views of insertion show a good deal of care and thought. Like many illustrations of intercourse, the penis barely penetrates so that the full length can be seen. While "Miss Jones and Bill" has a complete narrative arc, the force of the story and the depth of attention given to developing the visualization of penetration make that aspect of the pamphlet more successful than other aspects of the story.

Other sorts of objects show both skill in creating explicit depictions and a sense that sex spoke in multiple registers.[61] Prisoners used the materials at hand to create erotic objects, which yielded artifacts both mundane and sublime. A prisoner repurposed a peach pit in an old folk tradition of peach pit carving (illus. 62).[62] The carving features a masturbating monkey in place of a masturbating man. The monkey thumbs his nose with one hand and masturbates with another. The artist took advantage of the edge of the peach pit to make a tail that runs up the monkey's back and gave the monkey a hat with a pom-pom on top. In addition, he carved eyes, a nose, and a mouth that he then reddened. He also reddened the tip of the monkey's enormous penis. The penis is larger than any of the monkey's other limbs. The cheerful little figure, both thumbing his nose and masturbating, seems to mirror prisoners' reactions to prison officials' proscription against self-pleasure.

As these examples show, the subjects of penetrative intercourse, male genitals, and beautiful women became emblematic of sexuality and desire in general. Prisoners developed these subjects across a variety of media, using a range of materials and with varying levels of skill. Though less common, other subjects also appeared in prison pornography, showing that prisoners possessed an array of fantasies and ways of thinking about sex. The "Colgate Floating" carving discussed in the Introduction (see illus. 3), which shows

59 "Miss Jones and Bill," pamphlet, received 1963, Prison Material Box, 1, Series II, E.2, Folder 1, p. 3, North America: United States, 20th Century, Prison Art, Leavenworth Federal Penitentiary, Kansas, Kinsey Institute.

60, 61 "Miss Jones and Bill," p. 8. Kinsey Institute.

a woman copulating with a horse, provides one example of bestial longings refracted through a prisoner's art.[63] Perhaps softer and more romantic soap carvings existed, but if they did, the guards didn't confiscate them. Thus this carved bar of soap records an explicit vision that counters both the sentimentality of non-pornographic culture and the streamlined vision of sexuality found in pornographic magazines like *Playboy*.

While the themes in prison pornography might be disturbing, these objects nonetheless allow for an articulation of sex for those otherwise denied a voice. One set of materials comes with a statement from the warden. According to the letter by Warden T. W. Markley, an African American prisoner at Terre Haute had been sentenced to a reformatory under the Youth Corrections Act and then transferred to the federal penitentiary for "better control."[64] During a series of psychiatric interviews, the prisoner identified himself as homosexual. The warden describes the prisoner's diagnoses as "sociopathic personality disturbance, anti-social reaction, characterized by disregard of social standards, inability to form meaningful relationships, poor sexual identification and homosexuality, social and emotional immaturity." From the warden's letter, it looks like the state had pathologized the young man and had sentenced him to ever more coercive forms of control. The young man fought back with whatever limited methods he could muster, including the attempt "to destroy the contents of his cell (because of strict supervision and control)," a race-related disturbance, a food strike, and an assault. The State and the man were at war with one another, and the State was winning. The warden saw the man's homosexuality and creation of obscene materials as part and parcel of his sociopathic and antisocial behavior.

62 Monkey Pendant, Realia, [1940?], ISR931, carved peach pit, Kinsey Institute.

The two pamphlets he created, though pornographic, were not thematically gay as the warden's assessment of his character would suggest. The first one, titled "Uncle Fred and Sue gets caught and that's not all," was written on small pages, folded in half to form a booklet. It was hand-lined and hand-lettered and featured hand-drawn images in pencil and crayon. The pamphlet tells a complicated story of incest from the niece's perspective. The story begins with the aunt leaving. The niece, Sue, a post-pubescent woman, showers and then walks downstairs to make her uncle breakfast. However, the uncle has sex with her instead. When the aunt comes home unexpectedly and surprises the two in the act, the aunt and uncle's plot emerges. The whole morning was planned to embolden the niece into having sex with her uncle. The niece responds by having sex with the aunt. The writer ran out of room and had to add a note card on which he describes how the niece denounces the aunt and uncle for their lack of stamina. Instead of being seduced by aunt and uncle, all of the characters engaged in mutual trickery and deceit.

The second pamphlet is much less plot-driven. It features a hand-drawn set of cards featuring a black man and white woman. She fellates him. They have sex, and then he has anal intercourse with her. Interestingly, given the warden's assessment of the young man as an "obligatory homosexual," neither pamphlet features male–male relations. The two pamphlets detail a set of desires that are neither violent nor particularly misogynistic. These materials focus on the pursuit of sex and pleasure against social conventions that condemned interracial sex and incest. Though losing his battle with the state, the man used his pencils and crayons to articulate an antisocial vision of sexual pleasures, one that defied categories of sexual control at the time of his incarceration.

Many prisoners found inspiration in popular culture and comic books (illus. 63). One prolific artist produced a series of sketches, cutouts, handmade books, and other paper objects.[65] These materials focused largely on sex but had no single theme and remained untitled. Some were figure studies and some were studies of penetration. The prisoner also created a number of unfinished books that reveal his desire to create an illustrated volume. He was clearly familiar with pamphlets, comics, and encyclopedias of sexual knowledge. One "book" labeled the "Encyclopedia of Sex" by "Prof. I . . . W." was modeled after non-academic "believe-it-or-not"-style volumes that featured oddities and little-known facts. The cover of the proposed book featured a "Table of Contents" with "Illustrations: Comics; Cartoons; Paintings; Portraits; Commercial Art and Volumes: Sex Appeal; Sex Book; Sex Comic; Sex for Fun; Homosexuals; Unusual Sex; 500 Sex Sellers and many, many more."[66] These topics seemed simultaneously educational and lurid. The same artist traced pornographic photographs to create abstracted versions of an image and traced and then recreated pornographic versions of the comic-strip cells of *Blondie* and *Dick Tracy*.

Elements from the broader culture, including popular culture and world events, had enough of an erotic appeal that prisoners used those ideas for pornography. At a moment when people across America decorated their homes with images of the young and handsome JFK, one prisoner used Kennedy's image to create pornography. Kennedy's presidency symbolized a sense of arrival as Irish Catholics saw themselves as fully accepted in the American polity for the first time. In framed photographs, lithographs, newspaper articles, magazine covers and samplers, people used JFK to speak about their American patriotism, Irish pride, and their affiliation with the Democratic Party. In the prisoner's version, he mashed Kennedy's image with the popular song entitled "The Twist." The illustration, labeled "Let's do the twist, and around we fight" (illus. 64) features a nude pencil drawing of Kennedy. The drawing features the president in a recognizable three-quarter profile. His body has been poorly wrought by tracing the outline of his clothed figure and then trying to find the lines of the body underneath. Instead of successfully stripping Kennedy of his clothes, the artist has given him small and saggy breasts and thickened calves that follow the line of his trousered legs. Unable to draw Kennedy's bare feet, the creator has given him slipper-like flats. According to the caption that runs alongside the drawing, Kennedy says, "Khrushchev doesn't have everything is this old world as I got in my hand I have the light of life, say's the big bright light John F. Kennedy." Kennedy holds his enormous red, erect, and dripping penis in his right hand. The caption alongside his ejaculation reads: "old and new life just droping." Along the bottom, the note from the U.S. to the USSR finishes: "So don't forget we have a lot of life over here Khrushchev."[67] Apparently, a pornographic dance-off between Khrushchev and Kennedy over the quality of life in the two societies excited both the president and the artist. The idea of the twist as erotic appears in the man's other drawings. Another, titled "Let's go to the twist up and down and around we go," features a naked woman calling to a man in the distance: "Hey over here I'm ready I can lay or do it any way C—." A nude and erect man responds: "Oh Daren I have a Dick that is always up to date time, and is a real sweetheart R—."[68]

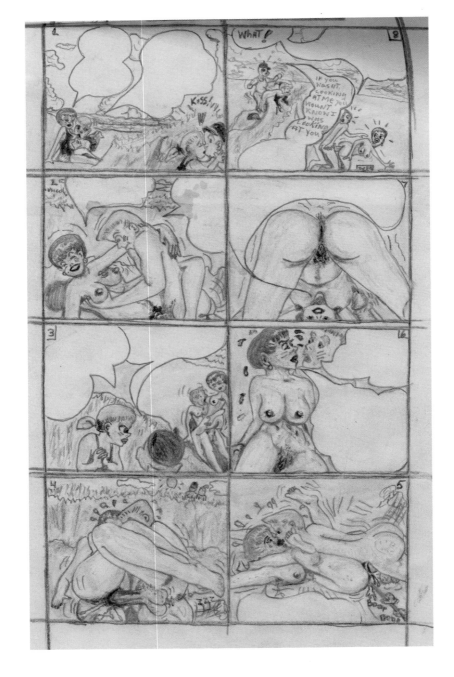

opposite:
63 "8 Cell Series
of Two Couples
Performing
Intercourse,"
item 2010.4.1.23,
North America:
United States,
20th Century,
Prison Art,
Baltimore,
Maryland,
received 1958–62,
Kinsey Institute.

Other sorts of fantasies about the meaning of world politics appeared in these materials. In the classic libertine tradition, pornographic renderings could have a political impact; in these versions, however, the meanings remain inchoate. In one image taken from a prisoner's cell, Jesus Christ kneels and fellates a Roman legionnaire while a fellow soldier smiles in the background.[69] The Roman pulls on Jesus' long hair, leans back with pleasure, and drools, as semen pools beneath Christ's mouth. The cross upon which Jesus will be crucified is etched with "U.S. Steel." A swastika is placed on Jesus' hip. In this rendering a Nazi Jesus is forced to pleasure the Roman state before being crucified on American steel. The artist clearly saw a message in this image, but the frisson of sexual energy seems to dissipate before the inchoate political renderings. Are we supposed to pity Nazi Jesus or laugh at him? Is he a figure of sympathy, repulsion, or longing? It is impossible to discern whether the image suggests sexual desire or sexual punishment. Is fellatio, like crucifixion, punitive? Or, like crucifixion, is it pleasurable for one and punitive for the other? The outlaw imagery combining swastikas and Christ might suggest that the creator saw himself as fighting against the state, religion, and industry, but it remains hard to read this as a political statement beyond an inchoate rejection of good taste. But the rejection of good taste and propriety was one of

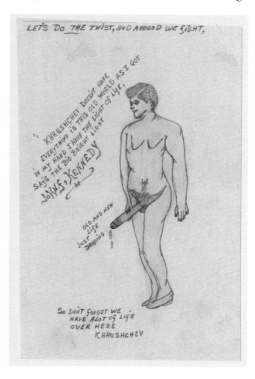

64 "Let's do the
twist, and around
we fight," item
2010.4.490, North
America: United
States, 20th
Century, Prison
Art, Baltimore,
Maryland,
Kinsey Institute.

the more telling ways for antisocial renderings to conceptualize sex. Some cultural critics have suggested that tastelessness itself was a radical act.[70] If so, then this drawing radically attacked the corporate, state, and religious status quos.

Some objects illustrated the ways that prisoners used pornography to communicate with each other, such as a confiscated valentine sent to one inmate from "Ricky." The heart-shaped card was made of cardboard, string, and crepe paper. When opened, a red-tipped erect penis decorated with a red crepe paper bow would rise toward the reader. Ricky had glued the following poem to the inside of the card:

> *To My Eskimo Pie*
> Your something face is just the thing
> that fills me with delight
> of your beady eyes and hungry grin
> I dream throughout the night.
> We have no secrets. I surely know
> A flute you work real fine
> High "C" and Low, you sure can blow
> So lick a tune on mine.[71]

Though a bit weak as poetry, the verses communicate a clear sexual desire. The obscene card, sent from one man to another, illustrates a vernacular tradition of communicating about sexuality that is wildly at variance with any Hallmark idea of the Valentine's holiday. Whether to read the card as sentimental or vaguely ominous depends upon the writer and receiver's relationship. The statement about the lack of secrets and the request to "lick a tune" might have indicated a consensual relationship awkwardly rendered. Alternately, it could have demanded oral sex for silence. Coercive sexual relationships were publicized by the press in the late 1960s, almost two decades after the confiscation of this card, though sexual relationships between men were of course taking place well before the press decided to make it the central issue of its reportage.[72]

Letters between prisoners that had been confiscated by guards shared a similar combination of roughness and intimacy. These notes were folded and refolded into compact forms and then taped into small, easily palmed and tossed parcels. Labeled with nicknames like Sleepy, Boo-Boo, Kitty Cat, Jelly Bean, Denver, or Dimples, these notes were passed from prisoner to prisoner as they hoped to communicate undetected by the guards.[73] Some writers straightforwardly valued the well-being of their partners over themselves. One begs his partner to stay out of trouble: "Please Dick don't get in trouble while you are up here, try to keep your parole date so you can get out of here. I will miss you when you go but I would rather miss you than have you in a place like this. I love you with all my heart."[74] Jimmy's sincerity allowed for the easy expression of sentiment. Other letter writers did not have a way to speak about their emotional attachment with other men. One writer, for example, lacked a language to speak of desire and affection and instead resorted to crude comparisons. "Hi Little Buddy, Look Bud I don't know just how to start this letter to you, I'm afraid I'm going to lose your friendship and as you know little Buddy I'd rather fuck my own mother, rather than ever lose your friendship."[75] This letter writer seems to mask his real sentimental attachment with the language of "mother-fucking." Underneath the gruffness and profanity, the writer searches for a language of care. In contrast, another letter writer mixed threats and love in equal measure. His relationship with "billy," the object of his desires, was very real to him at the same time as it was ominously coercive:

billy you think I don't know you are letting some guys up there fuck you and you ate my buddy up and he came down and told me so you can see why i am mad

you see baby i have known a lot of queers but i never fell in love with them as I have you i love you more than i love my whole family and thats saying a lot

billy if you write to me and say you will be mine only mine then nothing will happen to you but if i hear any more about some one up there fucking you Are you eating any one i'll fuck you.

i love you please understand that and as for moon I will see that
he gets whats coming to him when he comes in the yard.

. . .

Jonnie[76]

The combination of entreaties, declarations, demands, and threats under-
scores the complexity of Jonnie's attachments. While he might have felt
deeply about "billy"—something new in his emotional life—his demands
remained violent and coercive. Regardless of whether the emotional
attachments they describe are gentle or harassing, prison letters and prison
art exhibit a certain veracity, an honest reflection of their relations with
others, even if the sentiments that they display remain disturbing.

It should come as no surprise that some of these materials displayed a
willfully violent sexuality that refused to see the object of their desires as
autonomous subjects. Inmates housed at these prisons had been convicted
of committing criminal acts, including crimes of violence and sexual
crimes, though the anonymizing of their names makes it impossible to
connect their art with their criminal histories. Nonetheless, the extent
of rape fantasies in these materials demonstrates that coercive sexuality
was its own pleasure for a number of these men.

One hand-drawn pamphlet uses institutional scrap paper to create
an alternative version of a Dick and Jane children's story. The original
Dick and Jane story, first published in 1930, had become a staple by the
1950s in teaching children to read through imagining an idyllic white,
suburban middle-American family.[77] The prison version, confiscated from
Leavenworth Federal Penitentiary in 1963, describes the imprisonment of
Jane, her beating, and Dick's sexual dominance over her as he rapes her
vaginally, anally, and then orally, over her continual protests and cries of
pain. In a strange displacement given that it was rendered on scrap prison
stationery, the pamphlet documents Jane's eventual imprisonment and
bondage. As Dick says to her in a wordplay that might itself have derived
from prison culture, "you are in for a long fucking time or a long time
of fucking." Through the panels, Dick remains an outline, while Jane is

more fully drawn, with carefully colored red hair and a pinkish-hued body (illus. 65). To provide a setting, the writer carefully drew row after row of tiles, showing an attention to the institutional backdrop of the room.

As opposed to many prison-penned stories, this one provides a complete narrative arc. It begins with Jane's declaration of sexual and corporal virtue. According to her, she had never been spanked except by her father, and never been sexually active (though she has a boyfriend). Dick says that he looks forward to spanking her with a strap. He forces her to undress. He beats her, and the accompanying panel shows her reddened buttocks. He rapes and sodomizes her and eventually locks her in a cell with a shackle around her waist. The story is structured through a dialogue between Dick and Jane. The back and forth between the two characters is not set off in dialogue bubbles, sections, lines, or even quotation marks but runs as a continuous stream, differentiated only by call and response:

It will go all the way back to your stomack OK. Baby, here it comes. I am going to fuck you now. Oh. oh oh pleas pleas pleas that hurts ohooooo it going inside me. ohoooo, shut up I just got the head of it in you. Your cunt is tight. But it will loosen up. Just wiggle your ass baby. Wiggle it that better it is going in now. Oh that feel good to get

65 Jane and Dick narrative and pictures 8 rec'd from Leavenworth Federal Penitentiary 1-9-63, Box 1, Series II, Prisoner Erotica— Diaries. Fiction, Autobiographical Sketches—Male, Folder 1, E. Leavenworth, Kansas, Kinsey Institute.

one this tight for a change. I think I can ram it home now and really get to fucking. You. I got a hot head to put into your little cunt. Oh pleas I can't it hurts it hurts it hurt's it's hot it hurts oh. Oh shit, oh, oh pleas a please take it out take it out oh put it in-out ohooo get ready Baby I am ready to come.

The result of the back-and-forth dialogue is an almost omniscient stream of consciousness narration combining pain and pleasure, beating and being beaten, differentiated only by the shifts between Dick (powerful and in control) and Jane (raped and increasingly helpless). In the final panel, Jane is alone in the cell and Dick is no longer in the frame. She is shackled and he is free.[78] The gender dynamics of the pamphlet show an insistence on the brutal sexual exploitation and subjugation of women. This pamphlet's focus on Dick beating and raping Jane makes it clear that Dick's and the writer's pleasures come from her pain. It is not that the pamphlet ignores her subjectivity; instead the pamphlet details her subjective experience in concert with Dick's sexual pleasure. When she is reduced to a chained sex object in the final frame, the narrative has reached closure. For the producer of the pamphlet to detail another's violence, rape, and shackling as part of imprisonment even as he faced these possibilities as part of his own lived experience demonstrates either an eerie displacement of fears or an absolute refusal to acknowledge those fears by shifting vulnerability onto women. From reading the pamphlet, one cannot tell whether to be relieved that the author was incarcerated or whether his brutality emerged as a reaction to his incarceration.

In another disturbing example, a set of pamphlets shows a doubled consciousness in which seduction and rape serve as mirrors for each other in the author's mind. Two pamphlets—confiscated and produced by the same inmate in 1961—tell the same complicated story of street harassment, stalking, and rape.[79] The first pamphlet was hand-drawn with pencil coloration and hand-lettered on manila paper with a staple binding. The illustrations would have taken some skill and suggest the artist probably had consumed comic book images in the past, since the

pamphlet used that genre's renderings of perspective and figuration. The
first pamphlet begins with a man harassing a woman on the street. He rips
her dress off and tears at her bra. She escapes into a house and locks the
door. While she undresses, combs her hair, and gets into bed, he watches
through the window. She masturbates as he sneaks in through the window.
She protests that she is a virgin and offers to fellate him instead. He gets
Vaseline to "loosen her up" and then he rapes her in a variety of positions.
The second pamphlet is also staple-bound, hand-drawn in ink and pencil
with almost the same scenes. In this version, however, the two know each
other and embrace in the street. The woman says the man cannot come
in because of her nosy aunt. When he suggests breaking in during the
night, she laughs in response. After entering the house, she undresses
while looking at herself in the mirror. From the window, he watches her
as she looks in the mirror, a double gaze that feels vaguely ominous. He
sneaks in through the window. She protests that she's a virgin, she fellates
him, again he gets Vaseline to "loosen her up," and again they have sex in
a variety of positions. The core elements—the meeting on the street, the
sneaking into bed, the protests of a virgin, the fellatio, and then the use
of Vaseline—repeat in the two versions, suggesting a compulsive need
to revisit and envision a certain narrative structure. However, where one
booklet makes the encounter look like the mutual escape from the aunt's
surveillance, the other looks like harassment and rape, and the differences
between the two only register during a few points of dialogue. Their
similarities suggest the doubled way the man saw the same scenario. He
could see and articulate the mechanics of consent, just as he could imagine
the same scene as rape. Clearly, he found both visions of the scene erotic.
Rape and consensual relations literally looked the same to him. Reading
the two together suggests the ways the prisoner could move back and
forth between rape and mutuality, substituting volition for coercion and
acceptance for compulsion.

Another pamphlet that focuses on rape takes the violence even further.
This 1962 pamphlet illustrates the violent interracial rape of a young teenager.[80] The pamphlet was quite long, a full forty-five pages. Captioned and

illustrated in pencil and crayon, it was created on scrap office paper that had been cut into the approximate dimensions of a Tijuana bible—that is, wider than it is tall. The pamphlet begins with a blond teenage girl. As she returns from a babysitting job, she gets snatched by an adult African American man, who rapes her vaginally, orally, and anally. As the frames continue, more and more men are introduced so that the story becomes a matter of numbers as the interracial gang-rapes add up. With each type of rape, the girl responds with begging and crying that emphasizes her vulnerability: "Sob sob Please don't hurt me I'm a virgin," or "Sob Sob Please don't make me do it." Each sort of rape includes an illustration of the particular sexual act. The artist carefully penciled in the men so that their race is clear and included dialogue to emphasize the black on white rape, calling her "white bread" and "white pussy." Although the race of the artist is unknown and could have equally been a black or white man, the interracial nature of the rape was central to the writer-illustrator's sense of excitement.

Another pamphlet emphasized another type of interracial rape. This unillustrated story, called "I Was a White Slave for Mexico," details the descent into white slavery by a pretty eighteen-year-old hat-check girl who falls in love with an older man who drugged her when on vacation to Mexico. When she wakes up, she finds that men have invaded her room and are staring at her naked body. They rape her en masse. The strange combination of a growing number of men and shifting actors and locations makes it hard to understand the action of the story. For the writer, rape became a geometric progression:

> about twenty-four men came into the room. They looked at me and came over to the bed where I was . . . Fourteen men fucked me in the ass hole, six in my cunt and four in the mouth. And then they all took me again, they sure were giving me a fucking they all had me on my knees giving them head jobs. Then they took me over to the bed again and put me on my stomach, and one by one they got on my body again, putting their dicks in my ass hole.

The story becomes even more violent and at the same time abstracted by a numerical progression. From twenty-four men raping her, the numbers rise to thirty-six men and then to eighty men. The narrative also details beatings, Spanish fly injections, and lesbian sex. Despite the unemotional inflection of ever more desperate situations, the booklet ends with a strangely upbeat invitation by the girl to visit her in Mexico, "the girl in the whorehouse."[81]

This pamphlet describes sexual acts from the outside in a way that is strangely disembodied in that it focuses on the violation of bodily integrity. Rather than detailing what sex might feel like for men or emphasizing how it felt to inhabit a male body, the account focuses on the woman's penetration and fear. In "I Was a White Slave for Mexico," the narrator talks about "dicks in my asshole" rather than what it might feel like to put a dick in "her asshole." If anyone's body is inhabited in these descriptions, it is that of the subjugated female, who experiences no pleasure and instead describes what she wants not to happen. The articulation of types of rape and the geometric progression of perpetrators that ultimately becomes just a number per orifice—fourteen men here, six there, and four elsewhere—makes it clear that the writer cared less about the act than the massing of men. Rape gains meaning through numbers, as if the writer found something arousing through the removal of individuality. Perhaps the writer found arousing a mass extirpation of whiteness through racialized mass rape, or perhaps mass rape created male solidarity in the subjugation of women. Regardless, the geometric progression deepened a sense of watching sex rather than experiencing sex because the writer visualizes penetration through numbers.

For male prisoners who sought sexual relief from their own physical limitations in a psychological flight of imagination, these pamphlets offer a cramped and limited ideal of sexual happiness. Instead of focusing on male freedom, including the ability to imagine alternate locations or to consider a wide range of sexual partners, they document a sense of limitation—they narrow the field of vision rather than extend it. There are no bevies of women on moonlit tropical beaches. Instead, the creators of these documents chose to focus their miseries upon a single woman's body in a very limited space. Further, these pamphlets detail a strangely displaced sort of sexuality where pleasure comes not from the description of feelings in the male body but from the description of causing a woman pain, and then they escalate. The number of rapists edges up in a linear progression; vaginal rape builds to anal rape, and anal rape is followed by oral rape in a pattern denoting degradation. Sex looks less like male pleasure in these accounts than a form of male pleasure at causing female misery. These documents show little delight and instead suggest a desire to displace misery, captivity, and pain onto women.

While some pamphlets willfully embraced misery and pain as a leit-motif of sexuality, others drifted into a similar territory of pain and misery through a sense of distortion. Distortion could be cognitive, representa-tional, or both. One set of sketches from a Maryland prison by a single prisoner shows no clear sense of scale, no horizon line, no treatment of foreground. The sketches tend to treat the space as a single flat plane to be filled with objects. The lack of skill was compounded by significant mental illness that affected what the prisoner thought and how he saw the world. Loyal B. Calkins, the prison official who saved these materials, wrote in a note that "all of the drawings with the exception of the one on this page, were drawn by the same inmate who is a chronic schizophrenic with a very assaultive criminal record."[82] The prisoner's own renderings reference the disturbing nature of mental illness and medicine. One image, labeled "Hiden Madness," details three figures standing over an indistin-guishable bundle. The first figure prepares a carefully wrought hypodermic needle. His lab coat looks pristine and in his pocket he has three well-defined pencils. Behind him stands a larger figure with a monster's face. The huge, looming head twists to one side; one eye melts out of the socket while the other is rendered almost completely round, with a fully visible cornea staring back at the viewer. A third, possibly naked, figure stands behind the monster.[83] Madness and distortion affect the content and rendering of the vision. The prisoner titled his works, though common words like "birth" were misspelled as "Brith" and the more complicated words "Cleopatra" and "hurricane" were written as "Clopatia" and "Huecain," suggesting a limited literacy. The quantity of the drawings, numbering in the hundreds, demonstrates that these images were not the product of a simple confiscation by a guard. Instead, the prisoner devoted considerable time and care to his creations and prison officials knew of his pasttime, perhaps even encouraging it. The occasional inked correction of a mis-spelled title written in pencil shows that someone considered the materials and their meanings and might have even communicated with the prisoner to work out his intent.

The artist tried to detail a range of ideas about sexual pleasure and its meanings, ranging from the phantasmagoric, including "death freak," "ghost sex," and "ice-age sex," to the more mundane, like "morning love," "side sex," and "tabletop sex." They also range in the affective realm, from images labeled as "rape" and "Blood in the Moonlight" to balloons in the shapes of hearts called "Hearts for Love." One drawing of a series of vignettes, labeled "Sex manieacts" (illus. 66), shows at least eight couples drawn in red pencil across a single sheet of paper. A man in the middle of the drawing whips a woman as her severed foot flies up in the air. A woman manacled to the bed with her legs open, showing her vaginal opening, dominates the foreground, but it appears as if another person lies shackled beneath her. A box, possibly a coffin, shows the smiling head of a woman surrounded by what might be other body parts. A masked man penetrates a woman on her hands and knees. In the uppermost right, a man and woman lie in the missionary position, while an open door to the right shows just a portion of another standing man. Other figures are incorporated onto the page; while the scene and even the number of figures remains unclear and incoherent, the carefully rendered erect nipples and penises show the figures' excitement.

The images vary in detail and quality, with some showing sophis-ticated patterns of shading and perspective and others revealing problems with even simple renderings, which suggests that the prisoner might have experienced moments of serious cognitive impairment but also periods of relative clarity at other times. The same prisoner drew an eight-celled

comic book with care (see illus. 63). The artist had a very clear idea of how a comic should look and what went into each frame. He also drew coherent figures in the cells. One incomplete series showed two couples watching each other have sex. For the first six cells, thought bubbles dominate the space, but only one cell has the thoughts of the participants filled in. That cell shows two men standing, having sex from behind with two women on their hands and knees. The men yell at each other across the divide of their thoughts: "What!" The other man replies: "If you wasn't looking at me, you wount know I was looking at you." Despite the careful attention paid to drawing the thought bubbles, seven of them remain empty. Instead of working out how his characters might think and feel, the inmate filled in a yellow landscape with green hills in the distance and carefully drew the couples' complete bodies with arms, legs, and reddened erect penises, nipples, and vaginal openings. Clearly, the prisoner was more motivated by the coloration of excitement and display of sexual positions than by the development of dialogue that would speak to his comic book characters' inner lives.[84] He can only articulate how the dialogue between the men might begin, not where it might go or why. In other images, including one of guns and knives, the prisoner achieved remarkable clarity and even presented the subjects in schematics so that the viewer could see how bullets fit into the chamber of a gun.[85]

What does the proliferation of materials from this prisoner demonstrate? The 116 created and seized images show the wide range of the prisoner's sexual fantasies, from sexual dismemberment to phantasmagoric sex to sentimental sex. They also show the range of styles in the prisoner's visual lexicon. While not a skilled artist, he nonetheless brought in motifs from the surrealistic style (including melting limbs and eyes), sentimental popular culture (like heart-shaped balloons), comic books, and outlaw art (like the motifs of coffins and knives). He clearly drew from a variety of visual traditions to express himself. Further, certain subjects, like guns, brought a clarity to his renderings despite his cognitive impairment. Even though he could not articulate the expressive content indicative of an affective world in the comic's "thought bubbles," the form of the comic

66 "Sex manieacts," item 2010.4.1.49, North America: United States, 20th Century, Prison Art, Baltimore, Maryland, Kinsey Institute.

67 Nurse giving male injection, acquired 1963, item 2012.30.77, North America: United States, 20th Century, Prison Art, Kinsey Institute.

book and its value were clear. In other words, although he could not imagine what went on in the heads of others and could barely illustrate his own mental condition, he thought a lot about sex and found clarity in violent and comic book culture.

An awareness of psychiatry, psychologists, medicine, and doctors affected prisoners' fantasies and they saw themselves and their erotic fantasies as caught within a medicalized world (illus. 67). Prisoners saw themselves as constituted by and reflected back in the gaze of abnormal psychology. Prisoners not only represented their own madness as a subject in their art, they also saw a psychological foundation for their sexual proclivities, from the nightmarish characterization of medical violence in the drawings of the prisoner just described, to more foundational readings of their own psychology.

A story written by an inmate from Chino, confiscated in 1958, focused on a patient's relationship with his psychiatrist. Entitled "All for Love (A Study in Psychiatry)," this story creates a Freudian foundation for the author's own desires.[86] Clearly, the writer had studied Freud and had a working knowledge of the Oedipal complex. Even more impressive, however, is the way that the author created a narrative that successfully worked the notions of transference and counter-transference into the sexual plot of a pornographic short story.

The beginning starts with an almost noirish cadence. The narrator describes meeting a psychiatrist and deciding to enter into analysis: "I was in love with my doctor . . . Joyce Kimbrough was her name, I had met her through one of the business contacts that I have, we met at a party that was being given at one of the larger uptown hotels. I remember seeing her across the room, looking very calm, cool, and just a little bored." Growing intrigued by the aloof doctor, the patient schedules an appointment. In the psychiatrist's office, the patient/narrator shares the memory of his mother crying after his father had died. He had gone in her room to comfort her one day and ended up lying in bed next to her. He fell asleep and woke up with his mother caressing his belly and then his penis. Son and mother caress each other and undress. As he describes this scene, he looks at his psychiatrist, who has a peculiar look on her face. He becomes aroused. The patient continues his recitation, saying he knew it was wrong but his mother needed it. Mother and son begin to have sex.

> I began as she had told me but that peculiar sensation seemed to flood my being and I thought at first to be engulfed, almost with no violation [volition(?)] I began to bunch faster and try to drive my

dick deeper with each thrust. I wanted to get all of me inside that mass of quivering flesh. The world was reeling and she must have sensed it and told me "take it slow and easy, we have a lot of time."

The narrator/patient explains that they continued to have sex until his mother died seven years later. As he describes his sexual experiences with his mother, both the patient and psychiatrist grow aroused and the psychiatrist wipes his face with a handkerchief. Psychiatrist and patient begin to kiss and caress each other. They have sex. Then, as he performs oral sex on her, her secretary enters and performs fellatio on him. The story ends as both psychiatrist and patient orgasm.

The author not only had control over his prose, but showed originality in terms of foundational ideas and found a way to communicate multiple story lines in parallel. As the narrator tells of having sex with his mother, he also details the growing arousal of doctor and patient. Sex in the past leads to sex in the present. Further, sex with his mother led to his desire for his psychiatrist and to her reciprocation; Oedipal sex led to transference and counter-transference, all in a neat fictional package. In essence, his recounting of his past becomes the story of sexual fulfillment through psychiatry. Clearly, this prisoner believed that psychiatry and psychology spoke both about and to him.

Doctors and psychiatrists both functioned as the subjects of patient fantasies and provided explanations for their arousals. As the story above shows, the relationship between the scientific study of sex and pleasure ramifies in multiple directions. While prisoners were supposed to be subjects of study, they turned the relationship around and studied sexual science. They wrote back in response to what was written about them.[87]

Prisoners understood these hidden relationships between sexuality and scientific study. The seizure of pornographic images and the use of them for "scientific purposes" became just another aspect of governmentality, and the prisoners knew it. One confiscated illustration, "Psychiatric Interview S.Q. From Our Side" (illus. 68), notes the fervor of the psychiatrist looking to understand the prisoner's mind. The caption to the illustration,

which reads "Do you like squirrels? Have you read Dr. Kinsey? Hmmmmmm?" is an echo of the larger process through which documentation and articulation reinforced each other.[88] The prisoner knew that the document he produced would be used to peer into his mind. He used Kinsey's name as a codeword for sexuality, understood as key to the self. Ironically, the prisoner recognized the way that his drawing was being used to examine his thoughts, but all he could do was document the process. The image was then seized and shipped to the ISR's archives, bundled with all of the other articles of prisoner pornography, its criticism made irrelevant by being buried in the archives. Despite this clarity on the relationship of prison pornography to the legitimation of the scientific study of sex, prisoners could not effect change.

Kinsey and other members of the ISR saw themselves as expanding scientific knowledge, but they also earned a particular cultural legitimation from their work with prisoners, and they capitalized on that legitimacy when needed. Evidence for this claim comes from the Customs case *U.S. v. 31 Photographs*, which embroiled the ISR throughout the 1950s. The case began in 1950 when a new customs agent in Indianapolis raised the question of whether the ISR should be able to import materials considered obscene under the Tariff Act of 1930. The previous agent thought that a tacit dispensation for researchers should apply, but the new agent asked for direction from Washington, which found the imported materials grossly obscene.[89] (The materials under dispute included books in French and English, some handwritten notes, and commercial photographs. None of these materials related to prisons or criminal sexuality.) In 1957

Judge Edmund L. Palmieri upheld the ISR's right to import materials for scientific study that would otherwise be illegal.[90] According to Judge Palmieri's decision, pornographic materials should be considered in the context in which they were to be viewed. At the ISR, where access was limited to serious researchers who studied sexuality, community standards dictated that the materials would not be considered obscene even if they might be elsewhere.[91] Thus the ISR won the case, resulting in the so-called "Kinsey exception," which allows research institutions to import materials for scientific study that might otherwise be labeled obscene.

To make claims about the ISR's legitimacy, Kinsey's lawyers incorporated statements from prison administrators and state officials into the case evidence. Karl M. Bowman, MD, University of California Medical Center; Dr. Manfred Guttmacher, chief medical adviser for Baltimore City's Supreme Bench; and Harley Teets, Warden of San Quentin, provided affidavits. In fact, one-third of supporting materials came from prison administrators. When called upon to articulate why they worked with Kinsey and his team, officials wrote about the value of research with prisoners. Harley Teets, Associate Warden from 1946 until 1951 and Warden of San Quentin starting in 1951, summarized what he saw as the value of Kinsey's research for the prison system:

> During the period approximately from 1948 to 1954 and during which time Dr. Kinsey and his associates were doing research here I was in direct contact with you and appreciate the value of your research in actual management of prisons and/or people, wherever they may be, in relation to sex offenses, adjustment and the part played by sex in other than sex crimes.[92]

He provided a signed affidavit stating that a greater understanding of criminal sexuality would help administrators run prisons.[93]

Others touted the value of the study of prisoner pornography for what it might reveal about sexual aberrations. James V. Bennett, director of the United States Department of Justice, Bureau of Prisons, noted that

During the 20 years that I have served as Director of the Federal
Bureau of Prisons, I have been impressed by the need for increased
knowledge of many aspects of sexual behavior . . . Scientific studies
of sexual behavior have considered many modes of sexual expression
including the production of erotic material. It has been demonstrated
a great deal can be learned from the study of erotic materials, particularly as such materials may be a reflection of underlying mental
aberration in the persons producing it. Thus, our knowledge and
understanding of various pathological sexuality [*sic*] and of sexual
offenders has been enhanced by the study of the erotic productions
of these deviated persons.[94]

According to Bennett, the study of prison-made pornography could lead
to a better understanding of mental aberrations and sexual pathology.

The testimony from Bennett, Teets, and others legitimated the work
done at the ISR and was used to help sway the judge regarding the importance of importing erotica to the ISR, but frankly, the *U.S. v. 31 Photographs*
case itself was concerned with the importation of commercial materials
through customs and had little to do with prisoner pornography. Nonetheless, looking into the criminal mind was central to the way that Kinsey,
Gebhard, prison officials, and others justified access to knowledge about
sexuality. At the moment when the state intervened into sexual science and
tried to limit the circulation of illegal materials, Kinsey and others defended
themselves by citing the need to examine the fantasies of prisoners through
their pornography. Though prison pornography remained irrelevant to
the seized materials in the case, prisoner sexuality nonetheless was thought
of as central to the goals of scientific inquiry and was thus brought time
and again into the issue. The fantasies of prisoners, in part, justified the
ISR's exclusion from laws that limited the circulation of commercial goods.

The value of prisoner pornography came from the roadmap it provided into the fantasies and desires of criminals, according to members
of the ISR and prison officials. Gebhard himself explicated this ability in
his request for confiscated materials:

When we were working in the California prisons, the wardens periodically gave us the confiscated erotic material (mainly drawings, letters, and "cartoon books") which had accumulated. These are proving valuable to us, giving us insight into the desires and fantasies of inmates. Unfortunately I find we have very little of such materials from Soledad. This is our fault: we should have sought it more consistently. Frankly, I kick myself when I think of how valuable it would have been to have obtained a sample of erotic material from the general inmate body and compared it to material from the Z wing, but that opportunity has passed. At any rate, if you could arrange to have confiscated erotic material sent to us, we would be very appreciative.[95]

Kinsey, Gebhard, prison administrators, and others believed in the centrality of prison fantasies to sexual knowledge.

Although they might have thought of themselves as documenting, rather than intervening in, its production, there is evidence that the researchers did both. In innumerable ways, the study of prison fantasies and the articulation of those fantasies was reciprocal. As early as 1950, Kinsey and officials at San Quentin began to note that some materials collected came from the so-called "hot-room."[96] In a letter requesting confiscated materials from the warden of Minnesota State Prison, who had previously worked at San Quentin, Gebhard again referred to the "hot room":

I recently examined our collection of "hot room" drawings, letters, cartoons, etc. and, in the process, realized we haven't added a blessed item since our last trip to California. Consequently I have written to the wardens of all our old stamping grounds, attempting to persuade them to send us material—being careful to point out that I strongly doubt if they would run afoul of the postal authorities (especially since our favorable decision in the customs case).

In the Midst of this I suddenly thought, "My God, why haven't I been dunning Rigg for such data"! Hence this letter. If you are short on "hot room" material, we will send (free) paper, pencils, and crayons to your institution. Sorry, but we cannot provide models.[97]

Apparently, Kinsey and his team had been contributing art materials so that prisoners could document their fantasies. This donation of materials was integral to the incitement of sexuality; a pack of crayons and the paper to write on became the platform for the conceptualization of desire. But the name "hot room" implies a physical location as well as the supply of materials. Instead of creating an architecture of surveillance and thus forcing prisoners to repudiate obscene objects as Foucauldian ideas of the panopticon might suggest, Kinsey and the wardens created a safe space for creativity. In the process, they called forth all sorts of desires. Obscene materials were then shipped to the ISR so that its members could work to understand prisoner sexuality.

By making prisoners' desires into objects of study, Kinsey and prison officials fed obsessions both fantastical and scientific. Prisoners showed their obsessions with the hundreds of illustrations and innumerable stories they created. Members of the ISR showed their obsessions with the urge to collect and archive these materials. ("We have just completed the typing of all the text of the material which you contributed from the 'hot room'. We have all of the pictures mounted and classified.")[98] Even creativity served governmentality. The Foucauldian implications of the focus on prison pornography seem unavoidable. As Michel Foucault points out in *Discipline and Punish* (1975), power doesn't repress, it creates. In the case of prison pornography, prison administrators and members of the ISR incited the pervert/prisoner to articulate a hidden "truth of sexuality." As Foucault argues in *The History of Sexuality* (1976), the idea that sex is a central truth worth speaking of contributed to a discursive explosion on the subject of sexuality. Certainly, Kinsey's own works contributed to that eruption of discourse. His volumes and those completed by ISR members after his death made statistics the language of sexual science. Arguments about normative sexuality after the middle of the century took for granted a scientific and statistical foundation for claims about truth. But the discursive generation can also be seen in the thousands of pages created by prisoners.

The ISR continued to benefit from its associations with prisoner pornography. Once the Kinsey exception was established in court—in part because of the perceived value of peering into the criminal mind—the ISR used the ruling about customs regulations to justify the mailing and transportation of materials interstate, despite the dubious legality of this practice. (In obscenity law, customs regulations remained distinct from postal regulations.) Despite this distinction, Gebhard used the ruling on the ISR's case to ask prison officials to send materials within the U.S. In a letter to the California Institute for Men at Chino, Gebhard wrote: "I do not believe that you need to be concerned about postal regulations. The postal authorities have never interfered with our domestic mail, and since we recently won our case versus U.S. Customs, I imagine the postal authorities consider the Federal Court decision applies also to them."[99] Besides the dubious legality of this claim and the problematic ethics of Gebhard recommending that prison officials circumvent the law, there is also an intrinsic circularity to it. The ISR used testimony about the value of prison erotica as a justification for importing materials that had nothing to do with prisons and then used the Kinsey exception that applied to Customs to justify the transmission of more prison pornography across state lines. The supposed value of prison pornography trumped the law repeatedly. The weight of these claims seems too great for homemade prison pornography made by men who could barely read or draw stick figures, but apparently drawings of naked women, masturbating men, and intercourse, and the occasional violent pamphlet or fetishistic story, were too important to disregard. Homemade and handmade pornography promised to provide the key to understanding the crisis of expanding criminality at a critical moment in the carceral state.

Prisoners knew that the state seized and studied the representations of their deepest desires. Prison officials took prisoners' private notes to each other, took their photographs of girlfriends and striptease performers, and took their fantasies, written in longhand and drawn in crayon. Despite this foreknowledge, prisoners produced these materials; maybe they saw themselves as being in a constructive relationship with researchers, or perhaps the pleasures of a brand-new box of crayons were too hard to resist.

These seized objects can be considered part of the discursive explosion that tried to get to the "truth" of sexuality. The carceral state did not repress sexuality; it created it, and in the case of prison pornography it incited fantasies and then shipped them to archives. Once organized, typed, and accessioned, these materials were to wait until state-approved authorities could sort out the nature of desire in some sort of legitimate way. But strangely, after the ISR contributed to their creation, asked for their collection, used these objects to change laws, and then bent the law to allow for their shipping, these materials have gone largely unused. Kinsey's death, the loss of funding at the ISR, the shift from a zoological/statistical to a sociological/psychological perspective, and a retrenchment in prison culture all contributed to a shift in priorities. As a result, prison pornography as a set of materials has gone under-studied.

In many ways, prison pornography echoed the wider range of hand-made and homemade objects. In terms of themes and subjects, prison pornography reflected the larger world of sexual desires, rather than being atavistically set against it. Imprisoned men created images that mirrored subjects found both in commercial and homemade and hand-made pornography. Prisoners worked with available materials, although the media of expression in prison reflected a dearth of commercial culture and raw materials as compared with those used in the broader world at the moment. While outside prisons people might collage or alter magazines and newspapers, or craft erotic objects from wood or metal, in prison men relied more heavily on paper and everyday materials like soap and fabric sheets. Despite this difference, prisoners created objects remarkably similar to those found circulating more widely. The masturbating man made of pipe cleaners, for example, appeared in commercial productions, handmade and homemade renditions, and prison pornography. Pencil sketches likewise appeared both within and outside prisons.

Comic books and pamphlets remained a popular form regardless of where they were produced.

The styles in these productions and of these productions reflected the styles of the times. Men whether in or out of prison shared the vision of the woman with pneumatically endowed breasts from the 1950s pin-up. The brilliant red adornments given to the "fast" woman also transcended boundaries. Fantasies about the boss and secretary spread even to those segments of society who were not "bosses." The visual style of the comic book spread appealed so that even those who could not imagine how a story might progress or what characters might think or say in the individual cells would still create cellular divisions on the page. Other forms, like the "encyclopedia of knowledge" that shouted "strange happenings," made popular in books like *Ripley's Believe It or Not!*, showed up in prison pornography. Thus, in many ways, prison pornography belongs with the other assemblages of homemade and handmade pornography.

However, by its very definition prison art was outlaw art, art made by outlaws.[100] Imprisoned, monitored, and surveyed, these men lived in the heart of the physical and metaphysical panopticon. The state controlled what these men did, saw, and read, and confiscated those materials that did not fit into what were considered appropriate affective worlds. In illustrating and articulating their desires, inmates pitched themselves against the state. Each illustration of anal sex, incest, fellatio, or cunnilingus, every illustration of a woman, a tongue, and a martini glass, every raw illustration of a woman's body and a masturbating monkey countered state ideas of appropriate behavior and control of the self.

Prison pornography documents a refusal to check the self. Instead of a sexuality regulated by social demands, these materials document the pleasures gained from a rejection of social control. The pleasures can be seen in the willingness to explore and visualize unsanctioned sexual activities, from bestiality to incest to interracial sex. They can also be seen in taking pleasure in brutality to extremes, from the pamphlets showing a geometric progression in the number of rapists, to the labored and misspelled articulations of begging victims. These objects refused to follow the rules. At the same time, these materials acknowledged the consequences of breaking the rules when they wove together sexuality and the carceral state. Men took the ideas of limitation, confinement, and the carceral state and used them in their pornography. Physically imprisoned men extended the ideation of the prison into their sexual desires. Desire often looked like the imprisonment, shackling, and pain of others. Imprisonment and desire were woven together so firmly that they substantiated each other.

Though traditionally labeled as "outsider art," there is something very "insider" about prisoner pornography because it was produced by men incarcerated by the state, with state knowledge, for state concerns. Though generally treated as "outsider art," this selection of prisoner pornography might as well be thought of as state-generated, or at least state-encouraged, erotica. Instead of being timeless articulations of outsider fantasies, these objects were generated through the tension between incitement and repression, between scientific engagement and individual desires, and were used for extending governmentality before being boxed up and forgotten, a window into criminality for a population equally discarded.

4

The Postwar World and
the Making of a People's
Pornography, 1940s–1970s

Nowadays, libraries often let patrons bring drinks into reading rooms, but in the twentieth century beverages were forbidden, especially in archives and special collections because of the danger to rare books, manuscript sources, and other original materials housed inside. Given prohibitions against beverages, let alone food, the existence of a cookie in the Kinsey Institute archive seems surprising. This cookie, accessioned in 1952, is a crumbling remnant of the expansion of homemade and handmade pornography that occurred between the Second World War and the 1970s. Shaped like a penis and given pubic hair made out of brown chocolate sprinkles, this cookie seems out of place in multiple ways. Not only does it shock for its place in the archives, and not only does it seem rather fossilized by the longevity of its tenure, but cookies have an association with women's culture and female crafts. As this chapter will show, the postwar period saw the expansion in the number and type of erotic artifacts. Not only did more people create more types of handmade and homemade pornography, but new people produced them as well. Further, they did so despite a growing availability of commercial materials.

The expansion of a sexualized commercial market came in two phases. The early phase, which lasted through the late 1950s, saw a mass consumer culture shot through with erotic tensions. During the war and after, sexuality worked as a meta-language to speak about social needs during a critical moment in American society. Nonetheless, the state maintained censorship, limiting the circulation of commercial pornography. In response, people made their own pornography that exposed, leered, and laughed at latent erotic tensions. During the later phase, from the late 1950s until the 1970s, a liberal consensus began to form, contributing to a loosening of censorship and the development of a legal and explicit sexual consumer culture. Pornographic novels, films, magazines, photographs, and more proliferated. Despite the advent of legal pornography and the subsequent saturation of a sexualized consumer culture, people made amateur pornography in ever greater numbers in a growing number of media.

Across the time period, handmade objects built upon the long-established vernacular tradition, but the expansion itself transformed the nature of the amateur category. People increasingly felt like their own products had value and meaning, partly as a result of the DIY movement that saw making as part of a form of cultural democracy. As well, new sorts of handmade and homemade pornography began to appear as people knitted, sewed, and baked amateur obscenities. Makers, including women, gay and trans people, and African Americans, adapted old production methods to new ideas, tones, and subjects. As this chapter will show, despite the growing availability of commercial objects, handmade and homemade pornography flourished, becoming increasingly diverse in terms of its makers, subjects, and meanings, and ultimately creating a broad and politicized people's pornography.

The Wartime and Postwar World

During the Second World War, the state used sexuality to link patriotism to the home front, calling on men to be virile and suggesting that women would be their rewards. A commercial culture linked the war effort with sexuality and condoned sentimentalized sexuality as an expression of the "home fires" that would continue to burn. The massive movement of people allowed a greater anonymity for people to explore sexual desires that might have remained subsumed beneath social demands had the war not intervened. While overtly the war played off the longing to return home to the "girl next door," in practice new social conditions allowed for new sexual arrangements, from interracial sexuality in Britain to homosocial erotics in single-sex barracks.[1] This atmosphere created ripe conditions for pornographic expression.

Objects made by soldiers, prisoners of war, and local civilians, including pornographic objects, have been misleadingly labeled as "trench art," whether they came from trenches or camps. Craft objects fashioned from the remnants of industrial warfare, including wood, bone, cloth, hair, and metal, fall into the trench art category. Soldiers and civilians began fashioning art from industrial materiel in earnest during the First World War, though objects considered trench art also appear from the Boer War, the Franco-Prussian War, even the Napoleonic Wars, long before trenches became the defining position in warfare.[2] The scale of

69
Bottle opener from the Second World War, brass. Author's collection.

the two world wars, however, extended the magnitude of the category of trench art as tens of millions of men became combatants and great swaths of the world were affected by war. More people were taken out of daily life and thrust into industrial catastrophe as civilians and non-combatants were caught in war-torn regions, forced into agrarian and industrial labor, or herded into new regions and camps. Soldiers behind the lines, often bored, took industrial artifacts and transformed them just for something to do. Civilians searched battlefields and bombed-out areas for military materiel and made objects to barter and trade. People in concentration camps scavenged for resources that could be turned into items of value. POWs made objects to barter with the guards for supplies. Whereas the First World War on the Western Front was a war of immobility and stasis, allowing the construction of larger objects, the Second World War was largely a war of mobility and large-scale destruction. Soldiers, POWs, and civilians associated with the war still made art, but it tended to be small and more portable.[3]

Pornographic trench art from the Second World War includes a candelabra made from a brass shell casing with a sexy nude pin-up figure punched into the side; a metal inkwell with a wooden base ornamented with a carving of a nude woman; a wooden figurine of a nude woman carved on Iwo Jima; a dagger handle carved into a naked woman; a metal clipboard etched with the figures of two women, one topless, the other in lingerie; and a brass shell casing fashioned into a bottle opener attached to an erect penis and testicles (illus. 69).[4] Also considered trench art would be a coffin figurine that was carved in Sicily, no doubt to sell to the Allies during the Italian campaign. The figurine has a gruesome cast, with bare skull, articulated ribcage, prominent pelvic bone, and the mandatory erection pop-up, painted with a red tip.

That soldiers, sailors, and civilians made erotic objects is unsurprising given the sexual saturation of wartime culture. During the Second World War, commercial pin-ups were affixed to soldiers' and sailors' lockers as tokens of home and talismans of heterosexual desire.[5] Relatively tame pin-ups of Hollywood starlets were augmented by more revealing pictures of women in racier publications like *Esquire*. Planes were emblazoned with coquettish paintings and named with double entendres (illus. 70, 71, 72). Objects decorated with nude women fitted well into a culture that legitimated the proliferation of pin-ups; handmade objects made during the war featured the same arched-back, high-breasted, small-waisted archetype circulated in the drawings of Alberto Vargas and George Petty.[6] These public depictions of sexuality combined patriotism with a sense of home. As Marilyn E. Hegarty shows in her analysis of gender and war, women grew increasingly "enveloped in a discourse of sexual obligation" that suggested they owed it to men to keep up their sex appeal.[7] The saturation of men's culture with pin-up images was constituted through a shared conviviality over the idea of women's sexual accommodation. In this atmosphere, the extension of erotic commercial motifs into racier handmade objects seems unavoidable.

Trench art both unveiled such pin-ups and detailed much more imaginative fantasies. One group of images used the motifs of Second

World War propaganda and explicated implicit sexual messages.[8] A pencil sketch features a uniformed soldier on a bench with a woman, hinting toward all of the clichés about soldiers and their sweethearts canoodling in public during the war. In Hollywood movies and newspaper images, such embraces were given a romantic cast. This image, however, focuses on sexual satisfaction rather than romance and longing. The artist has drawn the woman lying face down on the soldier's lap and holding his erection. His hand reaches down to fondle her genitals. The artist provided the woman's side of the dialogue: "Feel me all you want soldier. While I 'blow your brains out,' but don't make me come, I want a 'Frenching job' as good as youre [*sic*] going to get, o.k." The physical intimacy of oral sex combined with the anonymity of not knowing each other's first names provides an alternative picture of sexual expression during the war from the limited ones circulated in Hollywood. Here, the orgasms matter and the promises made during the night have nothing to do with patriotism, the good fight, or returning from the war to conclude a romance.

70 "Cold Turkey," nose art, 1940s. Author's collection.

71 "Lassie, I'm Home," nose art, 1940s. Author's collection.

72 "Miss Manookie,"
nose art, Payne
Field, Cairo, Egypt,
1940s. Author's
collection.

A second pencil sketch by the same artist, featuring a doctor and nurse (illus. 73), plays upon the ways that Hollywood movies harnessed healthcare for warfare through romantic byplay. In the pornographic version, the doctor holds the nurse's bare breast in one hand. She swoons a bit to one side and holds his erect and bare penis. From her short curls and perky nurse's cap to his white lab coat and square jaw, the couple looks like the cover of a hospital romance novel set against the war. The dialogue, like the image, builds upon already established codes of breathless propaganda. "Nurse, your [*sic*] about due for and [*sic*] injection. In the arm, or buttocks. Doc? In the cunt, I believe Nurse. Oh Doctor! What a heavenly treatment." In this sketch, the artist replaced sentimental codes about sacrifice and duty with sexual demands and replaced coy banter with obscene language for sexual desires. These materials took the standardized articulations of heterosexuality harnessed for the good of the war and made them into much grittier expressions of desire.

As a group, handmade and homemade materials from the war reflect both earlier folk traditions and wartime commercial expressions. In terms of style and subject matter, coffin figures and penis bottle openers could

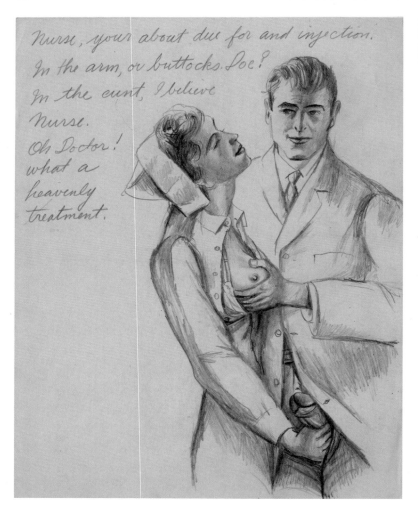

Nurse, your about due for and injection.
In the arm, or buttocks. Doc?
In the cunt, I believe
Nurse.
Oh Doctor!
what a
heavenly
treatment.

73 "Doctor and Nurse," [194?], item A630R A869a-f, Kinsey Institute.

have been made decades earlier. Though the war made brass, metal, wood, and bone more available for creative reuse, office materials also circulated. A celluloid "toothpick" that supposedly comes from wartime features a portly man with an articulated erection and dunce-cap-shaped toothpick (illus. 74). The toothpick and erection swivel on a brass fastener. Both the subject matter and style reach back in time. Although the context of production intrinsically defines objects, that context is barely written

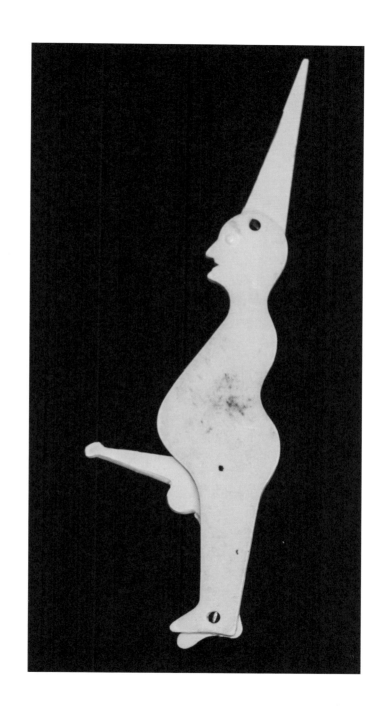

74 Celluloid tooth-
pick, articulated
figure, *c.* 1939–45.
Author's collection.

onto these wartime objects. No doubt, someone returning from the Italian campaign with a trench art souvenir would see his experiences wrought in it, but removed from their provenance, very little marks these objects as war-related. Other materials more concretely reflect the age of their creation by using the pin-up style and the breathless rhetoric of patriotism, marking handmade materials within a particular context. Even when parodying them—exclaiming "Oh, Doctor! What a heavenly treatment," for instance—such materials emerged from the same consciousness of patriotic sexuality during the war. Robert Westbrook notes that the famous photograph of a sailor kissing a nurse in Times Square during a victory parade in 1945 worked as "a representative kiss, manifesting in its mix of joy and violence the ambiguities of the moral contract binding protective men and protected women in a liberal state."[9]

The construction of more deeply sexualized images in homemade pornography suggests that the implications of that representation were well understood. Rather than just intimating sex, commercial constructions functioned as a public face of sex, without the more graphic sexual elements that were subsequently supplied by men through their own erotic artwork.

As well as adorning their airplanes with pin-ups or dressing as women in theatrical productions, men during the Second World War made erotic sketches, drawings, carvings, and other types of pornography. In sex-segregated communities, men made art about sex and desire and used the tools and materials they had at hand. In previous generations, men in lumber camps had carved wood and sailors had made sea ivory into scrimshaw; during the wars, soldiers used shells, casings, and paper to make trench art. Trench art continued traditions begun before the war but also recognized the commercialization of sexuality in erotic objects and made explicit the sexual tensions that were supposed to goad men into fighting.

After the war, during the decade between 1947 and 1957, reports about sex crimes, juvenile delinquency, and security risks in the federal government raised national fears about the consequences of sexual unorthodoxy.[10] These fears seemed like they would engender a new sexual conservatism. The possibility of Cold War blackmail led to the firing of thousands of government employees because of their sexual histories. The state continued campaigns against pornographers like Samuel Roth, a bookstore owner and publisher best known for his part in a later Supreme Court case about obscenity, who was arrested, tried, and sentenced to a five-year prison sentence. Overt attempts to stifle sexual degeneracy were joined by more covert actions; J. Edgar Hoover kept tabs for fourteen years on Irving Klaw, the photographer best known for his snapshots of Bettie Page.[11]

As well as cultural spectacles that kept the press focused on the dangers of sexuality came a series of shifts in practice. The U.S. Post Office coordinated the seizure of *Sunshine and Health*, the magazine of the nudist lifestyle, from the mails in Chicago, New York, Philadelphia, and other cities in 1947. In 1953, the Post Office used the local post office in Mays Landing, New Jersey, to seize the magazines where the publisher posted them, rather than at its end point, to cut off the circulation. Attacks on sexual degeneracy in the late 1940s and early 1950s looked like they would effectively keep obscenity at bay, despite the slight loosening of the courts in the *Ulysses* ruling in 1933, which had differentiated between the use of coarse language and materials meant to generate sexual arousal.

These tensions showed themselves most clearly in the battle over comic books. The distinction between pornography and comic books was never very clear. As Jill Lepore has shown in her book *The Secret History of Wonder Woman* (2014), Wonder Woman was born out of sexual radicalism; the creator, William Marston, idolized Margaret Sanger, the birth-control advocate, and lived in a joint marriage with two women, though the latter fact remained hidden until recently.[12] Public officials, psychiatrists, and religious leaders accused Wonder Woman and other comic book characters of perverting America's youth; across the country, cities and states banned the sale of comic books, including the *Wonder Woman* books, in the late 1940s.[13] Concerns had become so critical that a congressional hearing was called to examine the matter; chaired by Estes

Kefauver, the committee's mandate included an exploration of the link between pornography, comic books, sexual degeneracy, and juvenile delinquency.[14] The committee heard from child development experts and interrogated producers and distributors of pornography, including so-called "eight-pagers" or "Tijuana Bibles" that were often based on comic book characters like Blondie and Dagwood, Maggie and Jiggs, and other popular cultural figures. While commercial comic book characters like those in the DC Comics stable flirted with light bondage and sexual innuendo, eight-pagers bared all and showed the characters in all sorts of sexual hijinks and positions (illus. 75). As Mr. Chumbris, a Washington lawyer who gathered information for the Kefauver Committee, reported, "the 'Maggie and Jiggs' books are two-by-fours, they are books 2 inches by 4 inches; they are also known as 8 pagers, because they contained 8 thin pages. They are caricatures, they are cartoons. They usually take people from the comic strips, or famous movie stars, and they portray them in very lewd, perverted ways."[15] Comic strips in newspapers excited sexual fantasies, generating their own derivative forms of pornography. This excitement spilled into the homemade booklets.

At the simplest level, people traced comic booklets. Prisoners, whose access to commercial pornography remained limited, used tracing as a means of reproducing hard-to-get materials.[16] For example, one prison artist traced pornographic photographs, created abstracted versions of images, and traced and recreated cells of comic books. Though it might appear as if the prisoner has been using tracing as a way to replicate materials to sell to other prisoners, individuals outside prisons also traced pornography even though commercial pornography would have been easier for them to obtain; the process of tracing and recreating comic book characters must have brought its own pleasures. In the 1940s, a skilled artist who could sketch figures, wash with watercolors, and draw complicated sexual ideas nonetheless traced and copied a booklet called "Madame gets her morning douche." This booklet features a bellboy in uniform (with a small red cap perched at an angle, even when he is naked) at the service of his mistress. She bosses him around and controls their

75 "Tillie and Mac," n.d. Author's collection.

many sexual encounters, telling him what position ("now I ride you"), how many fingers to put in ("put three fingers into it"), and how to copulate ("don't play so much outside—start fucking"). Despite the artist's considerable skill, he traced the booklet rather than altering it. Other versions of the same traced pamphlet have also emerged.[17] Multiple sets of "Madame gets her morning douche" show that there was something appealing—whether sexual or financial—about tracing pornography. Eight-pagers and comic book pamphlets cost between twenty-five and fifty cents, so the appeal might have been either financial or creative.[18] In following the arc of bodies, reproducing the distinctive writing style of comics, and coloring in the erogenous zones, individuals might well have been participating in a creative act. In general, eight-pagers and comics with their simple line drawings and color blocking made tracing easier and allowed an individual to engage in creating pornography. Tracing might be one way to stamp erotic objects as one's own.

Some objects built off the latent erotic tensions in commercial productions. Barbie, Ken, and GI Joe dolls had an erotic element, as discussed in Chapter Two. Some people played with the latent eroticism by giving the dolls genitals and pubic hair and arranging them into sexual positions. Others remade the idea of Barbies altogether. A set called "Bare Naked Beach Bingo" created fully sexed figures with pubic hair, nipples, and vulvas (illus. 76). The set of sixteen figures came from a group of seventy that were found in a New England house, purportedly made by a man confined to his home.[19]

Other objects, like masturbating pipe-cleaner figures, spanned the commercial/homemade divide. They appeared in the interwar years, in prison art, and as both commercial and homemade objects after the war ended. The ease of manufacture meant that the figure was highly adaptable and could be applied equally to men and monkeys. One version, made with fuzzy pipe cleaners, has been commercially produced, as evidenced by the typeset poem that names him, "Jerkie Boy." Like most pipe-cleaner figures, Jerkie Boy smiles and waves when the box is opened. A poem suggests that he is a "self driving chap" who "greases his pole and provokes his own sap."²⁰ Jerkie Boy speaks about sexuality with an irreverent good humor that he shares with a homemade pipe-cleaner figure stamped "Nature Boy." Nature Boy sports black eyes, a dot nose and mouth, and reddened genitals. One arm wraps around to grasp the penis, while the other curls up like a monkey's tail. Like all such figures, a thread tied to the arm reaches through the back of the box, where it can be pulled to make the monkey-man masturbate.²¹ Jerkie Boy and Nature Boy both demonstrate a smiling self-satisfaction. They communicate a willingness to flip off the world, gesturing obscenely to everything beyond the box. Such novelties and homemade objects enlivened each other, providing subjects, technologies, and shared sensibilities toward sexuality.

The growing commercialization of Christmas made Santa Claus a frequent subject for bawdy humor.²² Santa Claus as a set of ideas and visual signs had only been codified relatively recently, through advertisements like Whitman's chocolates and Coca-Cola, and these ideas spread after the Second World War as a part of the idealization of the sentimental home. As the idea of Santa Claus developed, so did a pornography devoted to him. One pornographic Santa was made from pipe cleaners.²³ Like other pipe-cleaner figures, masturbating Santa is set into a box, but this small box is wrapped in Christmas wrapping paper with stylized poinsettias set on a bed of silver and white plaid. Inside the box, Santa has been given a head made from a large bead graced with a bit of white fluff for a beard. His fluffy red pipe-cleaner suit is interrupted with a large white penis made from a white pipe cleaner. When the thread attached to the arm is pulled through the back of the box, Santa masturbates. One can easily imagine the gift-wrapped, masturbating Santa making the rounds at a party, poking fun at the sentimental holiday season in the postwar world.

Whereas trench art and postwar objects built upon commercial and vernacular traditions that told men's stories about sexuality, feminized crafts, in contrast, tell a different set of stories about sex in a bawdy women's register. We can date such objects to as early as the 1940s, though no doubt some earlier obscene women's crafts have yet to be found. While the feminist movement gave women a political voice for demanding sexual

76 Bare Naked
Beach Bingo: sixteen
handmade erotic
"Barbie" figures,
New England,
c. 1950s–60s.
Courtesy of
Steve Powers.

agency and a cultural voice for calling attention to women's craftwork in
the 1960s and '70s, homemade and handmade erotic objects based on
feminized skills appeared decades earlier, although they went unnoticed
as feminized objects. One example, a penis warmer, provided a fluffy
feminine exterior for the masculine body.[24] This penis-shaped sock featured pink yarn for the testicles and tip of the penis, while white yarn
adorned the shaft. A drawstring along the base of the penis tightened the
warmer around the genitals and held the object on the body. The loose-
knit pattern and acrylic yarn show that the object had a greater decorative
value than a utilitarian one. This penis warmer really functioned as penis
adornment, and a decidedly frivolous one at that.

Other fiber art projects brought feminized skills to obscene objects
during the 1950s. A series of pot holders and aprons look like home

economics sewing projects gone wild. These objects feature kitchen linens with hidden genitals. One apron is designed to look like a pair of men's shorts (illus. 77).²⁵ Inside the fly, a fabric penis with a bright red tip—filled with synthetic padding for girth and heft—can be pulled out. The penis dangles from the shorts' fly if not held erect, making the apron more comical than threatening. The version here features an erect penis and then a smaller penis and vulva hidden in the pockets to either side. Another project has two matching pot holders, made in a male version and a female version.²⁶ The male pot holder contains a set of shorts with a padded penis hidden in the fly. The female pot holder opens to a nest of real pubic hair. There are a whole series of these, each with its own decorations, edgings, fabrics, and whorls of pubic hair, made with fabrics featuring Christmas plaid, kitty-cats in bow ties, and blue and gray hearts and vines. These objects, meant to provoke shocked laughter, look like novelties born of women's crafts (illus. 78). So do pornographic objects that came from kitchen arts in the postwar world, such as the cookie donated to the Kinsey Institute mentioned at the beginning of this chapter.²⁷ Shaped like a phallus, the head of the penis has been decorated with red circular sprinkles and an embedded chocolate-chip tip, while brown sprinkles have been used for pubic hair to adorn the cookie's testicles. While women's crafts produced erotic objects that might be labeled as novelties in the postwar world, the charm of the products should not obscure the ways that new makers made new products. These objects built on women's craft skills and lampooned the seriousness of sexuality.

Postwar handmade and homemade pornography thus built upon commercial foundations and used those foundations to mock sexual reticence and the postwar sentimental home. People in the postwar world made erotic objects using the lexicons at hand. Some used household materials like pipe cleaners or decorative edgings, while others came from well-established craft traditions. The range of objects testifies to the variety of ways in which people envisioned desires. There was no single model of how pornographic imagining might look or what sort of form it could take. Instead, what proves more notable is the DIY ethos, which erased

77 Phallic apron, 1960s. Author's collection.

the divide between novelty item and handmade object, homemade and commercial storytelling. The crossing and re-crossing of these borders suggests the mutual enrichment between the two categories, even as new people were brought into the production of erotic objects. The early expansion, though remarkable, only foretold the flood that followed over the next few decades that came in tandem with shifting obscenity codes.

A decade-long restructuring of obscenity codes remade the public realm of sexuality, and by the mid-1950s the conservative impulse against pornography had waned. In its place, a liberal consensus had begun to form that made "book-burners" look archaic. Even Dwight D. Eisenhower spoke against censorship.[28] By that time, the New York Society for the Suppression of Vice, Anthony Comstock's powerful organization that had successfully fought against Margaret Sanger and the circulation of birth control information, had lost all legitimacy and was moribund.[29] In 1954, a majority of judges affirmed that Post Office censorship raised important constitutional questions.[30] Kinsey's legal case with Customs and the eventual court victory by the Institute for Sex Research in 1957 showed that the courts recognized scientific necessity as a justification for the circulation of pornography and erotica. The plethora of cases reaching the Supreme Court demanded a rethinking of constitutional issues in obscenity law.[31]

In 1957, the U.S. Supreme Court heard *Roth v. United States* because of the lack of clarity on obscenity codes. The court decided that the First Amendment did not protect obscenity but that materials with "redeeming social importance" should receive protection. Although the courts stood firm that the First Amendment did not protect pornography, the new model allowed First Amendment protection for sexually explicit materials and began to pay attention to the concerns of "social value." The new

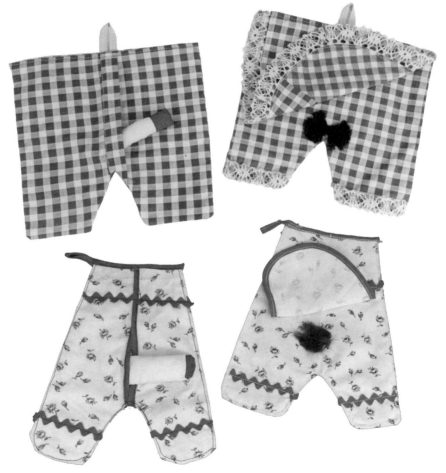

78 Potholders, 1960s. Author's collection.

standard left open a way to justify a wide range of materials if one could effectively argue that they had artistic, historical, or scientific value.

In some sense, the long search for respectability by sexual scientists, nudists, and literary elites came to fruition during this period. Despite Alfred Kinsey's own sexual experimentation, he maintained the outward appearance of a disinterested scientist.[32] Nudist resorts, which had pitched themselves as wholesome, family-friendly vacation spots for sunshine and exercise and restricted access to people of color and single men as a way to demonstrate their respectability in the postwar age, had become stodgy by the mid-1960s when protests began to feature public nudity to challenge the state's control over the body.[33] Even obscene literature found a new voice to explain itself; liberal challenges to censorship used the language of erudition to denounce prudery as old-fashioned.

The shift resulted in the growing legality of pornographic materials and the expansion of the sexual consumer realm. More people could find more types of materials in more places. Further, people could find materials that spoke in a variety of registers. In 1948, Kinsey had published *Sexual Behavior in the Human Male*; he followed up with *Sexual Behavior in the Human Female* in 1953, the same year that Hugh Hefner began publishing *Playboy*, the best-known racy magazine of the era. Bookstores displayed *Howl* (1956), Allen Ginsberg's poem that openly acknowledged male–male sexual desire. For less bohemian readers, the paperback revolution put inexpensive novels with lurid covers and titillating copy into stores and pharmacies.[34] More sex—straight, queer, and kinky—appeared in more places.

After the mid-1950s, commercial pornography expanded as obscenity laws eased. As courts began to articulate some grounds for the protection of sexual culture under the constitution, more commercial pornography became available. And after 1957 the market expanded even further as legal impediments diminished. Kinsey's books were joined by Masters and Johnson's *Human Sexual Response* and *Human Sexual Inadequacy* in 1966 and 1970, respectively. *Penthouse* magazine, founded in the UK, had migrated to the U.S. by 1969 where it was joined by *Hustler* in 1974.

Helen Gurley Brown's *Sex and the Single Girl* topped the best-seller lists in 1962. As the courts legalized materials because of their redeeming social or literary value, books long banned in the U.S. and UK finally appeared on the shelves, including D. H. Lawrence's *Lady Chatterley's Lover* (first published in 1928 in Italy), John Cleland's *Memoirs of a Woman of Pleasure* (*Fanny Hill*, first published in 1748–9 in England), and Henry Miller's *Tropic of Cancer* (first published in 1934 in France). These were republished in the U.S. starting in 1959. Their history and cosmopolitanism added to the perceived sophistication of these volumes. Further, a scholarly apparatus appeared simultaneously, offering people a way to speak about these volumes that countered mere prurience. Monographs like Peter Fryer's *Mrs. Grundy: Studies in English Prudery* (1964), Steven Marcus's *The Other Victorians* (1966), and David Foxon's *Libertine Literature in England, 1660–1745* (1965) provided a history for works previously considered obscene. The republication of works and the placement of them in a scholarly record happened conterminously, allowing for a new popular appreciation of them.

Thus, between 1957 and 1974, a liberal consensus on obscenity triumphed, at least momentarily, facilitating the expansion of the pornographic marketplace in numerous directions. Pornographic paperbacks, films, and magazines became mainstream, with mainstream theaters now allowed to show explicit sexuality in blockbuster movies. Grove Press republished previously banned pornographic classics like *Lady Chatterley's Lover* and promoted them in the mass market. Magazine publishers like Hugh Hefner, Larry Flynt, and Bob Guccione made headlines that advertised their status as *arrivistes*. *Midnight Cowboy*, an X-rated film, won Best Picture at the Academy Awards in 1969, the same year that Andy Warhol's *Fuck* (or *Blue Movie*) played in select theaters.

Paradoxically, the expansion of commercial culture further encouraged people to create their own. Homemade and handmade pornography changed as a result. Objects appeared in greater numbers as more people produced their own materials. They confronted sex and sexual diversity less with a "nod and a wink" and more with a shout. Objects still leered, but some materials also confronted sexual limitation and considered the political implications of sexuality. New types of people, who might have made pornography in the past using technologies of sublimation, began to associate themselves with sexuality in public and argue for the value of their desires. While commercial productions still had an impact on homemade objects, these later objects produced in the late 1950s, '60s, and early 1970s look less irreverent and more confrontational.

Handmade pamphlets, typescripts, and mimeographs increased in number and specialization. As Allan Bérubé demonstrates in *Coming Out Under Fire* (1990), an account of the history of gay military men and women in the Second World War, the mass movement of men and women during the war into broader homosocial spaces allowed for the expression of queer desires and the expansion of queer communities.[35] Members of emergent queer communities articulated sexual stories through typescripts and mimeographs as well as drawings and paintings. In *Out/Lines: Underground Gay Graphics from Before Stonewall* (2002), Thomas Waugh argues that these sorts of early fantasies connected members through the circulation of erotic objects. As Waugh writes, these visual sources "circulated clandestinely throughout North America and Europe during the first two-thirds of the twentieth century."[36] The stories ranged from just a few pages long to dozens of pages, typed in a single copy, copied via carbon paper, and mimeographed to create a form of cheap publication. Typescripts spanned the homemade/commercial divide. Some were made at home for the pleasures of spinning fantasy on paper, while others were sold from beneath the counter or even solicited to meet demand.

Individuals with desires not fully recognized by the commercial press turned to typescripts for the articulation of desires. For trans people, typescripts allowed them to take the desires they saw encoded in films such as *Some Like it Hot* (1959) to sexual conclusions. Typescript stories like "Robbie's Petticoat Discipline" featured boys forced to wear female dress. That story, typed on a standard manual typewriter, fit into the long line of trans fiction that was conterminously being recorded by activists like Louise Lawrence. Lawrence, who lived full-time as a woman from

1944 and was married to an army nurse, wrote the first medical article by a trans person about trans issues. She set up interviews for Alfred Kinsey with a variety of people, including transsexuals, cross-dressers, fetishists, drag queens, and transvestites. She also mentored others, including Virginia Prince, founder of *Transvestia* and co-founder of Phi Pi Epsilon, a national social organization.[37] Prince and Lawrence worked as community organizers and served as conduits for communication between the medical community, the press, and the queer community.[38] Lawrence's life's work focused on creating community and documenting that community for posterity.[39] She amassed an eleven-page list of materials with "male transvestite subject matter," according to its cataloging description. Most of the documents had been published, but some of them were circulating in typescript form.[40] Lawrence eventually typed more than 3,000 pages to send to Kinsey to document a variety of trans desires.[41]

For the gay community, mimeographs and typescripts allowed men to articulate desires that social and political organizing quieted.[42] Typescripts expressed desires set on baseball farm teams, naval bases, beach changing rooms, and so on.[43] They allowed gay men to see desire around them and to communicate fantasies that could then circulate more broadly. Handed from one person to the next, such documents articulated hidden subtexts even as they created hidden connections. As Waugh argues, "The impulse to desire, and to represent that desire, has motivated the embryonic gay cultures of the last century and a half—visual or literary, licit or illicit, appropriated or invented."[44]

Typescripts, like many other erotic objects from that moment, were situated somewhere between commercial and homemade objects. One collection shows the ways that the creator wedded commercial and original materials together. The 113-page collection was created on standard 8½ by 11-inch (letter) paper with three-hole binder punch-outs. The creator interspersed typescripts with glued-in illustrations. Two original stories were followed by an art sequence and then scrapbooked pages from men's magazines. The commercial foundations to the handmade stories showed themselves in materials, inspiration, and content. "Down on the Farm," a twelve-page typed story told in the first person, begins with a nostalgic gaze backwards toward an imaginary country life. The narrator learns about sex on the farm by watching his older brother receive oral sex from a farm girl and then joining in. His brother shows him "how many ways there are to use a cock" and teaches him to refine his talents as a "born cocksucker."[45] Beyond an initial framing that mentions egg gathering and milking stools, the story has little to mark it as rural. The nostalgic look back to country origins becomes a gesture toward incestuous desires as "country" becomes code for the pleasurably perverted.

The second typescript in the collection, "College Daze," self-consciously plays with the idea of situating gay sex within broader codes of commercial culture. One character invites another to make money through a magazine photoshoot. "Say, Kevin, you are built like a Greek Adonis, have you ever thought of making it pay off?" The college boys pose for athletic magazines, French postcards, and stag films. Interspersed with nude modeling, the characters engage in scenes of sexual abandon.[46] The temporarily abandoned camera in the following image (illus. 79) stood as a reminder that media linked men together and that the sharing and making of pornography allowed men to connect. In the story and in the practice of passing typescripts, pornography allowed men to construct desires and identities.

All-male spaces were relentlessly sexualized in illustrations of sex between prisoners, sailors, and inhabitants of the YMCA.[47] The illustrations to "College Daze" as well as "Down on the Farm" featured traced and then colored graphics. Print culture provided the artistic foundation for both sets of illustrations. The illustrations included figures of men drawn in a comic book style that was itself modeled on the physical culture and bodybuilding movements (illus. 80). The V-shaped shoulders, washboard muscles, bulging thighs, and artfully posed bodies showed the male form as an object of desire.

The spread of comic book culture made itself felt both in how people envisioned bodies and in the way that they read erotic tensions. Scrapbooked fiction positioned men's stories within queer culture, while the traced and colored illustrations transformed the male comic book body into an orgasmic wellspring. Men in these illustrations and stories were simultaneously both desiring subjects and objects of desire.

While people in earlier iterations had modeled their work on eight-pagers and placed the comic characters in explicit sexual positions, later homemade comic porn built upon latent tensions in the existing characters, stories, and series, and imagined the sexual possibilities that would emerge if characters were allowed to express a full range of desires. In part, this transition followed the shift from early funnies in newspapers that told serialized stories to larger comic books that allowed for longer plots and deeper character development, a change that had happened only in the late 1930s.[48] As comic book culture developed complexity, so did pornographic versions of comics, allowing for more socially and sexually subversive versions.

In one example of an exploration of the latent sexual tension between comic book characters, an artist considered the erotic triangle between Batman, Robin, and Catwoman.[49] Skilled at tracing and drawing, the artist took sexual elements of the popular series and extended them into a single culminating image. In the frame that the artist drew, Robin lies face up, manacled to a bench. He retains his cape, his boots, and his mask, but has lost his tights and shorts. Catwoman stands over him, about to engulf his enormous erection. She too wears only her boots, cape, and mask. Her erect nipples suggest her pleasure at this plot. Batman, meanwhile, stands shackled to an upright tree stump in the background. Wearing a cape, mask, boots, and his own impressive erection, he sports a smile. Despite the bondage overtones from the two men's shackles, the smiles on both men's faces and the lift to Robin's head and torso as he rises to meet Catwoman suggest a pleasurable union. Catwoman, in the artist's vision of the scene, has finally won the battle and been the victor over both men, to everyone's satisfaction. The tensions innate to the series, including those between the three characters, between the sexes, and even between sex and domination, are given life in the frame as the artist articulated the energies that animated comic book relationships.

juicy blow artist. As his face was plugged with four to eight inches of thick
dong, he moaned and groaned, and generally showed that he adored his hobby of
milking hot eager pricks of cocky, eager, pretty boys.

"Suck harder, Curt," encouraged Greg. "See if you can get a taste of this!"
Greg was ground to his balls in Kevin's bung and his glands were quivering and
twitching as volleys of gism warmed the love grotto. Kevin gasped as his hips
swayed to and fro, meeting Curt's mouth, sending his tool down his throat,
releasing a flow of starchy syrup to take the place of the load that was being
left in his behind. Curt had clamped his teeth into the root of the stalk in
his mouth and his throat muscles milked greedily. Kevin was squirming like mad
as his discharge poured out at the same moment as Greg's - his body barely
touched the floor mat as he tensed his muscles for the orgasm. To join in on
the fun, Robin, who had recovered sufficiently to part the cheeks of Curt's
cute ass, was running his tongue up and down the crease and into the tight bung
hole that quivered from the tickling sensation.

Dion had curled up near Kevin's ass and as Greg's slick penis squished out
of the hot hole, Dion took the jewels in his hand and licked and sucked all the
juice off and stuffed most of the flaccid dauber and empty sack of balls into
his mouth. When he was licked clean, Dion turned to the prostrate, exhausted
body of Kevin and ran his tongue over the sweaty butt, his nose parted the
handsome rear, and his long, broad tongue liked its job of licking and washing
from the crease of Kevin's ass the copious love juice. This was the first
time Kevin had ever been rimmed and he adored it. He just relaxed and purred
as he spread his legs and arched his hips. His butt had experienced some rough
treatment this past hour and Dion's soft tongue soothed and quieted the
twitching in his stretched cover.

Alan, too, was busy. His attention was turned to the prick of all pricks,
and his hands encircled Curt's long, pulsing wang, He held tight to the shank
and pumped his fists up and down, playing him off, sliding the loose skin on
his wang until it was bone-hard and throbbing. Alan continued to frig and jerk

Batman's dark side provided a popular screen for sexual fantasy, as another artist's consideration of the series demonstrates. This artist saw violence and competition between superheroes as central to their allure. In three handmade comic books, the artist, identified alternately as "Felix Lance Falkon," "Etienne," "Stephen," "Graewolf," and "Domingo Orejudos,"

plotted and illustrated superheroes with their "clothing removed and erections added," a redolent phrase provided by the cataloger.[50] One handmade comic book focused on Batman, Robin, and Green Arrow. The three superheroes hear calls for help from inside a nudist camp, where a rapist is attacking a woman. All three men strip, revealing their erections, before entering the camp. Despite the desperation of the circumstance, Green Arrow asks why they have erections, and Batman replies: "I always have a hard on when I chase rapists." Upon finding two men raping a woman, Green Arrow shoots one of the men in the penis. The superheroes vanquish the rapists and the grateful woman asks them back to her cabin for sex. Green Arrow convinces Batman that they cannot appear empty-handed, so they stop to adorn their penises with flowers. When they arrive at the woman's cabin, they find Robin already having sex with her. Batman then anally penetrates Green Arrow saying, "Shut up and take my dick, buddy, serves you right, for screwing us out of a fuck. Say, you're a pretty good piece of ass yourself . . . even tighter than Robin." The strip makes explicit the sexual pleasures of the chase and the fight, the reciprocal expectations of sex for salvation, and the homoerotic pleasures of competition and camaraderie. Sex is entangled with violence in the strip, which offers an extraordinarily fungible sense of pleasures and couplings. Batman is owed sex, and whether that comes from Green Arrow or the female nudist seems less relevant than satisfying that obligation. Rape, in this strip, shades into sexual pleasure, first when the woman's gratitude gives way to lust and then when Batman forces Green Arrow. Finally, according to the booklet, violence animates sex, creating desire in the first place when the three men grow aroused at the idea of violence and then animating each of the sexual interactions that follows. This artist saw an implicit sexuality in the fight scenes of superheroes and an implicit violence in the camaraderie and competitiveness between them, which he articulated in his own version of the comic book series.

The artist further explored the themes of sexual competition and fungibility in a strip devoted to rivalry between the Green Lantern and

Batman at the Justice League. The two compete over the relative merits of their pricks, trying to solve the problem first by fighting and then by putting themselves to a series of tests. Finally, Wonder Woman grows so annoyed that she hits them with love gas and they fellate each other. After a moment's pleasure, they continue their competition, fighting this time about the other's penile superiority. In these versions of Batman and the Justice League, Batman stands as a beacon for a certain sort of male–male sexual desire, one based in a competitive and brutal physicality. Fighting and fucking had an interchangeable appeal, and justice meant a sort of raw enforcement of a reciprocal sexual pleasure rather than a call to decency or hominess.

Homemade versions of comics built upon the visual styles, layout, and characters of comic books, explicating the erotics that were embedded in the strips. Each author then developed the erotic potential according to their own unauthorized readings. While one version saw Catwoman in an erotic triangle with Batman and Robin, another saw Robin sneaking in on Batman's territory, leaving the Caped Crusader to take his satisfaction out on the Green Arrow's body. While these versions directed the comic book characters' desires in different directions, both versions pick up on the implicit violence of the strip and the ways that violence and sexuality remain mutually constituted. These versions of comic book pornography abstract the straight, queer, and kinky sexual impulses that animate comic books and articulate a link between sex and violence. They shout about the generative impulses in popular culture in ways that other, more formal critiques of the media could not.

Another artist picked up on the same link between sex and violence in a satire, done in the style of *Mad* magazine. Part of the Entertaining Comics (EC Comics) stable, *Mad* debuted in 1952 and became a slick page periodical in 1955. *Mad* provided a template for satires of comic books, politics, and advertising throughout the 1950s, '60s, and '70s.[51] A pornographic twist on such a satire advertised a "self-raping" machine for girls.[52] Made with the distinctive smudges of a mimeograph copy—the cheapest form of reproduction before photocopying and digitization—this undated image hits all of the offensive stereotypes about what "girls" want (illus. 81). Illustrated with a drawing of a smiling woman as she administers a "self-violation" with the "Rape-all Frigging Machine" from "Douchebag Cuntucky," the advertisement describes all the benefits of the device. The machine lets women attach a picture of their favorite movie star to the "tit sucking stand" as the device shoots "electrically heated boiled starch for hot injections" through a penis-shaped reciprocator. A loudspeaker under the bed "emits grunts, groans, and endearing words from our special records." The satire shows what the author thought of as daring and subversive, although it is not clear whether the satire is directed at women for wanting to be violated or at men, whose chief contribution to sex seems to be grunts, hot starch, and tit-sucking. The illustration for the Rape-All labels parts of the machine, including the rheostat switch, the reciprocator, and the motor, making it as much a mechanic's joke as a pornographic satire. The satire seems to mock advertising copy, mechanical culture, men's understandings of women's desires, and women's desires themselves. The artifact documents a moment in which the language of violation, rape, and "meat cutting" were seen as daring and subversive and in which the frenzied and chaotic delivery of satire seemed cutting-edge. Moreover, the language of the satire—blunt, abrasive, and purposely offensive— demonstrates a way of seeing sex as embedded in a politics of politeness that the writer sought to attack. Rather than whispering, this object shouts about sex in an intentionally offensive way.

The satiric treatment of sexuality took on an even more overt political cast in another handmade object. This artifact captured the public rhetoric about Richard Nixon as "Tricky Dick," an insulting term that went back to a 1950 California newspaper editorial and gained salience in the 1970s when revelations about Watergate became public knowledge.[53] To make the appellation more pointed, one artist, an Indianapolis medical student, created "Tricky Dicky's Dick" in 1971.[54] The student cast a penis in plaster and then decorated it with the Stars and Stripes. Painting the shaft in white and red stripes and the head and scrotum blue, the student pinned silver stars of the kind that a teacher might paste to a child's graded paper

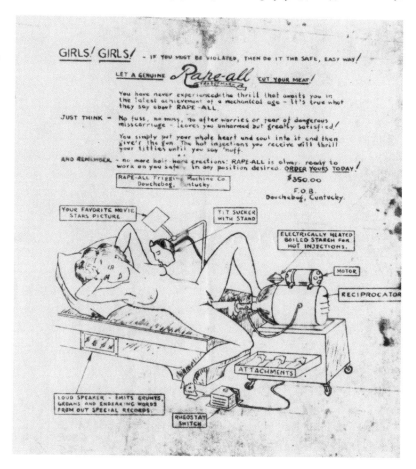

to the scrotum. Gold pubic hair made from Christmas tinsel completes
the figure. The note attached reads:

> Congratulations! You are now the proud owner of an exact replica
> of our powerful president's privates . . . better known as: "Tricky
> Dicky's Dick"! Be sure to handle it carefully and gently as you would
> any other symbol of our national heritage . . . During the playing of
> the National Anthem, it should be held erect.—Display it proudly
> on national holidays.

Mrs. Nixon comments on this replica: "It is an ever-expanding and growing symbol of what my husband represents to me, to this nation and to the world." It is a penetrating reminder of what this country stands for (or sits for, or lies down for, or whatever your position is on the issue.)

The satire combines political commentary and pornographic art. The piece plays on the multiple inflections of the term "dick," from the sexual to the abrasive, and suggests that Nixon has come to represent the negative connotations of the term. While the piece works as both a visual and a written satire, the scale of the piece raises interesting issues about how homemade pornography works as a practice. The dimensions of the sculpture including the testicles are 6¾ inches long by 2¼ inches in diameter (17 × 5.5 cm). That means that the penis is of roughly average size given that the penis is not fully erect, unsurprising given the mechanics of the casting process. To make the piece, the student must have cast it from life and probably used his own body as the basis. While making yourself a laughing stock as a way to mock the president makes sense at a public level for professional artists whose reputations rest on such gestures, to do so in private means making oneself the butt of a joke that reverberates only in one's own head. The joke becomes a statement about political allegiance rather than a persuasive tool to speak to others, though his donation of the artifact to the Kinsey Institute shows the value he placed on his satiric statement. These sorts of comic and satiric forms of pornography demonstrate how people engaged with public expressions of sexuality. People adapted popular forms (like the language of Tricky Dick) and ideas and made use of existing visual and literary vocabularies to express hidden meanings.

During this period, though, people also archived objects that might have been thrown away in the past. At some level, they began to value their own expressions. They began to see their own productions as attesting to something important about sex and bodies. One set of amateur paintings and drawings, for example, features 112 artifacts remarkable for their lack of skill.[55] The range of subjects includes figure drawings, sketches of intercourse, drawings of phantasms, and a storyboard for a film entitled "Sex at all Times" showing a group sex scene complete with light and camera setups. Done in India ink, marker, pencil, and watercolor on paper, the set of images shows what the artist thought noteworthy about sexuality. Clearly, the artist saw bodies as sexed, imagined the realm of the fantastic, and watched porn films and thought how he could do better with lighting and camera angles. The anonymous artist, identified as E.R.E.S., sought to illustrate a sexualized world, but however much the artist wanted to capture desire, the will to express exceeded the artist's skills of draftsmanship. As a result, the collection includes poorly wrought, badly executed watercolors (in which E.R.E.S. applied too much paint instead of working with the transparency of the medium) and sketches of disproportionate figures, misshapen bodies, enlarged heads, and disproportionate hands. Furthermore, E.R.E.S. knew about his or her own failures; most works are unfinished—figures were half-drawn and abandoned, others were half-inked as the artist tried various techniques with more or less success and then quit. As a group, they bring little to the history of artistic production, but as an archive they show the value accorded to individual sexual self-expression. The artist saved these objects and donated them—not because they were high art but because they documented the everyday expression of desire, no matter how flawed, ugly, and awkward.

Another artist produced two rough drawings, one in pencil and the other in ink, that also speak more to self-expression and self-realization than to skill.[56] The first pencil sketch offers the artist's so-called philosophy of sexuality.

My Philosophy is the philosophy of the **Prick** and the **Asshole** which is man's cunt. When you pull the foreskin back, it's all shit. That's what makes it an asshole. I wish I could fuck myself, but I can't. So I fuck little girls and boys. I WISH I COULD FUCK <u>YOU</u>, SAUL, BUT YOU WON'T Let Me. Someday you will learn. Even though I am 235 seasons old, I still have a hard prick in my dreams I LOVE YOU, Edward.

The artist wrote as a banner around the margins, "a page of almost poetry from my 68th and last sketchbook—written when I am drunk and dying." Despairing rather than beautiful, graphic rather than figurative, the page speaks to the artist's unrealized longings. The page looks as if "Edward" had created it quickly and with little deliberation. The lettering is uneven and hurried and the composition of the page is out of balance. The page looks like a screed about ways to articulate pain more than a composition that represents sexual actualization.

His second image, done in ink, uses a surrealist style to combine bodies into a series of melting masses. One figure, composed of a head, testicles, and fingers, has written beside it "I speak lies." In the middle of the page, another figure with an erect penis approaches a female horned devil, while to the left two swastikas have been drawn. Other figures fuse together sexual organs. The image is titled "'There is no God' For Saul, 1961." These figures show a sense of desperation in the combination of the imagery of evil with sexual organs as a way for Edward to speak of his own sexuality. If both the head and the testicles speak lies, what remains to speak the truth? The disturbing fusion of bodies and graphics articulates the artist's confusion and longing; Edward's desire for Saul is voiced in a register of despair. The strength of the two drawings comes from their honesty rather than skill; the two sketches are noteworthy for what they are willing to say, rather than the artistry of how they say it. During the postwar period a sociological sense of importance joined artistry as a reason for archiving materials.

In another example (illus. 82), a drawing of a sex circle shows skill, but the archiving of the image—which seems like an in-joke for friends—demonstrates the emerging value that people put on their expression of sexual ideas.[57] The quick line drawing illustrates a giraffe (labeled "Consago") licking a bunny's butt; the bunny fucks a pig called Riccio; the pig fellates another pig, McDermott; McDermott licks a woman labeled "Blondie from Dondie," and the woman fellates the giraffe. The very skilled draftsman who conceptualized and carried out the line drawing gave a sense of personhood to each animal even while showing them engaged in fantastical types of interspecies intercourse. Each animal seems to hint at a particular person who meant something to the artist and the artist's circle. The sex circle appears like an in-joke about sexual attributes, piggishness, and positions. While the illustration's charms allow it to work on its own, no doubt it meant even more in its social context, where McDermott and Riccio could be teased for their porcine qualities. The archiving of this image by the artist, rather than thumb-tacking it to a wall or burning it, for example, points toward an emerging revaluation of the individual in relation to society.

Another artist, known by his initials D. H., created angelic-looking figures in an array of sexual positions. The artist emphasized the curves of the body with delicate tinting that accentuates the rounded breasts and muscled arms on both sexes (illus. 83). Whether male or female, young or old, all of the models feature the same rosebud mouth with a gentle smile that softens the hard edges of their forms. Made in pencil and watercolor,

82 Consago (sketch), 1960, item 630.c7551, Kinsey Institute.

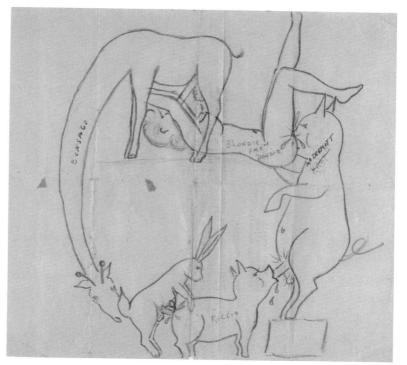

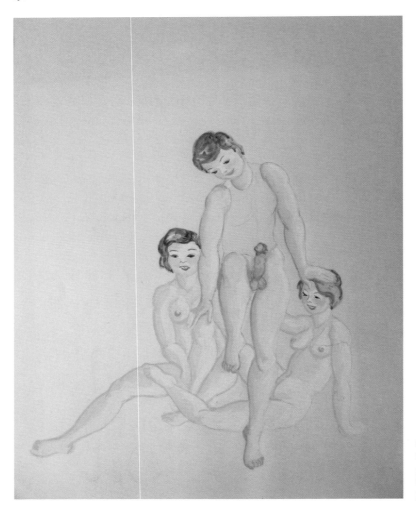

83 D. H., painting
in watercolor and
pencil, *c.* 1970s.
Collection of Jim
Linderman.

it seems as if D. H. added shoe polish or another form of whitening to
give the skin a luminous quality. According to Jim Linderman, a writer
and visual artist who collects and blogs about folk art, D. H. produced
stacks of these paintings at his summer cottage when he had told others
he'd gone fishing.[58]

The saving of these images, both by the artists themselves and by others,
shows the growing value placed on individual self-expression. Whether

these creations are poorly wrought or well wrought, their archiving attests to the increasing appreciation of private ideas about sex. They were saved and accessioned because they spoke to individual desires and philosophies; at a moment when the social sciences sought understanding about sexuality beyond statistics, the populace documented themselves as people with individuated desires. The half-finished sketches of an amateur artist, the despairing documents from Edward to Saul, and the in-joke about sex for a lost circle of friends worked as demonstrations of how sex spoke to distinct people. The articulation of the sexual self as meaningful swelled the Kinsey Institute archives and private collections as people began to want to document a history of themselves and how they saw sexuality.

Contributing to the preservation impulse was the growing recognition of outsider art and art brut (or raw art), categories developed by art historians for the artwork of untrained artists. One object, carved from a single branch, demonstrates an artist's view of women's sexual bodies (illus. 84). This object stands at the intersection of folk art and art brut, the term coined by Jean Dubuffet for art by outsiders such as psychiatric patients.[59] The creator of this carving was institutionalized as a teenager in the 1950s by his family when he began to hallucinate. Confined for six months and then released to his family home, he began carving erotic objects that he hid from his family to avoid their disapproval. Although his family destroyed most of his artwork, one of the few remaining carvings shows a celebration of sexuality and women's fecundity. The single carved cypress branch has been transformed into a 17-inch (43 cm) totem pole that repeats the motifs of women's breasts, bellies, and faces with two penises hanging down on the front and vulvas, breasts, and buttocks on the back.[60] The piece focuses on women's sexuality without being seductive or coy. Instead, the totem pole looks like a paean to fertility, with sets of swollen breasts, simple smiling features drawn on in black marker, and the popping belly buttons of pregnant women.

Also falling into the category of art brut would be the work of Henry Darger, discussed in Chapter Two, and the work of Dwight Mackintosh (1906–1999). Mackintosh suffered from brain damage. The state institutionalized him for fifty-six years from the age of sixteen until the age of seventy-two, when he was shifted to residential care during the wave of deinstitutionalization that took place beginning in the 1970s. Mackintosh took classes at Creative Growth, a center in Oakland, California, devoted to art for students with disabilities, where he drew mainly two subjects: human figures and motor vehicles. He used line drawings and rough, cursive-style calligraphy that was legible but nonsensical to create sexed human figures. The torpedo-like genitals given to the male figures marked the images as both sexed and sexual for Mackintosh. According to John M. MacGregor's description of Mackintosh's process,

> There is also an element of ritual involved in the process. For example, during the making of a drawing, the penis undergoes repeated "corrections," growing longer and longer as a result. Beginning with its small retracted state, a sequence of increasingly large forms are drawn, suggestive of the stages of erection, until the edge of the paper is reached. This takes place over considerable time, as Dwight returns to it again and again during the course of the drawing . . . At some stages fingers are then added, gripping the penis, and it becomes apparent that the boy(s) is (are) masturbating.[61]

When asked to title a drawing, Mackintosh volunteered that a row of figures showed "butt-fucking," a sexual activity that might have sprung from Mackintosh's lived experience as an institutionalized adolescent, according to John MacGregor. Mackintosh's sexuality, like those of other disabled and institutionalized artists, tends to be bracketed by the language of "difference," perhaps because of the awareness about the ways that disability has been translated into sexual degeneracy in the past. While it would be easy to dismiss the sexuality in Dwight Mackintosh's and Henry Darger's work, that impulse patronizes the artists, however unwittingly, as if they cannot create artifacts that speak to their own desires.

Other objects came directly from the folk art tradition. Though earlier objects had been created by a variety of people, the anonymity of the artists

84 Everett Edwards, Totem pole, c. 1960s. Author's collection.

masked their diversity. During the postwar period, however, collectors and dealers began to note the African American artists who made erotic art. For example, Steven Ashby, whose work has been collected by the Smithsonian and other important cultural institutions, became known as an artist after the death of his wife in 1960.[62] Ashby made sculptural assemblages using cast-off magazines, marbles, saw blades, pieces of trash, clothes pins, furniture, plywood, and so on. While some of his best-known pieces display a frank sexuality, many of his assemblages had no erotic content, including sculptures of dancing and self-portraits. Sex, in Ashby's work, was just another aspect of life. His erotic works combine a sly humor with grittiness. One sculpture features a nude, lactating woman with an enlarged vulva (illus. 85). She sits balanced over a sardine can. A phallus, emerging from the can, sidles next to her vaginal opening, making clear the pleasing erotics that can rise in response to fishiness and women.

85 Steven Ashby, *Woman and Sardine Can*, c. 1976. Collection of Robert A. Roth.

Another sculpture, of an animal-like man complete with glued on hair and polka-dot pelt, bends a woman over for intercourse (illus. 87). A third assemblage (illus. 86) features a woman and dog. Ashby has painted the woman's skin a bright pink. Her glued-on eyes and carved nostrils and mouth give her an expressive moue.

A final Ashby features a reclining woman (illus. 88). Her breasts are made from acorns, attached and then painted. Though not visible without magnification, the tips of the acorns function as erect nipples. Her vulva looks like it is painted on, but closer inspection shows that it is both carved and then painted black, giving it depth. Ashby left a small strip of wood bare of paint to hint at the vaginal opening.

Ashby decorated his yard with those objects fit for display in the neighborhood, keeping the more risqué ones under his bed. A resident of Delaplane,

Virginia, Ashby grew up farming in the small community alongside his father. An African American son of a freed slave whose family had been forced into labor, Ashby's work fits within the African American vernacular art tradition both for its techniques and for his focus on black culture. While other objects might also have been made by African American artists, a lack of provenance makes it impossible to know the race of their maker in many cases. Ashby's oeuvre makes it clear that African American artists had an interest in erotic arts and that they saw sex as a rich subject for humor and expression.

86 Steven Ashby, *Woman and Dog*, *c.* 1970s. Collection of Robert A. Roth.

Likewise, Mose Tolliver's works show the ways that sex fitted within the wide range of subjects among African American artists (illus. 89). Born to a tenant farming family in Alabama in the late 1910s or early 1920s before moving with his family to Montgomery in the 1930s, Tolliver made a living as a handyman, gardener, and tradesman. After a debilitating accident, Tolliver turned to painting starting in the 1960s. He painted portraits, animals, and Christmas trees. He also painted erotic panels featuring nude women and oral sex. Where Ashby's erotic artworks included both black and white subjects, Tolliver's focused more squarely on African Americans' sexual pleasure. In paintings like *Moose Lady with a Gentleman Named Charles Bailey*, *Lady in Love Finds John Duval*, and *Exercise Rock*, the subjects look back at the viewers while they receive sexual satisfaction, creating a triangular energy between those who give pleasure, those who receive it, and those who watch.[63] The viewers

87 Steven Ashby, *Woman and Centaur*, *c.* 1970s. Collection of Robert A. Roth.

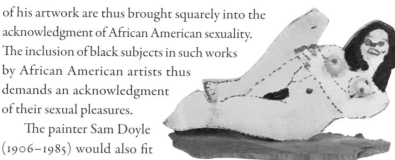

of his artwork are thus brought squarely into the acknowledgment of African American sexuality. The inclusion of black subjects in such works by African American artists thus demands an acknowledgment of their sexual pleasures.

The painter Sam Doyle (1906–1985) would also fit into this tradition. Doyle only found time to paint later in life, although he had always loved making art.[64] One of nine children, Doyle grew up on a small family farm on the isolated island of St. Helena, South Carolina. Family circumstances forced him to leave school before graduation. He worked as a porter, stock clerk, and in a Marine Corps laundry to support his family. After he retired, he painted using everyday materials like found wood and metal and house paint, rather than oils. Doyle painted famous figures like Martin Luther King, Jr. and Jimmy Carter, historical figures like Abraham Lincoln, family, friends, and members of his community. Having grown up surrounded by former slaves, Doyle understood the history of his community and its supernatural and religious traditions.

One of his erotic works, *Old Hag* (illus. 90), features a nude woman sitting on the face of a reclining person. While some describe the figure as a prostitute, others claim she is a supernatural being who "shed her skin and caused misery for her victims."[65] Thus, sexuality could be either pleasure or pain.

Artists like Sam Doyle, Steven Ashby, Mose Tolliver, and others including Jimmie Lee Sudduth, Henry and Georgia Speller, and John Schreiner, created art that depicted sexuality in the African

American community. Their art brought a variety of sexual traditions, beliefs, and visual frameworks into the fabric of the art world in the twentieth century which began to recognize older folk traditions.

The folk tradition that stretched back into the nineteenth century continued to influence craft production in the postwar world. Craftsmen made figurines, plaques, stamps, articulated figures and more. As Simon Bronner explains, "carvers were customarily men . . . strong associations were evident between masculinity and and working in the hardness of wood."[66] Carved wooden objects made in the folk tradition include fishing lures (illus. 91) and animals engaged in copulation (illus. 92). These objects hark back to older models of handmade objects when artists found inspiration in the natural world.

90 Sam Doyle, *Old Hag, c.* 1977. Collection of Robert A. Roth.

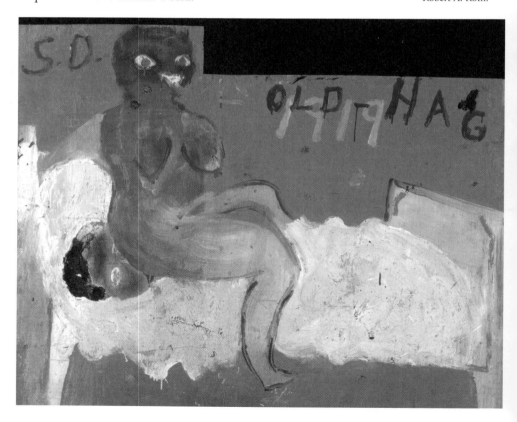

Also in this tradition would be surprise objects, which continued to be hallmarks of the handmade tradition. Another Santa Claus (illus. 93) has been made from plywood and dowels. Santa is caught with his pants around his knees. The size of Santa's erection shows that he is jolly for a reason. Another object seems like a box, but when the door is opened, one sees a hairy man masturbating while he sits in the outhouse, his pants pooled around his ankles (illus. 94). He happily looks at his own handmade and homemade pornography in the form of a portrait of a naked woman tacked to the wall. These objects provoke a surprised bark of laughter in us as viewers when we see what we're not supposed to, like Santa's penis or someone masturbating in the crapper. They dislocated sexuality from the discretion of the bedroom and placed it where it wasn't supposed to be. Instead of purifying sex, they offered it up with a whiff of older traditions. By poking fun at sentimental ideals of sexuality, such objects continued the older tradition of folk art with its pop-up penises, coffin figures, and other surprises.

Traditional folk art, embedded in a folk culture, merged with a folk art revival. The revival of folk art as a category brought it to museums, galleries, and classrooms in the 1960s and '70s.[67] Professional artists with craft skills created their own handmade erotic objects. William Accorsi, best known for his children's books, also made erotic craft objects, some of which were featured in *Hardcore Crafts*, a catalog of erotic craft work produced in 1976. One piece, entitled "Saturday Night," works as a freestanding puzzle in which people and animals fit together in a

91 Fishing lure: A gift to a barber, sold by his wife in an estate sale, western Pennsylvania, *c.* 1955. Collection of Mark Rotenberg.

92 Dogs, Realia, wood carving, donated *c.* 1960s, item 63OR A403.1, Kinsey Institute.

Saturday-night orgy. Men fit with men, women fit with men, and animals fit with both in a continuous mass. Accorsi deepens the effect by using untinted maple for both people and animals and gently watercoloring eyes and hair. Bodies have "innies" into which "outies" fit, regardless of gender and where they belong in the natural world.[68] The puzzle shows how all are made of the same stuff.[69]

Pottery by Louis Mendez (1929–2012), a member of the faculty at Ohio State University and the Philadelphia College of Art, played with erotic motifs.[70] A professional artist who helped transform pottery from a craft to an art, according to his obituary in the *New York Times*, Mendez exhibited work at the Victoria and Albert Museum in London and the Florence Biennale in Italy, among other international venues.[71] Mendez produced pitchers with penile spouts, vases made in both the male and female form, and sculptures of naked men, women, and sexual parts.[72] Michael Bennett, a sculptor who teaches at Kishwaukee College in Illinois, created *Penis Pot* in 1971 (illus. 95). Bennett works with all sorts of media, from found objects like sticks, to low-fire clays, to metalwork. *Penis Pot* features a pair of high-gloss, metallic-glazed penises emerging from a sturdy white ceramic pot. The penises, breaking through stodgy ceramics, offer a gentle ribbing of traditional pot making. Artists like Mendez and Bennett brought erotic craft forms to a professional level.

Female professional artists also reworked the craft tradition as part of the broader feminist movement during the late 1960s and '70s.[73] While handmade, these pieces came as part of a craft revival movement and received serious public attention as a result. The artists used sexual bodies, sexual acts, and even sexual clichés as inspiration for works that then appeared in galleries and museum exhibits. The activists remade crafts that had been labeled as women's hobbies into serious art. The fiber arts tradition, for example, proved a rich area for feminist reconsideration. Rhett Delford Brown created a sexual tapestry in the 1970s using sewing, beading, embroidery, and appliqué

93 Santa, *c.* 1980. Collection of Mark Rotenberg.

94 Outhouse, made by an engineer at Grumman Aerospace, *c.* 1960. Collection of Mark Rotenberg.

to provide a textured vision of bunnies copulating in the grass (illus. 96).[74]

Joanne Mattera's labia pillows are constructed from a variety of yarns, including hand-dyed, hand-spun fibers that were then woven, stitched, and filled so that the pillows reproduce the natural variation in the color of pubic hair. In one piece (illus. 97), Elaine Bennett, a graphic designer, used fabric and beads to create labia and then placed them into an ornamental copper box. The lid's embellishment with the profile of a woman and the word "BITCH" reclaims the linguistic disparagement of women's sexuality into a beautiful little package. Another artist, Shari Urquhart, created *Doctor Rug*, a multi-panel hooked rug with home-dyed yarn of couples "playing doctor" and then copulating, in the 1970s.

Feminist craft artists emphasized a sexuality anchored both in folk traditions and in nature, and their creations tried to strip sex of the artifice and the slick, laminated surfaces representative of popular culture. Surfaces that called for tactile appreciation linked the physicality of sex with the physical appreciation of craft products as objects to be enjoyed and used. Mattera's labia pillows asked viewers to sink into them. Bennett's work invites you to open the box and run a finger across the sculptural interior. These objects call for an engagement with sexuality at a tactile level. In Delford Brown's wall hanging, roly-poly bunnies copulating in the grass under blue skies and butterflies offer sex as an idyllic activity to while away the afternoon.

These erotic objects emerged from a larger feminist tradition. As Angela C. Fina, a ceramicist, has explained, she began her examination of sex by creating large phalluses that were cast from life in reaction to what she saw as male artists' obsession with breasts. "Later on, I sought to defuse the taboo about portraying female genitalia by being light-hearted and humorous in my work, and by making the forms look beautiful and unthreatening."[75] Female folk artists produced art that focused on sexuality in ways that reworked the vernacular tradition. Feminist theory of the time emphasized the need for women to take control of their own bodies and their own sexuality. Artists like Fina, Brown, and Mattera remade sexed figures in ways that explicitly and self-consciously responded to the male

artistic tradition. Instead of carving, sculpting, and welding, they made use of those craft traditions typically associated with women; instead of modeling the female figure on pin-ups or Playboy Bunnies, they focused on the female labia or humping bunnies. In the process, they radically transformed the meaning of handmade erotica.

95 Michael Bennett, *Penis Pot*, 1971. Artist's collection.

Though in some ways professional folk artists radicalized handmade pornography by incorporating new voices and developing new ways to see sex, they also polished away its harsh edges. Folk artists as a group took the vernacular tradition and made it slicker for public consumption. Rather than poorly wrought figures and half-finished sketches, professional folk artists used real and noteworthy skills to create sophisticated products. Folk art produced by professional artists took the handmade out of the home and into the studio, art galleries, and the consumer market, transforming its relationship to capitalism.

Out of mass war came a mass pornography. Old standards like the masturbating pipe-cleaner figure and movable copulating couples continued to be produced. These objects focused on uncovering the hidden realms

96 Rhett Delford Brown, *Very Busy Bunnies*, 1970s. Courtesy of Carol Cone.

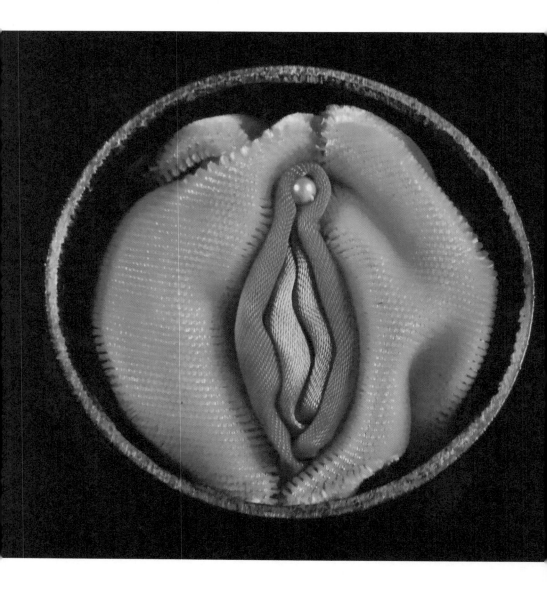

of sexuality and acknowledging sexuality in everyday life. Objects that exposed masturbation, uncovered sexual organs, and recovered hidden sexual histories tended to work through shock value, as if their goal would be a surprised bark of laughter. In articulating sex through a wink and a leer, homemade and handmade objects portrayed a sexuality both unsentimental and knowing. They undercut ideas of reverence, showing the sexual roots of sentimental culture, whether coming from national holidays or Hollywood. The objects mocked more than they confronted, and they depicted a sort of sexuality that might have emerged from the novelty market had the mass market produced vernacular sexuality. Rather than imbricating sex with violence, the objects suggest a flippancy toward sexuality and toward the society that kept sex covered up. In making these objects, people articulated a sexuality defined by irreverence, an emotional stance that itself refused the seriousness of state demands during or after the war.

With changes to obscenity laws during the 1950s and '60s that rolled back restrictions on sexual materials, more sorts of commercially produced erotica and pornography began to circulate. The widening circulation of commercial artifacts, including novels about sexuality, photographs, paintings, films, and tracts, opened the door to a range of ideas about and approaches to sex. Sexually inflected materials from the faintly leering to the frankly kinky, from naturist to queer, began to appear in a range of places. Paradoxically, as commercial materials proliferated, so too did homemade and handmade objects. Saturation did not bring satiation. Instead, people amped up the production of handmade and homemade pornography. More people made more objects. And new people, or at least people who can now be identified, made pornography. Women and African Americans began to produce such objects in their own craft traditions with their own subject matter. They began to articulate their own visions of sexuality.

The sorts of objects that people made show a continuity with earlier folk traditions as well as the influence of commercial culture. Intercourse, beautiful women, and masturbating men, three prominent themes in prison pornography, showed themselves to be popular in the outside

97 Elaine Bennett, *Bitch Box*, 1980. Artist's collection.

world as well. As increasingly different kinds of people made new kinds
of objects, an appreciation for the value of individual expressions of sexuality emerged. Homemade and handmade pornography followed the
larger DIY movement that gradually redefined "making" from practice to
politics. Anti-consumerism became its own justification, and DIYers pitted
themselves against consumerism by seeing self-definition, individualism,
and competence as promoting a kind of cultural democracy. This shift
came in tandem with a change in the tenor of homemade and handmade
materials. Radical politics, the women's movement, the demand for civil
rights and recognition, and the folk movement contributed. The demands
for fundamental social change called for a rethinking of sexuality and
gender roles, and this began to reverberate into the realm of handmade
objects. Whereas women's crafts made earlier tended to comprise erotic
objects like cookies and potholders that could fit into the home, by the
later period, women as artists began to claim authorship of artistic folk
objects in galleries and displays. Sex, formerly a place of laughter and
scorn, soon became a place for pleasure, joy, and political intervention.
Sex began to carry new meanings. It became a means of self-expression
worthy of holding on to and savoring; it became violent, so that violent
themes in commercial culture could be explored in handmade objects; and
it became professionalized as craft culture entered museums and galleries.
Concerned with issues of race and sex, inspired by consumer culture,
inclusive, navel-gazing (both literally and figuratively), self-referential,
violent, and political, a people's pornography had finally arrived.

5

Marketing Authenticity, 1970s Onward

G rayson Perry, the British potter, has become the public voice for outsider art. He creates ceramic pots featuring explicit content, with titles like *Kinky Sex* and *Moonlit Wankers*, and routinely cross-dresses as his alter ego Claire in bold, Alice in Wonderland-style clothes. Perry received the Turner Prize in 2003 and was named Reith Lecturer for the BBC in 2013, the same year he was made CBE (Commander of the British Empire, an honorary award) in recognition of his contribution to the arts. In a video created for the exhibition "Provincial Punk" at Turner Contemporary in Margate, Kent, in 2015, Perry, dressed as Claire, declares that "contemporary art is the R&D department of capitalism. Deal with it."[1] When an honored, cross-dressing British potter tells the world that erotic outsider art feeds capitalism, we know something foundational has changed.

To understand this change, this chapter considers two intertwining phenomena: the development of new technologies for the creation of amateur pornography and the commercialization of handmade and home-made objects. These two phenomena are intertwined. Although people continued to make objects by hand, instant cameras, camcorders, and digital cameras transformed what people understood as amateur pornography. Increasingly, amateur pornography meant images. Simultaneously, as amateur pornography became mechanized, handmade and homemade objects became elevated into folk art, outsider art, and art brut, and moved into galleries, museums, and collections. Once understood as art, handmade and homemade pornographic objects lost their immediacy and their disruptive potential, becoming instead ossified articulations of human authenticity. Thus as new technologies began to define homemade pornography, handmade objects were reconceptualized as culturally legitimate. Both of the two newly defined areas—mechanically produced amateur porn and handmade erotic art—were marketed as real and authentic. In both iterations, commercialization rendered marketable the amateur articulation of the sexual self.

In many ways, the marketing of amateur objects is unsurprising and has been raised by art historians. As the journalist Adam Cohen stated in an article on the work of Mose Tolliver, "capitalism alters everything it touches."[2] Art historians have discussed the relationship between the market and authenticity, but historians of pornography have not. Because historians have largely focused on commercial pornography, the topic of authenticity, amateur productions, and emerging markets has not been carefully considered. This chapter thus tries to bring historians into a conversation about an emerging commodification of amateurishness as a marker of sexual authenticity.

Two sets of chronological frameworks need to be taken into account to consider amateur erotic materials: when people made the objects, and when cultural institutions began to recognize the objects. The first four chapters of this book consider the chronologies of when people made objects. This chapter explores the relationship between making and recognition. It considers the impact of Polaroid and video technologies on the making of amateur pornography and the belated cultural recognition of certain forms of art making. The process of recognition is ongoing and by no means complete. Objects made years earlier have gained recognition as the definitions have shifted.[3]

Issues of recognition and differentiation are exacerbated for sexual artifacts where social class and social context differentiate high-art nudes from low-art nakedness.[4] Erotic objects have been divided into separate marketplaces and institutions. The divisions are arbitrary, reflecting the viewers' relationships to those objects as well as the objects themselves. Whereas similar claims have been made about folk art and outsider art in general and hinge on connoisseurship,[5] when placed in the context of erotic objects, these same divisions point toward something else. To be an art connoisseur suggests something about aesthetic appreciation and taste, at least to those outside the collecting community; to be a connoisseur of pornography says something about sexual desire to outsiders, though many collectors and dealers see this appraisal as capricious and misleading. In general, visual materials go to one market (art) while written works and paper works go to another (erotica), but even that principle falls apart. Henry Darger made books but has been classified as an artist, and his works have been shown at the Tate Britain in London, while "Sex Doll Polaroids," a set of visual artifacts, was sold by an erotica dealer. Whereas materials defined as art garner shows at art galleries, generate appreciation, and get channeled into museums, materials defined primarily as erotic move into the erotica trade and get funneled onto a distinct and less remunerative track. Whereas items defined as art have provenance, a record that documents the history of the object in the world, items defined as pornography generally have no trail and any identifying information will have been scrubbed from the records.[6]

Erotica, even if rare and handmade, has little value in comparison to art. The "Sex Doll Polaroids" collection, discussed at the beginning of Chapter Two, was brought to a store in San Francisco called The Magazine, where Ivan Stormgart worked. The front half of the store sold "fashion, art, architecture, gossip, movie star stuff. The back half is all porn—gay on the right, straight on the left." Trash pickers, often homeless people, would bring in ephemera for sale. Someone brought in the Polaroid collection for sale and, according to Stormgart and his associate, Cynde Moya, "We liked them so much, we scanned them for people to see."[7] Trash pickers are important to the preservation of erotic materials because erotica and pornography often get dumped when family members die. As Dorian Gomez reported to Steve Bornfield in 2011 about the opening

of the Erotic Heritage Museum in Las Vegas, "A lot of people who donate
to the Trust want to get rid of it before the family has to go through it
(after their death). A lot of these pieces are better off in a trust. A family
may not understand the value and sell it off at a swap meet."[8] Mark Rotenberg, a dealer and authority on antique erotica, reported that many of
his favorite handmade and homemade objects came from venues such as
flea markets, swap meets, and online auctions. Even clearly "old" erotic
objects are hard to appraise. Rather than moving from pocket to pocket,
or even from garbage to gallery, erotic objects circulate wildly if they join
the market at all.

Throughout the nineteenth century, the erotica market was dominated
by new publications, the finer and fancier the better. Indeed, "fancy"
became a term almost synonymous with "obscene," and vendors used the
term to indicate the quality of the book or the illustrations.[9] Both flash
and fancy markets dealt in commercial productions, while used books
sometimes made it back onto commercial registers. Handmade objects
went into an alternate stream that remained hidden until the twentieth
century. Only as nineteenth-century objects themselves became antiques
and only as ephemeral and outsider objects became art did these objects
begin to attain value and provenance.

Much rests on definitions. This chapter deals with objects that might
be alternately labeled as erotica, folk art, folk erotica, folk pornography,
amateur art, amateur erotica, amateur pornography, vernacular art, art
brut, raw art, outsider art, and/or any combination of these terms. The
labeling of artifacts has real consequences in terms of who sells the objects,
who buys them, and how much they are worth. In essence, definitions
affect the relationship between art and commerce.

Further, these definitions have changed over a relatively short period of
time. The emergence of new models for understanding art have concerned
the community of critics, gallery owners, and art historians as even basic
definitions have been debated for folk art, vernacular art, outsider art, and
self-taught art. Julia M. Klein, a cultural reporter and critic, believes that
"the struggle over terminology" can be dated to the "American modernist

discovery of folk art in the 1920s," which continued with the promotion of "outsider art in the 1970s."[10] While Klein sees the years between the 1920s and 1970s as critical for the acceptance of folk and outsider art, according to Joan M. Benedetti, an art librarian, the matter has taken on greater urgency since the 1970s.[11] John Michael Vlach, director of the folklife program at The George Washington University, in reviewing the field of folk art and its scholarship, claimed that definitions were grounded in a "body of syrupy and nostalgic catch phrases that have taken the place of clearheaded thinking."[12] As David Brody argues in his consideration of the American Folk Art Museum, "the labeling of artistic categories is a messy business," and the definition of folk art in America has been particularly untidy given the combination of jingoism and market forces. As Brody recounts, art historians pitch folk artists against professional artists and state that folk art connotes a more timeless collectivity while modernism connotes a time-bound individuality.[13] Scholars point toward folk art as emerging from its cultural milieu rather than from the creativity of the individual academically trained artist.

Despite the supposed timelessness of folk art, the appreciation of it emerged at a particular moment in history. The folk revival emerged in Europe against the growing dominance of industrial cities in the nineteenth century. The process began with the desire to document regional languages, folk tales, and folklore before they were lost to national and modern consolidations of culture. Intellectuals spread out from city centers, gathering and documenting the language of pre-literate peasants and country people.[14] Beginning in the last quarter of the nineteenth century, folklorists attempted to document the patterns of cultural life that existed before the emergence of the modern nation-state.

By the early twentieth century, the pattern of documentation began to give rise to movements celebrating folk revivals with folk dancing, arts and crafts movements, and folk costumes.[15] As documentation shifted into revival, the "folk" became the "authentic voice from the past" that channeled the innate essence of a people. Folk revivals took on political connotations as a gesture toward the rejection of modern life.[16] Nazis in

Germany channeled the *Volk* in any number of ways, with women appearing in folk costumes at political rallies and artists reimagining folk themes like the harvest in state-celebrated paintings.[17] Folk or *Volk* became the antithesis of urban, international decadence in its connection to the notion of innate cultural categories of people. The folk supposedly spoke to timelessness in these renditions, and as such the nod toward folk became a political statement about anti-modernism. That is, the term "folk" was deployed, whether cynically or not, as a strategic rejection of modernism as part of the political platform.

Both contributing to the rising fascination with folk culture and becoming fodder for the political machinations of those enamored with the folk was a generation of modernists who functioned as tastemakers. Modernists grew entranced with the representations made by primitive peoples, whether those people were the folk, children, those with mental illnesses, or the colonized, all groups conceptualized as more "emotional" and therefore more "in touch" with the essential self. They studied the art and adopted the techniques of such primitives and supported the artwork of untrained artists. Modernists, whether in literature or in the visual arts, also celebrated the exploration of psychology and consciousness through which the artwork of institutionalized individuals became seen as particularly revealing of an essential self. This strand of artwork later began to be labeled art brut in Europe and outsider art or visionary art in America.[18] Fascist states in Europe sought to separate the pure "folk" from the more corrupted "degenerate" and modern elements that supposedly contaminated it, though clearly the realms interacted throughout the early twentieth century.

In America, folk art collecting had been tied to decorative and craft traditions in the nineteenth century. Art historian Kenneth Ames sees this collecting as part of an antiquarian impulse by affluent East Coasters that resulted in nineteenth-century collections, exhibitions, and publications and in the formation of museums and study programs in the twentieth century.[19] Over the course of the twentieth century, the term "folk" connoted primitivism and naive art in America. The 1920s and '30s saw a brief flirtation with folk art concomitant with other projects that sought to document the diversity of American culture, like the Federal Writers' Project's Slave Narrative Project and the Farm Security Administration's photography program. Folk art in America began to gain serious attention when the Whitney Studio Club launched a show in the 1920s and the Museum of Modern Art and the Newark Museum had major folk art shows during the 1930s.[20] In 1951 Winterthur, one of the premier museums in American decorative arts, was established in Delaware, and the following year it began its material culture program.

Interest in folk traditions returned in the 1960s and '70s, invigorating the arts. The 1961 opening of the Museum of American Folk Art in New York signaled the deepening of interest and was followed by folk art shows at a number of major galleries and exhibitions.[21] As one critic of a 1974 show at the Whitney Museum stated, folk art, "by virtue of its instinctive, intuitive quality, provides a more basic vision of the world. It is both purer and cruder."[22] The curator of the Brooklyn Museum suggested that folk art "might be defined, I think, as the naive expression of a deeply felt reality by the unsophisticated American artist."[23] The linking of folk art to feelings and authenticity made qualities other than technique the hallmark of artistry.

According to Elizabeth Manley Delacruz, "in the early 1970s, there were only two commercial galleries in the field. By the mid-nineties, 'there were as many as ten thousand collectors of twentieth century folk art, and there was an army of pickers supporting more than a hundred galleries.'"[24] Between the 1970s and the 1990s folk lost its association with politics and gained an apparatus for legitimation. No longer the province of radicals, folk art could hark back toward an ideal of authenticity.

Erotic folk art has begun to be incorporated into the larger corpus of folk art, though the process is incomplete and many erotic folk objects remain separated from more traditional sorts of folk art. For example, Steven Ashby, the African American artist discussed in the previous chapter, has eight objects in the Smithsonian Institution; his erotic materials, however, are kept by private collectors like Bob Roth, founder of the

Chicago Reader and an important collector of outsider art. The same separation holds true for the works of Mose Tolliver. However, volumes like *Souls Grown Deep: African American Vernacular Art of the South* (2000) placed sexual artifacts alongside other works by folk artists.[25] To combat the segregation of erotic folk art from other forms of folk art, the gallery owner and art dealer Carl Hammer mixes erotic works with other pieces of contemporary art when he participates in the Armory Show. He believes that erotic folk artists are major American artists who deserve recognition.[26]

As folk art gained popularity and marketability, venues began to show and sell materials by artists whose work had little to do with shared community, traditions, or histories—the traditional hallmarks of folk art.[27] Vivian Raynor, the *New York Times* art critic, noted in 1988 that

> Time was when "folk art" meant work made in innocence of industrial reality and intended to serve a purpose—furniture, trade signs, portraits and the like. Now, the term covers just about anything made by the untutored and largely for self-expression. Purists grind their teeth in vain, but naiveté for its own sake is a business that is here to stay.[28]

Raynor, in this review, railed against the extension of the category of folk to include other sorts of untrained artists. According to the broadening of the category, folk artists were lumped together by what they were not—not "insiders," not trained by art schools, not elite. "Outsider art" as a term has become a bit more accepted, though these works have also been labeled as "art brut," "outsider art," "visionary art," and "self-taught art."

As the term "outsider art" caught on, the art world developed the language, the inventory, and the marketing strategies for this new style of art. The Outsider Art Fair, an annual event begun in 1993 in New York and joined by a Paris offshoot in 2013, has become increasingly remunerative.[29] A tension between commercialism and art appreciation has marked shows and reviews of outsider art. One gallery owner, for example, would only sell pieces to people who would "love the art" as opposed to those would see it as an economic investment.[30] Love of the art has not slowed sales, as the critic Holland Cotter pointed out in a review of the Outsider Art Fair in 1998. After noting the commercial successes of the field in the 1990s, Cotter writes that "The deeply felt expressions of inner lives and of an authentic popular culture are wrapped in a disarmingly warm but acquisitive and potentially distorting embrace."[31] Gallery owners, art critics, and art historians use artists' life histories and stories to add resonance to the art (consider the treatment of Dwight Mackintosh and Henry Darger in chapters Two and Four of this book). Inner lives and authenticity marked outsider art as real.

Commentators and reporters have spoken of the pricing of outsider art with a sort of stunned amazement. An article in the *San Francisco Chronicle* reported that the cost of Dwight Mackintosh's figure drawings went from $5 to $300 in just a few months and that his large canvas drawings were selling for up to $2,500 in 1992.[32] By 1993, a year later, his drawings were valued at between $500 and $5,000.[33] In 1999 Creative Growth, the center where Mackintosh made art, changed its mission. It began to gear its shows toward "Manhattan gallerists, rock stars, and international dealers," those who began to buy outsider art, according to journalist Nathaniel Rich. The center responded by staffing with professional artists and art administrators. Outsider art—associated with an authentic, untainted drive to create—became a valuable commodity. As Rich explains, "the fantasy of the notion of professional purity persists. It does more than persist. It sells."[34]

A Christie's outsider art sale in 2003 signaled a new era in which outsider art "broke the 'grass ceiling,'" according to a contemporary commentary. At that auction, a work by Martín Ramírez sold for almost $100,000.[35] The positioning of outsider and folk art as noteworthy areas for preservation, collection, and display has created a market for materials that had little value in the past. Erotic objects that fit into the purview of outsider and folk art benefited from recognition and began to command substantial revenues.

The monetization of Henry Darger's books and drawings demonstrate what can happen between love and money. When he left his rooms to move into a nursing home, all of his possessions went to Nathan Lerner, his landlord and a fellow artist. Lerner saw art beneath the piles of Pepto-Bismol bottles and stacks of ephemera. According to all accounts, Lerner worked tirelessly to interest critics, collectors, museums, and psychologists in Darger's art. By 1977, with Lerner's assistance, the Hyde Park Art Center in Chicago mounted the first Darger show. According to a report in the *Chicago Tribune*

> At first, none were for sale. But in about 1979, the Lerners began selling to collectors, initially at about $1,000 each. "He saw dollar signs," says Michael Boruch, who was hired by Lerner to catalog the contents of the room shortly after Darger's death. "Nathan evolved from, 'These should be protected,' to 'My gosh, people would buy these things and I own them.'"[36]

The Lerners donated drawings to the Collection de l'Art Brut in Lausanne, the most famous art brut museum in the world, as well as some to other museums, keeping the remaining drawings and books in their control. The opening of a show on Darger at the American Folk Art Museum in 1997 cemented his reputation.[37] By 2000, collectors were paying up to $100,000 for Darger's drawings and a museum paid $2 million to acquire a substantial body of his work.[38] By 2014 a drawing by Darger, *Sans titre*, sold at Christie's auction house for $745,076.[39]

The triumph of folk art, art brut, and outsider art transformed the artists' treatment of erotic subjects. As these types of art moved into galleries, museums, and collections, they became rarified. Though still considered as "authentic" and "real" in their expressions of internal life, they no longer signified as erotica or pornography. In many ways these objects, removed from the grittiness of their making, lost a rawness as they garnered appreciation. Their construction by amateur, untrained artists became part of what made them real and valuable, and their amateur status marked them as legitimate expressions of sexuality. But as they grew more accepted, their status as erotic became subsumed to their place as art. Darger's acceptance by the art world muted concerns about his sexuality—in their place came discussions of his technique and his context. Similarly, discussions of Steven Ashby's works place them in the context of his locality, Ashby having lived his whole life in the same place where his family had labored in slavery. They do not discuss the rouged tips to the penises he painted, or the bulging eyes of a horse staring at a nude woman. Sex became secondary to other sorts of explanations that validate ideas of authenticity, like methods, emotions, and communities.

Further, their rough qualities blunt criticism of their sexual content. In some sense, folk and outsider artists' naiveté as artists suggests a sort of sexual naiveté as well. As Carl Hammer said in an interview, "It softens the blow that it's done naively, as opposed to [Robert] Mapplethorpe. People think that the eroticism is somehow more acceptable. Viewers are given the green card because it's naive. It feels less confrontational."[40] However, as Hammer also pointed out, the willingness to accept artistic naiveté as sexual naiveté falters when artists venture into more complicated sexual themes: "There's a problem when it goes beyond a simple figure." Although folk artists produced more explicit depictions of sexual activity and sexual desire, those objects, according to Hammer, are kept "hush hush."[41] Segregating the nude from more explicit depictions of sexual activity allows viewers to maintain the "folksiness" of folk art and so allows viewers to contain ideas about the nature of sexuality. The incorporation of more simplistic ideas of sexuality into canonical art and the segregation of more challenging ideas about sex into private collections in some sense neuters folk art and outsider art.

Part of the acceptance of these forms of art emerges from the mistaken belief that folk and outsider art stand outside commercial culture. Although both fields gained value and moved into the commercial market as art objects, their status as uncommercial and even anti-commercial expressions of sexuality remain more important. These objects are thought to speak to some sort of sexual expression unpolluted by commercial culture. In some way, by placing these materials as outside commercial culture, the ideas about sexuality embodied in them are perceived as more innate, more intrinsic, more real. However, authenticity itself has become a marketable quality, and this process of valuation of the authentic and the amateur was replicated within the realm of photography.

Simultaneous to the "discovery" of folk and outsider art came new forms of amateur pornography. The invention of Polaroid instant cameras and camcorders allowed the category of amateur pornography to be transformed. The legitimation of outsider and folk art and the mechanization of amateur pornography happened concurrently and seems to attest to a shared search for authenticity and need for expression. Further, the two shifts ultimately end at the same place, with the commodification of authenticity. Though assessment of the full impact of the Polaroid and the video recorder remain beyond the scope of this project (given their mechanical rather than handmade nature), their impact on homemade pornography deserves some recognition.

Before the 1970s the camera had limited utility for homemade pornography because of the need to process film and print images. Thus, in some sense, the Polaroid camera created the category of amateur pornography. As the sociologists Charles Edgley and Kenneth Kiser have noted, "Prior to the development and mass distribution of the Polaroid camera, homemade pornography was almost impossible to achieve, unless one of the participants had access to a developing laboratory and the skill with which to process his own prints."[42] Using a commercial printing house to process film always opened one up to exploitation and possible blackmail. Mail order houses promised confidentiality, but if that guarantee was broken there was little one could do.[43] Reputable houses would not handle materials they deemed obscene or thought might be illegal. The Eastman Kodak Company, for example, confiscated materials thought to contravene postal regulations for obscenity.[44]

Roadblocks to the widespread photographic production of amateur pornography disappeared with the invention of the Polaroid camera. The Polaroid process removed some of the dangers of taking pornographic photographs. By creating a print without negatives, Polaroids minimized the risk carried by the easy duplication of prints, which could allow one's personal experiments to become public commodities. By getting rid of the need for processing, the Polaroid allowed a private process of picture-taking to remain private. Users could circumvent commercial locations and use photography in a more controllable and circumscribed way to explore their sexual desires. In the process, Polaroid remade amateur pornography. Introduced in 1947, the Polaroid became available to the American consumer in 1948. As Thomas Waugh discusses, Sam Steward, a professor turned tattoo artist, bought the first version of the Polaroid on the market so that he could film himself with his friends having sex. He and his friends acted out their fantasies and looked at the results with amazement.[45] Since a Polaroid camera remained an expensive piece of equipment, people used it to document sexuality but in relatively small numbers. During the 1960s, the police in one East Coast city confiscated roughly sixty Polaroids showing men who were nude and having sex.[46] Early Polaroid processes allowed for the mechanization of amateur pornography, but the numbers were dwarfed by handmade objects like sketches, which were themselves dwarfed by commercial productions.

The development of a one-step process in the early 1970s and the creation of the inexpensive sx-70 model made Polaroids widespread. By the late 1970s, the Polaroid was the biggest-selling camera in history. By 1983, almost half of American households had one.[47] As Jonathan Coopersmith notes, the sx-70 seemed to stand for SEX, and its first inexpensive model was named "The Swinger."[48] In *Fully Exposed* (1989), an overview of the male nude, Emmanuel Cooper noted that "The Polaroid photograph has become so identified with private pictures and the erotic image that the two have become almost synonymous." In 1982 Edgley and Kiser detailed a number of examples in which people made "use of instant photography devices to create homemade pornography."[49]

Despite the ease and privacy that Polaroids brought to amateur pornography, dangers remained. In one case, Virginia courts sentenced a couple to a two-year prison term and placed their children in foster care for taking nude photographs and filming their own sexual intercourse. The couple came to the attention of the police when the children brought the images into school for show-and-tell.[50] In a 1993 case a man's grandson threw eleven Polaroids onto the lawn during a domestic dispute. After the police asked him about the photographs, the man put them in his pocket, saying they were private photos—only to be charged with possession of pornography. According to newspaper reports, the images showed a "woman standing nude in the shower, nude in her bedroom and lying spread-eagled on her bed. Other shots depict the woman fondling herself and close-up views of her crotch. But the most objectionable photo from prosecutors' point of view shows [the man] apparently penetrating the woman with his hand."[51] As long as amateur pornography stayed private, it allowed people a way to explore and articulate ideas about sexuality to themselves. However, when these materials went public, these materials crossed into the realm of obscenity.

That dangerous crossing of documents into the public realm became part of the erotic appeal of the instant photograph. The circulation of sexual displays photographed in private became built into swinger culture, according to periodicals devoted to the practice. Edgley and Kiser have documented how the exchange of Polaroids became standard after people established contact via correspondence pages. According to their analysis, the exchange of images guaranteed safety by promising mutually assured destruction: both parties had nude and potentially damaging photographs that could be circulated in case of information leaks and which could be used for mutual extortion if necessary. Instead of limiting the spread of Polaroid photographs and keeping them private, the dangers of display began to generate their own erotic frisson. A 1977 advertisement in *Hustler* magazine called for "Polaroid photography enthusiasts." It promised introductions to those who liked to photograph, be photographed, or buy photographs from other amateurs. The *Hustler* section titled "Beaver Hunt" institutionalized the amateur mail-in as part of its monthly magazine.[52]

By the late 1970s, Polaroid instant cameras had transformed amateur pornography by cementing the idea that pornography was not only visual but photographic. Polaroids made it easy and relatively inexpensive for people to document themselves and each other in sexual positions and allowed people to play with sexual display. As amateur photographic pornography grew in popularity, it became incorporated into commercial productions. Questions about who or what constitutes an amateur began to haunt these materials. What was amateur pornography? Was it more truthful than commercial pornography? Were photographers really taking pictures of their girlfriends or were they professional photographers using amateur technologies to fake images of the "the girl next door?" If the person photographed was a professional sex worker, was it still amateur pornography? Questions about whether the images were produced by amateurs of amateurs remained relevant and would underlie discussions of amateur pornography even as the technologies and platforms for homemade pornography changed.

While Polaroid photography did much to transform amateur pornography, it rendered sexuality onto the still image. It took the availability of the camcorder and video recorder to capture the moving image for the amateur market. A few amateur pornographic films preceded the video revolution, but these materials were rare. The issues of secrecy and potential extortion around the processing of pornographic film were magnified in cases of moving images because even the basement darkroom was not sophisticated enough to process and print film.[53]

The video revolution changed pornography by transforming both the production and the consumption of commercial pornography before it began to affect amateur materials. When commercial pornographic films had only a limited number of outlets (fewer than eight hundred at the height of the "golden age" in the 1970s), the economics of showing film remained an algebraic equation. If eight hundred theaters demanded roughly fifty-two new films per year and the production of each film cost roughly $100,000 to $150,000, then the total cost of commercial production would be $5–10 million. Videos, in contrast, cost somewhere around $15,000 to shoot and could go directly to the home market, bypassing the theater entirely.[54] Producers could be far less technically skilled and a

video could be filmed in as little as a day or two. In short, video expanded
the market while simultaneously saving money on production costs.

In the home, the consumption of video technology was gendered
male, akin to photography, ham radio, and other sorts of technological
hobby-crafts. This association was strengthened by the early adoption of
pornographic materials in video. Though Hollywood stalled the transfer
of movies to video for the home market, the pornography industry threw
itself into the breach, copying its back catalog into video loops and then
videos for sale and rent.[55] Male video hobbyists met a market in pornography organized for men. By 1987 the number of theaters showing
pornography had fallen to 250, while the market for X-rated video rentals
swelled to 100 million units per year.[56] Home video had a clear place in
the consumption of commercial pornography, and home video pornography helped anchor the development of the independent video store.

The production of amateur video pornography took slightly longer
to develop because of technological constraints. By the mid-1970s video
recorders had become available, but these were expensive, bulky, and hard
to operate. Early recorders needed separate microphones, tapes, and
cameras, and as a result their impact on homemade pornography remained
negligible. Not until the 1980s did camcorders offer an "all in one," light-
weight way of taping.[57] The introduction of the camcorder transformed
amateur pornography by allowing people to capture their own sexual
activities without processing, printing, or public exposure.[58] The extent
of amateur video pornography remains unknowable and stories about its
adoption remain underdocumented and anecdotal.[59]

Very quickly, the distinction between private videotaping of amateur
sex and the public circulation of commercial pornography began to break
down. Labeled "DIY pornography" or "amateur pornography," homemade
video pornography quickly became its own niche in the market, with its
own journal, *Amateur Video Guide*, and conventions.[60] Scholars suggested
that the appeal of amateur video pornography lay in the desire for the real.
According to Niels van Doorn, for example, amateur video and "the desire
for 'real', authentic sexual practices formed a response to the increasingly

spectacular, silicon-enhanced artificiality of commercial feature-length pornography."[61] The desire to see "real" pleasures by "real" people helped create the market for recycled homemade footage. Jonathan Coopersmith has identified only a single company that distributed amateur pornographic videos in 1980, but he notes that by 1991, amateur pornography reached 30 percent of new offerings in the video industry.[62] As Laurence O'Toole remarks, "After panicking, the porn industry's more measured response to amateur was to swallow it up. The majors started distributing it, or running their own ranges, as well as mimicking its style."[63]

The line between amateurs and professionals remained nebulous. One woman interviewed in 1987 for an article in the North Carolina business press described her experience of moving from home-movie maker to amateur pornography marketer. "It started out just kind of for kicks. I mean, we never even considered wife-swapping or swinging or whatever, you know, but we'd made these tapes of us, uh, fooling around, and it was a turn-on, knowing that other people were watching us." After being contacted by a video label, she and her husband decided to sell other people's traded videos. "We didn't want to sell ours, you know, the ones of us, but we got to thinking, 'Why not sell the ones we traded for?'"[64] By selling other people's home movies, the couple made enough money to put a down payment on their house. The ease of making money from amateur pornography was noted by others. Detective Robert Hoxter of the San Diego sheriff's department categorized the field of non-professionals making and circulating pornography as a "cottage industry."[65]

The popularity of homemade pornography encouraged people to sell videos intended for home use as commercial pornography. Leaked and stolen tapes of celebrity home videos like "Pam and Tommy Lee" (1997) and "Tonya and Jeff's Wedding Night" (1994) were sold commercially without the consent of the participants. Pamela Anderson and Tommy Lee attempted to sue the company that distributed their pirated movie, but their efforts failed. Tonya Harding's ex-husband, Jeff Gillooly, sold a tape of the couple's sexual relations.[66] Though these were amateur tapes made at home for home use, their movement onto the commercial market demonstrates the lack of distinction between homemade and commercially made pornography by the 1990s. As Minette Hillyer suggests in her analysis of these home movies, "Probably the most explicit point of communion between pornography and the home movie, as ersatz genres of film production, is the promise that they both attempt to reveal the 'truth.'"[67]

This trend of leaking private materials to the public realm continued as digital technologies overtook the video market. The fascination with "the real" promoted an interest in celebrity sex tapes as well as reality-based amateur markets. By the 1990s, according to van Doorn, the mass media had become fascinated by the lives of everyday people, resulting in the rise of reality TV and the search for the "real" and the "authentic."[68] The line between amateur and professional remained nebulous in other ways as well. The so-called "gonzo" subgenre of pornography used video cameras and desktop video editing. The hand-held camerawork made it appear more authentic. In gonzos, professionals interact with "amateurs," or newcomers to the adult video scene, according to film scholar Chuck Kleinhans.[69] Even amateur-based franchises like the "Girls Gone Wild" series made use of professional cameramen, though cameramen emphasize their own efforts as amateurish.[70] Commercial and amateur productions mutually constitute each other in both hidden and obvious ways.

The so-called "pornographication" or "pornification" of culture moves in multiple directions. More people supposedly see pornography than ever before, affecting people's definitions of standard sexual practices and changing people's ideas of desirable bodies. Porn stars' practices supposedly influence teenage girls' grooming habits and are said to shape teenage boys' desires and expectations. In these ways, commercial pornography affects the habits of the populace. At the same time, amateur practices have commercial applications, and the difference between commercial culture and amateur culture remains indistinct. People hack into celebrity phones and leak the nude images to the press, for example, while teenagers take pictures of themselves to trade. YouTube has been joined by YouPorn, an Internet site devoted to user-uploaded materials.

The shocking ease of uploading and delivering digital materials has joined the revolutionary nature of home photography. Amateur photography and cheap computers together allow for amateur pornography in its current form. Online digital pornography has become the current standard, making earlier delivery systems appear quaint.

Handwritten pamphlets, hand-drawn images, and handmade carvings have moved into the realm of nostalgia, as if the technological distance blunts them as pornography. This point is worth underlining. The change in technology has transformed our understanding of amateur pornography and created a nostalgic appreciation for older forms of amateur pornography, as if those who made porn in the past did not really understand sexuality in all of its permutations. From the vantage point of uploaded YouPorn images, handmade scrimshaw carvings look almost chaste. This nostalgic appreciation can be maintained because we rarely see the range of pornographic artifacts available. A single nude drawing on a gallery wall looks like an individual's expressive consideration of the body. Multiplied by a hundred, it begins to look more like an obsession; add in sexual penetration and it begins to look like pornography. People rarely see the full range of artifacts and thus conceptualize only the most accessible forms of pornography—which currently feature digital close-ups of shaved bodies—as real porn. Though online video might be the current form of amateur pornography, it is not the only one, as this project has tried to show. Pornographic carvings, prints, pamphlets, stories, cartoons, plaques, and coins testify to peoples' sexual desires and were just as dirty, problematic, odd, real, and authentic as today's amateur pornography.

Though capitalism has intervened to exploit amateurness as a quality, the search for authenticity and truth demonstrates something about people's desires. People long for an unmediated form of sexuality. They seek a sense of sex that precedes consumer culture. They see in amateur creations something real, even if that realness is dubious and problematic. This longing for the real has dominated the world of art and the world of pornography since at least the 1970s. The rise of folk, vernacular, and outsider art and amateur pornography were concomitant, shaped by different forces but arriving at the same place. Their trajectories point toward the same longing by people who want to experience an unmediated expression of truth and who want to have a sense of sexuality not wrapped in artifice and not shaped by commercialism. Amateur works seem real, authentic, and personal while commercial pornography seems somehow laminated and plasticized. Unfortunately, that longing for the real opened a marketplace for the "real" as exploitable as any other. Pornographers sold amateur porn as a subfield of the market. Dealers marketed outsider art for its emotional truth and folk art for its expression of an unmediated folk culture. The longing for truth has a commercial potential, and the qualities of amateurness remain exploitable, with the art world and the world of commercial pornography monetizing that longing.

The recognition of that process does not make pornographers or art dealers evil, nor does it make consumers stupid. Instead, the recognition of the ways in which capitalism consumes authenticity speaks to the persuasiveness and adaptability of capitalism; as noted by Karl Marx and Friedrich Engels more than a century ago when they wrote the *Communist Manifesto*, "All that is solid melts into air." It also testifies to the depths of people's longings. People know full well that reality TV and beaver-shot photo spreads are curated versions of the truth, but the longing for stories about how people live and how they look encourages consumers to engage in the willful suspension of disbelief. Consumers recognize that these artificial interventions affect content, but they nevertheless seem to be choosing partial truth over no truth at all. Further, beneath the desire to watch and understand the "reality" and authenticity made by others is the continued impulse to make pornography, even if people today are employing new technologies to do so. The making still matters.

Along with the making are the objects being made, which provide testimony beyond their makers' life span, a point suggested by Ivan Stormgart when he handed me a handmade scrapbook of dead porn actors called "Porno Angels in Heaven."[71] The scrapbook featured death notices and biographies opposite magazine photos and tear sheets of male porn stars. The anonymous producer of this volume detailed lives sadly shortened by AIDS in page after page of the scrapbook. Though we often think of an individual's immortality as existing in forms such as Shakespeare's plays or through Kant's writings, perhaps immortality can be wrought smaller, reflecting the ways that most of us live. Though not everyone would want to be remembered through a pornographic scrapbook that shows one's orgasmic pleasure, some people have lived erotic lives and would prefer their tributes to be messy and vibrant and human. An immortality achieved by making and celebrating sexuality in all its physicality and awkwardness seems particularly sweet given the alternative, which is that we forget people as individuals with all of the passions that drove them. Such objects, which testify to a little death in the face of a larger death, stand as markers of people's compulsion to create and their originality in doing so.

References

Introduction: Alternative Sources for American Sexual History

1 Leon Rosenstein, *Antiques: The History of an Idea* (Ithaca, NY, 2009), p. 37.
2 Scrimshaw tooth, 1879, item 2007.7, Mystic Seaport Museum, Mystic, Connecticut.
3 Tristan Hopper, "'It's All Fake': Vancouver Exhibit's 'Whale Bone Porn' Is Not 19th-Century Scrimshaw, Former Museum Director Says," www.nationalpost.com, March 30, 2013.
4 Zoophilia with horse, Realia, [196?], ISR 731, Kinsey Institute (formerly the Institute for Sex Research), Bloomington, Indiana.
5 Walter Kendrick, *The Secret Museum: Pornography in Modern Culture* (Berkeley, CA, 1996), p. xiii.
6 Thomas Waugh, *Hard to Imagine: Gay Male Eroticism in Photography and Film from their Beginnings to Stonewall* (New York, 1996), p. 8.
7 For discussions of Anthony Comstock and censorship, see Nicola Beisel, *Imperiled Innocents: Anthony Comstock and Family Reproduction in Victorian America* (Princeton, NJ, 1997), particularly Chapter Three; and Paul S. Boyer, *Purity in Print: Book Censorship in America* (New York, 1968), pp. 1–11. Elizabeth Haven Hawley mentions the confiscation and subsequent destruction of business records: Elizabeth Haven Hawley, "American Publishers of Indecent Books, 1840–1890," PhD dissertation, Georgia Institute of Technology, Atlanta (2005), p. 417. For discussions of Sumner, see Jay A. Gertzman, *Bookleggers and Smuthounds: The Trade in Erotica, 1920–1940* (Philadelphia, PA, 1999), pp. 103–33. Donna Dennis discusses the extent of the destruction using anti-vice organizations' annual reports. She notes the "staggering" amount of destruction as compared with the "scarcity" of materials that remain. The destruction was tallied in poundage rather than by piece. For example, the 1900 report, which tallied over years of destruction, noted that 78,608 pounds of books and sheet stock were destroyed as well as hundreds of thousands of images, thousands of photographic plates, and tens of thousands of pounds of stereotype plates. See Donna Dennis, *Licentious Gotham: Erotic Publishing and its Prosecution in Nineteenth-century New York* (Cambridge, MA, 2009), pp. 275–6.
8 Douglas M. Charles, *The FBI's Obscene File: J. Edgar Hoover and the Bureau's Crusade Against Smut* (Lawrence, KS, 2012), p. 4.
9 Hawley, "American Publishers of Indecent Books," pp. 138, 10; see also Dennis, *Licentious Gotham*, p. 275.
10 Helen Lefkowitz Horowitz, *Rereading Sex: Battles over Sexual Knowledge and Suppression in Nineteenth-century America* (New York, 2003), p. 10. Jesse Battan details the battle as a war of words that sought to affect the populace at the level of consciousness. Jesse F. Battan, "The Word Made Flesh: Language, Authority, and Sexual Desire in Late Nineteenth-century America," *Journal of the History of Sexuality*, III/2 (October 1992), pp. 223–44.

11 The idea of pornography as a secret got a boost from the memoir *My Secret Life*, one of the most famous pornographic documents of the nineteenth century. The book, published in Amsterdam and smuggled into England, cost between £40 and £100 and was printed in an eleven-volume set. See Lisa Sigel, *Governing Pleasures: Pornography and Social Change in England, 1815–1914* (New Brunswick, NJ, 2002), p. 88. There is also Walter Kendrick's *The Secret Museum*. A TV miniseries entitled *Pornography: The Secret History of Civilization* (1999), produced by Channel 4 in the UK, also capitalizes on this language.

12 Jessica Yu, *In the Realms of the Unreal: The Mystery of Henry Darger* (New York: Wellspring Media, 2004), DVD; Jim Elledge, *Henry Darger, Throwaway Boy: The Tragic Life of an Outsider Artist* (New York, 2013); Michael Bonesteel, *Henry Darger: Art and Selected Writings* (New York, 2000); John MacGregor, *Dwight Mackintosh: The Boy Who Time Forgot* (Oakland, CA, 1992).

13 See, for example, Jonathan Coopersmith, "Do-it-yourself Pornography: The Democratization of Pornography," in *PrOnnovation? Pornography and Technological Innovation*, ed. Johannes Grenzfurthner, Gunther Friesinger, and Daniel Fabry (Vienna, 2009), pp. 48–55; Minette Hillyer, "Sex in the Suburban: Porn, Home Movies, and the Live Action Performance of Love in 'Pam and Tommy Lee: Hardcore and Uncensored,'" in *Porn Studies*, ed. Linda Williams (Durham, NC, 2004), pp. 50–76; Zabet Patterson, "Going On-line: Consuming Pornography in the Digital Age," in *Porn Studies*, ed. Williams, pp. 104–23; and Susanna Paasonen, "Labors of Love: Netporn, Web 2.0 and the Meanings of Amateurism," *New Media and Society*, XII/8 (2010), pp. 1297–312.

14 Jonathan Coopersmith, "Pornography, Technology and Progress," *Icon*, 4 (1998), pp. 94–125: p. 94.

15 See for example Hillyer, "Sex in the Suburban," pp. 50–76; and Patterson, "Going On-line,"

pp. 104–23. Dwight Swanson discusses amateur collections of adult movies. These films were professionally produced but owned and shown by amateurs. Dwight Swanson, "Home Viewing: Pornography and Amateur Film Collections, A Case Study," *The Moving Image*: *The Journal of the Association of Moving Image Archivists*, V/2 (Fall 2005), pp. 136–40. For a discussion of amateur online pornography, see Paasonen, "Labors of Love." Though her work does not consider pornography per se, Patricia Zimmerman's book on amateur film is nonetheless worth thinking about in this context: Patricia R. Zimmerman, *Reel Families: A Social History of Amateur Film* (Bloomington, IN, 1995), pp. ix–xv.

16 Joseph Slade, *Pornography and Representation: A Reference Guide*, vol. II (Westport, CT, 2001), p. 677.

17 Raphaella Baek, "Dan Savage on Porn, Amateur Porn, and Porn about Fluffers," www.washingtoncitypaper.com, March 20, 2014.

18 For a detailed analysis of the printing methods and costs for the "flash press," see Patricia Cline Cohen, Timothy Gilfoyle, and Helen Lefkowitz Horowitz, *The Flash Press: Sporting Male Weeklies in 1840s New York* (Chicago, IL, 2008), pp. 48–9. While men bragged that they could make fast money, a lack of cash reserves, an inability to find good printers, lawsuits for libel, ink freezing in an unheated warehouse, and a quick rise and quicker fall from wealth seem indicative of under-capitalization rather than ready profits. Reports of enormous fortunes made from such publishing ventures cloud the issue. See Donna Dennis, "Obscenity Regulation, New York City, and the Creation of American Erotica, 1820–1880," PhD dissertation, Princeton University, New Jersey (2005), p. 235. However much the claim that fast money outwitted the dull police was popularized in the texts, publishers lived precariously. Hawley, "American Publishers of Indecent Books," p. 418. The divergence between claims about great wealth and available evidence that

points toward much smaller profit-making continued into the 1920s and '30s. See Gertzman, *Bookleggers and Smuthounds*, p. 37. Gertzman points out that the dealers were actually Jewish immigrants or children of immigrants.

19   Robert Darnton, *The Literary Underground of the Old Regime* (Cambridge, MA, 1982), pp. 207–8; Lynn Hunt, ed., *The Invention of Pornography* (New York, 1993).

20   See for example Julie Peakman, *Mighty Lewd Books: The Development of Pornography in Eighteenth-century England* (Basingstoke, 2003), and Sigel, *Governing Pleasures*.

21   After the Second World War, new magazines reflecting American cultural experiences began to dominate the pornographic marketplace at home and abroad. Recent work by Elizabeth Fraterrigo has demonstrated that *Playboy* articulated a lifestyle for single men that spoke to distinctly American consumer aspirations. Elizabeth Fraterrigo, *Playboy and the Making of the Good Life in Modern America* (Oxford, 2009); see also Barbara Ehrenreich, *The Hearts of Men: American Dreams and the Flight from Commitment* (Garden City, NJ, 1983). *Playboy* started in the 1950s, *Penthouse* began in the 1960s and *Hustler* in the 1970s, creating a triad of semi-legitimate displays of sexuality. Both Ehrenreich and Laura Kipnis see the magazines as developing carefully articulated rejections of feminine and feminist culture, though Kipnis sees the working-class *Hustler* as the more Rabelaisian of the two. Laura Kipnis, *Bound and Gagged: Pornography and the Politics of Fantasy in America* (New York, 1996).

22   Klara Arnberg, Joseph Slade, and Whitney Strub have demonstrated the ways that pornographers lagged behind innovations in marketing and production, in the context of Swedish magazine sales (Arnberg), film production (Slade), and print culture in the age of film (Strub). Klara Arnberg, "Under the Counter, Under the Radar? The Business and Regulation of the Pornographic Press in Sweden, 1950–1971," *Enterprise and Society*, XIII/2 (June 2012),

pp. 350–77; Joseph Slade, "Eroticism and Technological Regression: The Stag Film," *History and Technology*, XXI/1 (March 2006), pp. 27–52: p. 32; Whitney Strub, *Perversion for Profit: The Politics of Pornography and the Rise of the New Right* (New York, 2011), p. 5.

23   See Patrick Kearney, *The Private Case: An Annotated Bibliography of the Private Case Erotica Collection in the British (Museum) Library* (London, 1981).

24   Linda Williams, "Porn Studies: Proliferating Pornographies On/Scene: An Introduction," in *Porn Studies*, ed. Williams, pp. 1–23: p. 2.

25   Frank Rich, "Naked Capitalists: There's No Business Like Porn Business," www.nytimes.com, May 20, 2001.

26   Adam Sandler, "Adults Only, Big Business," *Variety* (January 19, 1998), p. 5.

27   Dan Ackerman, "How Big Is Porn?" www.forbes.com, May 25, 2001. Accessed on December 22, 2013.

28   Emmanuelle Richard argues that neither the *New York Times* editorial nor the *Forbes* article has been skeptical enough about its figures. Richard quotes Bill Margold, a performer, who stated that the media should have been more wary: "In an industry predicated on screwing, you're going to get f*****. You honestly expect us to tell the truth about what we're making?" Emmanuelle Richard, "The Perils of Covering Porn: Rash of Recent Dotcom-angle Stories Perpetuate Myths about the Industry," USC Annenberg *Online Journalism Review*, www.ojr.org, April 3, 2002.

29   See for example Carmine Sarracino and Kevin M. Scott, *The Porning of America: The Rise of Porn Culture, What It Means, and Where We Go from Here* (Boston, MA, 2008), and Michael Kimmel, *Guyland: The Perilous World Where Boys Become Men* (New York, 2008).

30   Mary Eberstadt, "Is Pornography the New Tobacco?" *Policy Review* (Hoover Institution), CLIV (April 1, 2009), www.hoover.org.

31   Pamela Paul, *Pornified: How Pornography Is Transforming Our Lives, Our Relationships, and Our Lives* (New York, 2005), pp. 262, 275.

32 As Gail Dines and Robert Jensen wrote in a debate column in the *New York Times*, "Pornography is the industrialization and commodification of sex, and like all big industries, its product is generic, formulaic and plasticized." Gail Dines and Robert Jenkins, "A Habit that Can Destroy Lives," in the Room for Debate series, "Should Pornography Come out of the Closet?" www.nytimes.com, November 11, 2012. Dines explicates this position further in Gail Dines, *Pornland: How Porn Has Hijacked Our Sexuality* (Boston, MA, 2010).

33 Despite the advent of reader-response theory, there are very few studies that document how people read pornography. Clarissa Smith, *One for the Girls! The Pleasures and Practices of Reading Women's Porn* (Bristol, 2007), Chapter Three, provides one exception. Feona Attwood, Clarissa Smith, and Martin Barker have conducted an online survey about how everyday people use pornography via an opt-in online survey called the "Porn Research Project." In *Making Modern Love: Sexual Narratives and Identities in Interwar Britain* (Philadelphia, PA, 2012), I have tried to create a model of reading for materials about sexuality.

34 Historians have not been able to connect pornography as a business with consumer demand because records from both pornographers and consumers are missing. According to Elizabeth Haven Hawley, "The apparent silence within the historical record about how publishers of indecent books did business in nineteenth-century America is formidable." Hawley, "American Publishers of Indecent Books," p. 3. Scholars have tried to reconstruct production practices from police records and catalogs—see for example Colette Colligan, *A Publisher's Paradise: Expatriate Literary Culture in Paris, 1890–1960* (Amherst, MA, 2014)—and have tried to read consumer reactions from the relationship between pornography and the broader culture, for example Fraterrigo, *Playboy and the Making*

of the Good Life in Modern America, and Kipnis, *Bound and Gagged*. However, the gulf between production and consumption remains formidable. Very few historians have approached pornography as a business in their studies; exceptions might include Joseph W. Slade, "Pornography in the Late Nineties," *Wide Angle*, XIX/3 (July 1997), pp. 1–12, and Arnberg, "Under the Counter, Under the Radar?"

35 Alexander C. Halavais, "Small Pornographies," *ACM SIGGROUP Bulletin*, special issue on virtual communities, XXV/2 (February 2005), pp. 19–22. See also Blaise Cronin, Garry Milius, and Betsy Stirratt, *Private Eyes: Amateur Art from the Kinsey Institute Collection*, exh. cat., Kinsey Institute (Bloomington, IN, 2010), p. 5.

36 For this book I interviewed antiques dealers including Carl Hammer, Steve Powers, Patrick Bell, and Arthur Liverant. I also spoke at length with Mark Rotenberg, Jim Linderman, and Ivan Stormgart, who collect and sell folk objects, books, photographs, and antique erotica. I interviewed collectors, including Bob Roth and another collector who chooses to remain anonymous. I have communicated with Milton Simpson, Elaine and Michael Bennett, Barry M. Cohen, Justin Engers, Brian Emrich, Kirk Landauer, and Louis Picek. I have visited the Museum of Sex in New York, the Mystic Seaport Museum and Library in Connecticut, the Milwaukee Museum of Art, and Intuit Gallery in Chicago. I have consulted with the Nantucket Historic Society and archivists at the Smithsonian Institution. I have most extensively worked with the Kinsey Institute in Indiana. I have also corresponded with any number of collectors online.

37 Materials held in private collections often have little provenance. Likewise, many of the materials at the Kinsey Institute were donated anonymously. Thus the archives can provide no names, dates, locations, pricing, or history. Materials at the Kinsey Institute confiscated from all-male prisons form a corpus of works with a provenance and backstory that can be

helpful, but scholars should be careful not to use prison materials to make generalizations about how "men" conceptualize sex.

38 Alfred Kinsey's training as an entomologist, rather than a historian, shapes the Kinsey Institute's various collections in particular ways. He did not collect the sorts of data that historians see as essential and he organized the collections in ways that historians find problematic. For example, the photograph collection was originally organized by sexual position, rather than country of origin.

39 When presenting a version of this paper at the "Erotica, Pornography, Obscenity in Europe" conference (University of Warwick, April 10–12, 2013), Stuart Campbell of National Museums Scotland told me that they had a number of hand-cast and hand-etched artifacts that had been found in archeological sites around Scotland.

40 Horowitz, *Rereading Sex*, p. 25.

41 Regina Kunzel, *Criminal Intimacy: Prison and the Uneven History of Modern American Sexuality* (Chicago, IL, 2008), p. 5; see Christopher Hensley, Cindy Struckman-Johnson, and Helen M. Eigenberg, "Introduction: The History of Prison Sex Research," *Prison Journal*, LXXX/4 (December, 2000), pp. 360–67; Catherine D. Marcum, "Examining Prison Sex Culture," in *Sex in Prison: Myths and Realities*, ed. Catherine D. Marcum and Tammy L. Castle (Boulder, CO, and London, 2014), p. 6.

1 Carving Out a Vernacular Sexuality, 1830s–1930s

1 Phone interview with the collector, who chose to remain anonymous, April 30, 2014.

2 Jean Stengers and Ann van Neck, *Masturbation: The History of the Great Terror* (New York, 2001). Materials as diverse as *Aristotle's Masterpiece* (1690), *Sexual Behavior in the Human Male* (1948), *The Awful Disclosures*

of *Maria Monk* (1836), and *The Memoirs of a Woman of Pleasure* (1748–9) share a seriousness in their treatment of sexuality even though they developed from very different genres and traditions.

3 Iain McCalman, *Radical Underworld: Prophets, Revolutionaries and Pornographers in London, 1795–1840* (Cambridge, 1988). See also Lynn Hunt, ed., *Eroticism and the Body Politic* (Baltimore, MD, 1991); Robert Darnton, *The Forbidden Best-sellers of Pre-Revolutionary France* (New York, 1995); Lisa Sigel, *Governing Pleasures: Pornography and Social Change in England, 1815–1914* (New Brunswick, NJ, 20022), Chapter One.

4 Elizabeth Haven Hawley, "American Publishers of Indecent Books, 1840–1890," PhD dissertation, Georgia Institute of Technology, Atlanta (2005), pp. 16–17.

5 Ibid., p. 122.

6 Patricia Cline Cohen, Timothy Gilfoyle, and Helen Lefkowitz Horowitz, *The Flash Press: Sporting Male Weeklies in 1840s New York* (Chicago, IL, 2008); Timothy Gilfoyle, *City of Eros: New York City, Prostitution, and the Commercialization of Sex, 1790–1920* (New York, 1992); Amy Gilman Srebnick, *The Mysterious Death of Mary Rogers: Sex and Culture in Nineteenth-century New York* (New York, 1995), pp. 53, 191; Helen Lefkowitz Horowitz, *Rereading Sex: Battles over Sexual Knowledge and Suppression in Nineteenth-century America* (New York, 2003), Chapters Six and Eight.

7 Hawley, "American Publishers of Indecent Books," p. 88.

8 John D'Emilio and Estelle B. Freeman, *Intimate Matters: A History of Sexuality in America* (Chicago, IL, 1988), p. 131.

9 Judith Giesberg, *Sex and the Civil War: Soldiers, Pornography, and the Making of American Morality* (Chapel Hill, NC, 2017). D'Emilio and Freeman, *Intimate Matters*, p. 131.

10 Janet West, "Scrimshaw and the Identification of Sea Mammal Products," *Journal of Museum Ethnography*, 11 (March 1991), pp. 39–79: p. 39.

11 Margaret Lentz Vose, "Identification of the Origins and Sources of Selected Scrimshaw Motifs in 18th and 19th Century Contemporary Culture," PhD dissertation, New York University (1992).

12 Scrimshaw objects, whether pornographic or not, were rarely signed. Richard C. Malley, "Graven by the Fishermen Themselves: Scrimshaw in Mystic Seaport Museum," *Log of the Mystic Seaport*, XXXV/1 (1983), pp. 16–21: p. 17.

13 Scrimshaw, [19??], ISR 630R A75.1, Kinsey Institute (formerly the Institute for Sex Research), Bloomington, Indiana.

14 Milton Simpson, *Folk Erotica: Celebrating Centuries of Erotic Americana* (New York, 1994), pp. 36–7.

15 Ibid., p. 30.

16 Email correspondence with Stuart M. Frank, June 29, 2016.

17 For a brilliant overview of the transition from whaling to whaling museums see James M. Lindgren, "'Let Us Idealize Old Types of Manhood': The New Bedford Whaling Museum, 1903–1941," *New England Quarterly*, LXXII/2 (1999), pp. 163–206. In the UK, major collectors of pornography have been identified, while in the United States, ownership is still hidden. British collectors include Henry Spencer Ashbee (1834–1900) and George Mountbatten, 2nd Marquess of Milford Haven (1892–1938). Collectors have meticulously kept track of ownership of such volumes. See, for example, the attention given by John Studholme Hodgson to a volume owned by a previous, but unspecified, Duke of York. Peter Mendes, *Clandestine Erotic Fiction in English, 1800–1930* (Aldershot, 1993), p. 43, n. 10.

18 Andrew Burnett, *Coins* (Berkeley, CA, 1991), p. 7.

19 William Monter, "Gendered Sovereignty: Numismatics and Female Monarchs in Europe, 1300–1800," *Journal of Interdisciplinary History*, XLI/4 (Spring 2011), pp. 533–64: pp. 533, 534.

20 Robert Garson, "Counting Money: The U.S. Dollar and American Nationhood, 1781–1820," *Journal of American Studies*, XXXV/1 (April 2001), pp. 21–46: p. 22.

21 William Hunting Howell, "A More Perfect Copy: David Rittenhouse and Reproduction of Virtue," *William and Mary Quarterly*, 3rd ser., LXIV/4 (2007), pp. 757–90: p. 779.

22 Quoted in Benjamin H. Irvin, "Benjamin Franklin's 'Enriching Virtues,'" *Common-Place*, VI/3 (April 2006), www.common-place.org.

23 "A collection of 13 U.S. coins dating from 1812 to 1849 that have been altered to read 'ONE CUNT' instead of 'ONE CENT,'" Altered Currency, Novelties, Kinsey Institute.

24 "A One Cent Coin, 185?," Altered Currency, Novelties, Kinsey Institute; "A one cent liberty coin, 1930," Altered Currency, Novelties, Kinsey Institute.

25 Catherine Johns, *Sex or Symbol? Erotic Images of Greece and Rome* (New York, 1982), pp. 15–17.

26 For a discussion of winged phalluses, see ibid., pp. 68–72.

27 Will Fisher, "Queer Money," *ELH: English Literary History*, LXVI/1 (1999), pp. 1–23: p. 3.

28 "American silver dollar inscribed 420 grains, 900 Fine. Trade dollar, 1877," Altered Currency, Novelties, Kinsey Institute.

29 "French Ecu, inscribed BENEDITUM 1756 SIT," Altered Currency, Novelties, Kinsey Institute.

30 "French Five Franc piece, 1875," Altered Currency, Novelties, Kinsey Institute.

31 Lynn Hunt, "Hercules and the Radical Image in the French Revolution," *Representations*, 2 (Spring 1983), pp. 95–117: p. 111.

32 Edwards Park, "The Object at Hand," *Smithsonian* (October 1995), www.smithsonianmag.com.

33 Cane, private collection, undated. This cane has been featured in Simpson, *Folk Erotica*, p. 40, and now resides in a private collection in Pennsylvania. See Lisa Sigel, "Flagrant Delights," *Antiques Magazine* (July/August 2014), pp. 104–11. Phone interview with anonymous private collector, April 30, 2014.

34 Simpson, *Folk Erotica*, p. 41.
35 Novelty movable figures [19??], ISR 759, Kinsey Institute.
36 Man in a barrel [19??], ISR 480, Kinsey Institute.
37 Folk art [19??], ISR 1525, Kinsey Institute.
38 Coffin figure, held in the collection of Mark Rotenberg, Milford, New Jersey, viewed July 13, 2015; Simpson, *Folk Erotica*, p. 39.
39 In general, families and neighbors took care of the dead, and taking care of the body was a woman's task. The professionalization of death began with the Civil War. The South lagged behind the North in the adoption of professionalized death services, and rural death practices showed even slower adoption of professionalization than in urban centers. Charles R. Wilson, "The Southern Funeral Director: Managing Death in the New South," *Georgia Historical Quarterly*, LXVII/1 (1983), pp. 49–69; Spencer E. Cahill, "The Boundaries of Professionalization: The Case of North America Funeral Direction," *Symbolic Interaction*, XXII/2 (1999), pp. 105–19; Georganne Rundblad, "Exhuming Women's Premarket Duties in the Care of the Dead," *Gender and Society*, IX/2 (1995), pp. 173–92.
40 Coffin couple, n.d., from the collection of Justin Enger.
41 Though no one has written on fore-edge erotica, these materials circulated among the wealthy. I saw one example in an antique bookstore in London in 1993. Steve Powers, a New Jersey antiques dealer, is an authority on erotic snuff-boxes and his collection illustrates the fineness of the medium. Email with images embedded, Steve Powers to Lisa Sigel, May 7, 2014. Donna Dennis mentions erotic snuffboxes and music boxes that circulated in Boston in the 1840s. Donna Dennis, "Obscenity Regulation, New York City, and the Creation of American Erotica, 1820–1880," PhD dissertation, Princeton University, New Jersey (2005), p. 42; The price for erotic albums, pictures, snuffboxes, and music boxes in the 1830s ranged from $25 to $60. Hawley, "American Publishers of Indecent Books," p. 229.
42 See for example Jason Peacey, "The Print Culture of Parliament, 1600–1800," *Parliamentary History*, XXVI, part 1 (2007), pp. 1–16; and Eric Slauter, "Reading and Radicalization: Print, Politics, and the American Revolution," *Early American Studies: An Interdisciplinary Journal*, VIII/1 (Winter 2010), pp. 5–40.
43 Quoted in Alison Piepmeier, "Why Zines Matter: Materiality and the Creation of Embodied Community," *American Periodicals: A Journal of History, Criticism, and Bibliography*, XVIII/2 (2008), pp. 213–38: p. 214.
44 Ibid., p. 235.
45 "A Pretty Girl's Companion and Guide to Loves [*sic*] Sweetest Delights," n.p., n.d. [1900–1910?], Kinsey Institute.
46 Kahn's Museum operated for decades in the late nineteenth and early twentieth centuries as a museum of semi-licit thrills, linking medicine with houses of horror and sensation. Indeed, the illustration that fronted Dr. Kahn's catalog used a skull and crossbone motif. "Dr. Kahn's Museum of Anatomy, Science and Art: 294 Broadway, above Houston Street, New York City: Gotham's greatest attraction, open day and evening from 9 A.M. . . . only to men" (New York, n.d. [1880]). This version of Dr. Kahn's Anatomical Museum in Manhattan was built after a crackdown on the original museum in London. When Dr. Kahn's was prosecuted in 1873, the collection was shipped off to the Bowery, where the museum was reborn. See A. W. Bates, "Dr. Kahn's Museum: Obscene Anatomy in Victorian London," *Journal of the Royal Society of Medicine*, XCIX/12 (December 2006), pp. 618–24: p. 623. See also A. W. Bates, "'Indecent and Demoralising Representations': Public Anatomy Museums in mid-Victorian England," *Medical History*, LII/1 (2008), pp. 1–22; Dr. Kahn's Anatomical Museum, Lower East Side History Project, April 16, 2011, http://leshp.org, accessed September 4, 2016; Harriet Palfreyman, "Visualising Venereal Disease in London," PhD dissertation, University of Warwick (2012).

47 "A Pretty Girl's Companion," p. 13.

48 Ibid., p. 1.

49 Ibid., p. 4.

50 Ibid., p. 19. Edward Kelly notes the popularity of the leather dildo: Edward Kelly, "A New Image for the Naughty Dildo?" *Journal of Popular Culture*, VII/4 (1974), pp. 804–9: 804. Descriptions of dildos are littered throughout pornography; for example, *The Pearl,* a serialized nineteenth-century British pornographic publication has numerous such references to dildos. *The Pearl* (1897, reprint; New York, 1968), p. 279. The politics and history of dildos make fascinating reading; see for example Patricia Simons, *The Sex of Men in Premodern Europe: A Cultural History* (Cambridge, 2011); Heather Findlay, "Freud's 'Fetishism' and the Lesbian Dildo Debates," *Feminist Studies*, XVIII/3 (1992), pp. 563–79.

51 This collection was anonymously donated in the mid-1960s. The catalogue states that many of the materials in the collection came from the 1940s, but the bindings, content, and paper date some of the materials earlier.

52 Lord Byron, "The Enchantment," Miscellaneous Poetry Series, BEM Erotic Manuscript Collection, Kinsey Institute; "The Merry Muses of Caledonia, 1768," Miscellaneous Poetry Series, BEM Erotic Manuscript Collection, Kinsey Institute.

53 Harmon Jenkinsop, "The Footman and the Lady," Thread Bound Series, BEM Erotic Manuscript Collection, Kinsey Institute.

54 Respectively, Jenkinsop, "The Footman and the Lady," "French Maid," Beige Humiliation Series; Erlon Mareston, "Animal Lovers," Beige/Blue Series; "Rape is the Penalty for Beauty," 1963, Rape and Torture Series; and Jean de Pavanne, "Crimson Passion." All BEM Erotic Manuscript Collection, Kinsey Institute.

55 Some documents in the collection detail the erotics of office work and suggest the depth of boredom that inspired such productions. "The New Girl: An Office Idyll" is wrapped by brown paper and joined with a single brass fastener. The poem was typed on paper with a side heading that read "New Zealand Military Forces. War Diary or Intelligence Summary. (Erase heading not required.) Summary of Events and Information. War. Form N.Z.—375.) (In pads of 100.)" "The New Girl: An Office Idyll," New Zealand, n.d., Top Bound Series, BEM Erotic Manuscript Collection, Kinsey Institute. The rhyme scheme and the simple story of boss and secretary suggest that emotion, art, and erudition were less important than the subversive act of typing pornography at the office.

56 Horowitz, *Rereading Sex*, p. 4.

2 Adapting Commercial Culture into Handmade Objects, 1910s–1970s

1 www.alta-glamour.com/gallery.php, accessed August 21, 2019.

2 Jean Baudrillard, *Simulacra and Simulation*, trans. Sheila Faria Glaser (Ann Arbor, MI, 1994). See also Douglass Kellner, "Jean Baudrillard," in *The Stanford Encyclopedia of Philosophy*, ed. Edward N. Zalta, Summer 2015 edition, http://plato.stanford.edu.

3 Michael Emery and Edwin Emery, *The Press and America*, 6th edn (Needham Heights, MA, 1996), pp. 158–9.

4 Ibid., p. 163.

5 David C. Smith, "Wood Pulp and Newspapers, 1867–1900," *Business History Review*, XXXVIII/3 (Fall 1964), pp. 328–45.

6 Emery and Emery, *The Press and America*, p. 293.

7 R. D. Mullen, "From Standard Magazines to Pulps and Big Slicks: A Note on the History of U.S. General and Fiction Magazines Author(s)," *Science Fiction Studies*, XXII/1 (March 1995), pp. 144–56.

8 Erin A. Smith, "How the Other Half Read: Advertising, Working-class Readers, and Pulp Magazines," *Book History*, III (2000), pp. 204–30: p. 204.

9 Jay Gertzman, *Bookleggers and Smuthounds: The Trade in Erotica, 1920–1940* (Philadelphia, PA, 1999), Chapter Two.

10 For an analysis of the genealogy of hoarding, see Scott Herring, "Collyer Curiosa: A Brief History of Hoarding," *Criticism*, LIII/2 (Spring 2011), pp. 159–88. Susan Lepselter suggests that "hoarding speaks to and about our moment. In the manic depression surrounding crashes, foreclosures, and the secular jeremiads on consumer folly and greed, all occurring against years of confident neoliberalism and globalization, the hoarder's monstrous accumulations loom with an increasingly ambivalent fascination." Susan Lepselter, "Disorder of Things: Hoarding Narratives in Popular Media," *Anthropology Quarterly*, LXXXIV/4 (2011), pp. 919–47.

11 For an exploration of the complicated negotiations around censorship and control of Hollywood sexuality, see Francis G. Couvares, "Hollywood, Censorship, and American Culture," *American Quarterly* (December 1992), pp. 509–24. Whitney Strub demonstrates that such ideas should be considered in light of distribution patterns and local meanings. He shows that materials banned for obscenity might reflect local politicking and concerns. This model complicates any idea of a Hollywood-generated sexuality and a broad reaction. However, the existence of altered images shows an impact of the circulation of material culture. Clearly, individuals saw these materials and these starlets in certain ways. Whitney Strub, "Black and White and Banned All Over: Race, Censorship and Obscenity in Postwar Memphis," *Journal of Social History*, XL/3 (2007), pp. 685–715.

12 Altered Photographs Collection, Kinsey Institute (formerly Institute for Sex Research), Bloomington, Indiana.

13 "Rocky's Got it, Tony Wants It," original from International Photo, Altered Photographs Collection, Kinsey Institute.

14 Michael Cooper, Obituary: "Tony Zale," *New York Times*, March 27, 1997.

15 For a review of scholars who write about Marilyn Monroe's sexuality, see Dean MacCannell, "Marilyn Monroe Was Not a Man," *Diacritics*, XVII/2 (1987), pp. 114–27.

16 Altered photograph of Marilyn Monroe, Altered Photographs Collection, Kinsey Institute.

17 Joanne Meyerowitz, "Women, Cheesecake, and Borderline Materials: Responses to Girlie Pictures in the Mid-twentieth Century," *Journal of Women's History*, VIII/3 (Fall 1996), pp. 9–35: p. 9.

18 Paul Gephard to E. J. Dingwall, April 10, 1959, Correspondence, Kinsey Institute.

19 Meyerowitz, "Women, Cheesecake, and Borderline Materials," p. 13.

20 Julia Pine, "In *Bizarre* Fashion: The Double-voiced Discourse of John Willie's Fetish Fantasia," *Journal of the History of Sexuality*, XXII/1 (2013), pp. 1–33. Jane Garrett, "*Bizarre* Exchange: Postwar Fetish Art and Publishing in Japan and the United States," unpublished paper (2019).

21 Thomas Waugh, *Hard to Imagine: Gay Male Eroticism in Photography and Film from their Beginnings to Stonewall* (New York, 1996), p. 217.

22 Whitney Strub, "Challenging the Anti-pleasure League: Physique Pictorial and the Cultivation of Gay Politics," in *Modern Print Activism in the United States*, ed. Rachel Schreiber (Burlington, VT, 2013), pp. 161–74, p. 166.

23 Whitney Strub, "The Clearly Obscene and the Queerly Obscene: Heteronormativity and Obscenity in Cold War Los Angeles," *American Quarterly*, LX/2 (June 2008), pp. 373–98: pp. 378–9.

24 "Altered magazine *Physique Pictorial*," Gallery, www.alta-glamour.com, accessed September 6, 2019.

25 *Physique Pictorial*, IV/3 (Fall 1954), cover.

26 See Karl Toepfer, *Empire of Ecstasy: Nudity and Movement in German Body Culture, 1910–1935*

(Berkeley, CA, 1997); Michael Hau, *The Cult of Health and Beauty in Germany: A Social History, 1890–1930* (Chicago, IL, 2003); Chad Ross, *Naked Germany: Health, Race and the Nation* (Oxford, 2005).

27 Jessica Yu, dir., *In the Realms of the Unreal: The Mystery of Henry Darger* (New York, 2004); Jim Elledge, *Henry Darger, Throwaway Boy: The Tragic Life of an Outsider Artist* (New York, 2013); Michael Bonesteel, *Henry Darger: Art and Selected Writings* (New York, 2000).

28 Roberta Smith, "Folk Museum Gets Work of a Self-taught Artist," *New York Times*, October 4, 2000, p. E3.

29 N. F. Karlins, "The Past, the Ironic Present, or Passion?" *Art Journal*, LVI/4, Performance Art: (Some) Theory and (Selected) Practice at the End of This Century (Winter 1997), pp. 93–7.

30 Sarah Boxer, "He Was Crazy Like a . . . Genius? For Henry Darger, Everything Began and Ended with Little Girls," *New York Times*, September 16, 2000, p. B7.

31 Mary Trent, "Henry Darger's Reworking of American Visual Culture," *American Art*, XXVI/1 (Spring 2012), pp. 74–101: pp. 99–100, n. 1.

32 Ibid., p. 80; See also Michael Bonesteel, *Henry Darger: Art and Selected Writings* (New York, 2000); Leisa Rundquist, "Pyre: A Poetics of Fire and Childhood in the Art of Henry Darger," PhD Dissertation, University of North Carolina at Chapel Hill, 2007; John MacGregor, *Henry Darger: In the Realms of the Unreal* (New York, 2002).

33 Kate Butler, review of Kevin Kavanagh show "The World Needs a Narrative," *Sunday Times*, October 5, 2008.

34 Elledge, *Henry Darger*, pp. 38–48.

35 Bonesteel, *Henry Darger*, p. 8.

36 Henry Joseph Darger, U.S. Draft Registration Card, Chicago, IL, June 2, 1917, National Archives and Records Administration, at www.ancestry.com.

37 MacGregor, *Henry Darger*, p. 65.

38 Darger, Excerpt from "History of My Life by Henry Joseph Darger," in *Henry Darger*, ed. Klaus Biesenbach (Munich, 2009), p. 300.

39 Biesenbach, ed., *Henry Darger*, p. 13.

40 Nathan Lerner recognized the artistry of Darger's work and both generated attention for and documented Henry's life. He invited documentary filmmakers to record images of Darger's room and eventually donated the room to Intuit: The Center for Outsider Art, Chicago. For the film of Darger's room in 1973, see Colleen Fitzgibbon, "Henry Darger's room, 1973," https://archive.org, accessed September 3, 2019.

41 Klaus Biesenbach dates the start of the series to 1916 in Klaus Biesenbach, *Henry Darger: Disasters of War* (Berlin, 2004), p. 208; Michael Bonesteel dates the beginning as earlier either 1910 or 1912. Bonesteel, *Henry Darger*, p. 23.

42 See for example "At Jennie Richee: Trapped in lighted part of cavern they tried to elude Glandelinians surrounding them," in Biesenbach, ed., *Henry Darger*, pp. 126–7.

43 "Part two: Break out of concentration camp killing and wounding enemy soldier guards," in Biesenbach, ed., *Henry Darger*, p. 106.

44 Ephemera Boxes, Henry Darger Collection, Intuit: The Center for Intuitive and Outsider Art, Chicago, Illinois.

45 Darger, "Child Slaves," selection from volume III of *Realms of the Unreal*, in Bonesteel, *Henry Darger*, p. 82.

46 *Child Life: The Children's Own Magazine*, May 1939, and *Child Life: The Children's Own Magazine*, June 1943, Ephemera Boxes, Henry Darger Collection, Intuit. Materials in the boxes date some of the ephemera.

47 Darger, "The History of My Life," in Bonesteel, *Henry Darger*, p. 236.

48 Darger, "Child Slaves," a selection from volume V of *Realms of the Unreal*, in Bonesteel, *Henry Darger*, p. 99.

49 Darger, "So Sweet a Temper," a selection from volume IV of *Realms of the Unreal*, in Bonesteel, *Henry Darger*, p. 129.

50 Darger, "Introducing the Story of the Vivian Girls, in What Is Known as the Realms of the Unreal, of the Glandeco-Angelinian War Storm, Caused by the Child Slave Rebellion," a selection from volume I of *Realms of the Unreal*, in Bonesteel, *Henry Darger*, p. 39.

51 Doris Yvonne Wilkinson, "Racial Socialization Through Children's Toys: A Sociohistorical Examination," *Journal of Black Studies*, v/1 (September 1974), pp. 96–109.

52 See Ralph L. Pearson, "Charles S. Johnson and the Chicago Commission on Race Relations," *Illinois Historical Journal*, LXXXI/3 (Fall 1988), pp. 211–20; Naomi Farber, "Charles S. Johnson's 'The Negro in Chicago,'" *American Sociologist*, XXVI/3 (Fall 1995), pp. 78–88; and Charles S. Johnson, *The Negro in Chicago: A Study of Race Relations and a Race Riot in 1919* (New York, 1968).

53 Amber Holst, "The Lost World," *Chicago Magazine* (November 2005), www.chicagomag. com, June 26, 2007.

54 Biesenbach, ed., *Henry Darger: Disasters of War*, p. 15.

55 Henry Jose Dageris, World War II Draft Registration Card, April 27, 1942, Chicago, IL, National Archives and Records Administration, at www.ancestry.com, accessed January 20, 2016.

56 Darger, "History of My Life," in Biesenbach, ed., *Henry Darger*, pp. 281, 289; see David Roediger, "Race, Ethnicity and White Identity," *Encyclopedia of Chicago*, www.encyclopedia. chicagohistory.org, 2005.

57 Darger, "History of My Life," in Biesenbach, ed., *Henry Darger*, p. 288.

58 Darger, "The History of My Life," in Bonesteel, *Henry Darger*, p. 241.

59 Biesenbach, ed., *Henry Darger*, p. 12.

60 Karen Halttunen, "Humanitarianism and the Pornography of Pain in Anglo-American Culture," *American Historical Review*, C/2 (April 1995), pp. 303–34: p. 325.

61 Richard von Krafft-Ebing, *Psychopathia Sexualis: A Medico-Forensic Study*, first unexpurgated edition in English (New York, 1964), case 57, pp. 137–8.

62 Ethel Spector Person, ed., *On Freud's "A Child is Being Beaten"* (New Haven, CT, 1997), p. 4.

63 Halttunen, "Humanitarianism and the Pornography of Pain in Anglo-American Culture," p. 334.

64 Colette Colligan, "Anti-Abolition Writes Obscenity: The English Vice, Transatlantic Slavery, and England's Obscene Print Culture," in *International Exposure*, ed. Lisa Sigel (New Brunswick, NJ, 2005), pp. 67–99: p. 84.

65 Ibid., p. 83.

66 Mary Ting Yi Lu, "Saving Young Girls from Chinatown: White Slavery and Woman Suffrage, 1910–1920," *Journal of the History of Sexuality*, XVIII/3 (September 2009), pp. 393–417.

67 Brian Donovan, *White Slave Crusades: Race, Gender, and Anti-Vice Activism, 1887–1917* (Urbana and Chicago, IL, 2006).

68 Shelley Stamp Lindsey, "'Oil upon the Flames of Vice': The Battle over White Slave Films in New York City," *Film History*, IX/4 (1997), pp. 351–64.

69 Cecily Devereux, "'The Maiden Tribute' and the Rise of the White Slave in the Nineteenth Century: The Making of an Imperial Construct," *Victorian Review*, XXVI/2 (2000), pp. 1–23: p. 1.

70 James Bronson Reynolds, "International Agreements in Relation to the Suppression of Vice," *Social Hygiene*, II/1 (January 1916), p. 233.

71 Darger, "Child Slaves," selection from volume V of *Realms of the Unreal*, in Bonesteel, *Henry Darger*, p. 99.

72 Consider, for example, the extraordinary popularity of Shirley Temple films during this period in which Temple acted, danced, and sang as the female lead paired with adult men. Kristen Hatch argues that the early twentieth-century focus on children had different inflections than it does today. See Kristen Hatch, "Discipline and Pleasure: Shirley Temple and the Spectacle

of Child Loving," *Camera Obscura*, XXVII/79 (January 2012), pp. 127–55.

73 Margot Hillel, "'She Makes Them Tingle All Over': Eroticising the Child in Twentieth-century Australian Picture Books," *History of Education and Children's Literature*, VI/1 (2011), pp. 199–214.

74 Quoted in Kathleen McDowell, "Toward a History of Children as Readers, 1890–1930," *Book History*, XII (2009), pp. 240–65: pp. 240, 242.

75 Gary Cross and Gregory Smits, "Japan, the U.S. and the Globalization of Children's Consumer Culture," *Journal of Social History*, XXXVIII/4 (Summer 2005), pp. 873–90: p. 875.

76 A pornography of childhood might be conceptualized as a type of pornography that details the sexuality of children as part of the narrative. I use this term to differentiate the literature about childhood from "child pornography," which has become a term to signify photographs, films, and videos of children engaged in sexual activity.

77 Hillel, "'She Makes Them Tingle All Over,'" pp. 199–214.

78 "3 at Aronburg run, Via Glorinia" (detail), n.d., in Bonesteel, *Henry Darger*, pp. 202–3.

79 Interview with Kiyoko Lerner transcribed in Biesenbach, *Henry Darger: Disasters of War*, p. 17.

80 Quoted in Bonesteel, *Henry Darger*, p. 21.

81 Dageris, World War II Draft Registration Card.

82 Bonesteel, *Henry Darger*, p. 20.

83 "Annie Aronburg Appears to Henry Darger," selections from Darger's journals, in Bonesteel, *Henry Darger*, p. 200.

84 Darger, "Introducing the Story of the Vivian Girls," a selection from volume 1 of *Realms of the Unreal*, in Bonesteel, *Henry Darger*, p. 43.

3 Men and Time: Prison Pornography, 1940s–1960s

1 Kaitlin Throgmorton, "The Freedom of Reading," *American Libraries Magazine*, https://americanlibrariesmagazine.org, October 31, 2016.

2 Early models of sexuality left sexologists open to the criticism that their theories reflected aberrant and perverted desires, and not the practices of more reputable members of society. Kinsey's great achievement, according to the press, was that his statistical findings reflected the practices of society as a whole. John D'Emilio and Estelle B. Freedman, *Intimate Matters: A History of Sexuality in America* (Chicago, IL, 1988), p. 286; Elizabeth Fraterrigo, *Playboy and the Making of the Good Life in Modern America* (Oxford, 2009), p. 38. For an extended discussion of the impact of Kinsey's work, see Miriam Reumann, *American Sexual Character* (Berkeley, CA, 2005). Despite this reputation in the press, Kinsey relied on the prison population to round out his statistical picture of sexual behavior among the non-college-educated population. According to James Jones, Kinsey knew that his case histories relied too heavily on prisoners, college students, and gay men. James M. Jones, *Alfred C. Kinsey: A Public/Private Life* (New York, 1997), p. 522.

3 Wardell Pomeroy, *Dr. Kinsey and the Institute for Sex Research* (New Haven, CT, 1972), p. 71.

4 Ibid., pp. 202–3.

5 Ibid., p. 202.

6 "Emotional Security for the Sex Offender," Emotional Security Program, Metropolitan State Hospital Norwalk, California, March 1954, distributed with permission. SO1, Folder 1A, Sexual Offenders Collection, Kinsey Institute, Bloomington, Indiana.

7 See for example "Outstanding and Unusual Aspects of the Program", Norwalk, 1953, SO1, Folder 1A, and "The Emotional Maturity Society," mimeographed sheets, received 12/1955, SO1, Folder 1B, Sexual Offenders Collection, Kinsey Institute.

8 Joseph F. Fishman, *Sex in Prison: Revealing Sex Conditions in American Prisons* (New York, 1934), p. 23.

9 Carolyn Strange and Michael Kempa, "Shades of Dark Tourism: Alcatraz and Robben Island," *Annals of Tourism Research*, XXX/2 (2003), pp. 386–405.

10 Lieutenant Charles G. Flett, Chino, California, to Alfred Kinsey, April 24, 1955, Correspondence, Kinsey Institute; letter from Paul Gebhard to Mr. E. J. Oberhauser, California Institute for Men, Chino, CA, April 11, 1958, Correspondence, Kinsey Institute.

11 Douglas Rigg, Warden, Minnesota State Prison, Stillwater, Minnesota, to Paul Gebhard, Bloomington, Indiana, April 14, 1958, Correspondence, Kinsey Institute.

12 New York Department of Mental Hygiene, "Report on Study of 102 Sex Offenders at Sing Sing Prison (Albany, NY, 1950), p. 11.

13 Bureau of Criminal Statistics, Department of Justice, "California Prisoners 1956 and 1957: Summary Statistics of Prisoners and Parolees," (Sacramento, CA, 1958), p. 1.

14 Ibid., pp. iii, v.

15 Offenses by Age Group Chart, Atascadero, 1956, S01, Folder 1C, Sexual Offenders Collection, Kinsey Institute.

16 Bureau of Criminal Statistics, Prepared for the Department of Corrections, "California Prisoners 1954: Summary Statistics of Prisoners and Parolees," (Sacramento, CA, 1955): pp. 11, 22.

17 According to their own records, the Institute for Sex Research collected information from Indiana Women's Prison, the Ohio Bureau of Juvenile Research, and the Kruse School for Girls, but no collections of women's prison pornography have been identified. See "USA vs 31 Photographs," case file compiled by Greenbaum, Wolff & Ernst, June 16, 1959, United States District Court, Southern District of New York, United States of America, p. 19.

18 Phyllis Kornfeld, *Cellblock Visions: Prison Art in America* (Princeton, NJ, 1997). For example see Lee Michael Johnson, "Jail Wall Drawings and Jail Art Programs: Invaluable Tools for Corrections," *International Journal of Criminal Justice Sciences (IJCJS)*, II/2 (2007), pp. 66–84; Melissa Schrift, "Angola Prison Art: Captivity, Creativity, and Consumerism," *Journal of American Folklore*, CXIX/473 (Summer 2006), pp. 257–74; David E. Gussak and Evelyn Ploumis-Devick, "Creating Wellness in Correctional Populations through the Arts: An Interdisciplinary Model," *Visual Arts Research*, XXX/1 (2004), pp. 35–43.

19 Schrift, "Angola Prison Art."

20 Kunzel, *Criminal Intimacy*, p. 5.

21 Ibid., p. 8.

22 The issue of the carceral state, for example, has been the focus of a special issue of the *Journal of American History*, CII (June 2015). But while same-sex desire is broached in the issue in an essay by Timothy Stewart Winter, other sorts of sexual matters remain unexamined. Timothy Stewart Winter, "Queer Law and Order: Sex, Criminality, and Policing in the Late Twentieth-century United States," *Journal of American History*, CII (June 2015), pp. 61–72.

23 See Christopher Hensley, Cindy Struckman-Johnson, and Helen M. Eigenberg, "Introduction: The History of Prison Sex Research," *Prison Journal*, LXXX/4 (December 2000), pp. 360–67.

24 Joseph F. Fishman, *Sex in Prison: Revealing Sex Conditions in American Prisons* (New York, 1934), pp. 11–14.

25 Ibid., p. 26.

26 Ibid., p. 33.

27 Prison Questionnaire, *c.* 1943, prepared and given by John R. Russell, Vertical File, Kinsey Institute.

28 Fishman, *Sex in Prison*, p. 138.

29 Lieutenant Charles G. Flett, Chino, California, to Alfred Kinsey, April 24, 1955, Correspondence, Kinsey Institute.

30 Benjamin Karpman, "Sex Life in Prison," *Journal of Criminal Law and Criminology*, XXXVIII/5 (1948), pp. 475–86. A law review article from 1977 noted the total sexual deprivation, including masturbation, as one

of the defining features of prison life. James B. Jacobs and Eric H. Stelle, "Sexual Deprivation and Penal Policy," *Cornell Law Review*, LXII/2 (January 1977), pp. 289–312.

31 Jean Stengers and Anne Van Neck, *Masturbation: The History of the Great Terror* (New York, 2001); Thomas Laqueur, *Solitary Sex: A Cultural History of Masturbation* (New York, 2003).

32 Catherine D. Marcum, "Examining Prison Sex Culture," in *Sex in Prison: Myths and Realities*, ed. Catherine D. Marcum and Tammy L. Castle (Boulder, CO, and London, 2014), p. 6.

33 David Merritt Johns, "Free Willy: Should Prison Inmates Have the Right to Masturbate?" www.slate.com, January 10, 2012.

34 Kunzel, *Criminal Intimacy*, p. 156.

35 "Prison Mail Censorship and the First Amendment," *Yale Law Journal*, LXXXI/1 (November 1971), pp. 87–111.

36 Prison Photographs, Box 1, Maryland Penitentiary, 59920, Kinsey Institute; Prison Photographs, Box 1, Maryland Penitentiary, Pautuxent, 9/63, 59968, Kinsey Institute; Prison Photographs, Box 1, Orange County Jail, 59932, Kinsey Institute.

37 Prison Photographs, Box 1, Orange County Jail, images confiscated 1954, 59928, 59929, 59930, Kinsey Institute.

38 Prison Photographs, Box 1, California Federal Prison, Lompoc, 59907, Kinsey Institute.

39 Prison Photographs, Box 2, San Quentin State Prison, 60006, 60016, Kinsey Institute.

40 Prison Photographs, Box 2, nudist magazine, Sunshine Book Company, San Quentin State Prison, 60020, Kinsey Institute.

41 Prison Photographs, Box 2, San Quentin State Prison, images confiscated December 12, 1954, 60023, Kinsey Institute.

42 Prison Photographs, Box 1, Orange County Jail, 599935, Kinsey Institute.

43 Prison Photographs, Box 2, T.I., 1952–5, San Quentin State Prison, 60631, Kinsey Institute.

44 Prison Photographs, Box 1, Folsom Prison, 599913, Kinsey Institute.

45 Prison Photographs, Box 1, Folsom Prison, 5/55, 59916, Kinsey Institute.

46 Prison Photographs, Box 1, California Federal Prison Lompoc, 59908, Kinsey Institute.

47 Prison Photographs, Box 1, Maryland Penitentiary, 11/58, 59917, Kinsey Institute.

48 Prison Photographs, Box 1, California Federal Prison, Lompoc, 59910, Kinsey Institute.

49 Paul Gebhard, John Gagnon, Wardell Pomeroy, and Cornelia Christenson, *Sex Offenders: An Analysis of Types* (New York, 1965), p. 676.

50 Ibid., p. 670. For a discussion of participants and methods, see Chapter Two.

51 Prison art, Realia, [1965?], ISR 905, Kinsey Institute.

52 M.L.M, Jr., 1954, item 2011.50.12.11113, North America: United States, 20th Century, Prison Art: San Quentin, California, Box 1, Kinsey Institute.

53 M.L.M, Jr., 1954, item 2011.50.12.11110, North America: United States, 20th Century, Prison Art: San Quentin, California, Box 1, Kinsey Institute.

54 Set of images, 1949, items 2011.50.1.50 XVI-3, 2011.50.1.51 XVI-4, 2011.50.1.53 XVI-6, 2011.50.1.54 XVI-7, 2011.50.1.55 XVI-8, 2011.50.1.56 XVI-9, 2011.50.1.57 XVI-10; North America: United States, 20th Century, Prison Art: San Quentin, California, Box 1, Kinsey Institute.

55 Male with enlarged genitalia, Realia, donated 1952, ISR 730, Kinsey Institute.

56 Masturbating figure, Realia, [196?], 1 piece: paper, pipe cleaner, col.; 5" h. × 3" w. × 1¾" d., ISR 732, Kinsey Institute.

57 Crayon drawing, item 2011.50.1.120A XXXIV-4, North America: United States, 20th Century, Prison Art: San Quentin, California, Box 1, Kinsey Institute. This image is reproduced in Blaise Cronin, Garry Milius, and Betsy Stirratt, *Private Eyes: Amateur Art from the Kinsey Institute Collection*, exh. cat., Kinsey Institute (Bloomington, IN, 2010), p. 16.

58 See ibid.

59 Crayon drawing, item 2011.50.1.123A XXXII-7, North America: United States, 20th Century,

Prison Art: San Quentin, California, Box 1, Kinsey Institute.

60 Pamphlet, Leavenworth, Kansas, 1963, Prison Material, Box 1, Series II, Prisoner Erotica—Diaries. Fiction, Autobiographical Sketches—Male, E.2, Folder 1, Kinsey Institute.

61 Monkey pendant, Realia, [1940?], carved peach pit, ISR 931, Kinsey Institute.

62 A charming overview of peach pit carvings by R. V. Dietrich entitled "Peach Pit Carving" can be found online at http://stoneplus.cst.cmich.edu, revd March 23, 2009.

63 Zoophilia with horse, Realia, [196?], 1 piece: soap, yellow; 3½" h. × 2" w. × 3½" d., ISR 731, Kinsey Institute.

64 Note from T. W. Markley, Warden, United States Penitentiary, Terre Haute, Indiana, May 12, 1964, Prison Art: Terre Haute, Indiana, Kinsey Institute.

65 Items 2010.4.3–2010.4.51, North America: United States, 20th Century, Prison Art: Baltimore, Maryland, Kinsey Institute.

66 "Encyclopedia of Sex," item 2010.4.44, North America: United States, 20th Century, Prison Art: Baltimore, Maryland, Kinsey Institute.

67 "Let's do the twist and around we fight," item 2010.4.490, North America: United States, 20th Century, Prison Art: Baltimore, Maryland, Kinsey Institute.

68 "Let's go do the twist," item 2010.4.493, North America: United States, 20th Century, Prison Art: Baltimore, Maryland, Kinsey Institute.

69 "Taken from E.......'s cell," A-61269A, 2012.27.19 IV-1, North America: United States, 20th Century, Prison Art: Vacaville, California, Box 1, Kinsey Institute.

70 Laura Kipnis, *Bound and Gagged: Pornography and the Politics of Fantasy in America* (New York, 1996), p. 133.

71 Ricky, "'To My Eskimo' valentine card," North America: United States, 20th Century, Prison Art: Terre Haute, Indiana, Kinsey Institute. A photograph of this card is reproduced in Cronin, Milius, and Stirratt, *Private Eyes*, p. 3.

72 Regina Kunzel, *Criminal Intimacy: Prison and the Uneven History of Modern American Sexuality* (Chicago, IL, 2008), Chapter Five.

73 Unopened Letters, Letters between Prisoners, Prison Materials: California, Vacaville, Box 1, Series I, C.1, Folder 3, E, Kinsey Institute.

74 Letter from Jimmy to Dick [copy of letter found on A7682 Isolation Unit, June 10, 1951], Box 1, Series I, Prisoner Correspondence-Male, C.1, San Quentin State Prison, Folder 2, Kinsey Institute.

75 "Hi Little Buddy," [1949–50], Box 1, Series I, Prisoner Correspondence-Male, C.1, San Quentin State Prison, Folder 3, Kinsey Institute.

76 Letter from Jonnie to Billy, 1954, Box 1, Series I, Prisoner Correspondence-Male, C.1, San Quentin State Prison, Folder 1, Kinsey Institute.

77 An extensive literature about *Dick and Jane* exists in relation to Toni Morrison's creative reuse of the books in *The Bluest Eye* (1970). See for example Debra Werrlein, "Not So Fast, Dick and Jane: Reimagining Childhood and Nation in *The Bluest Eye*," *MELUS*, XXX/4 (Winter 2005), pp. 53–72; Adelaide Morris, "Dick, Jane, and American Literature: Fight with Canons," *College English*, XLVII/5 (September 1985), pp. 467–81; Phyllis R. Klotman, "Dick-and-Jane and the Shirley Temple Sensibility in *The Bluest Eye*," *Black American Literature Forum*, XIII/4 (Winter 1979), pp. 123–5.

78 Jane and Dick narrative and pictures 8 rec'd from Leavenworth Federal Penitentiary 1-9-63, Box 1, Series II, Prisoner Erotica—Diaries. Fiction, Autobiographical Sketches—Male, Folder 1, E. Leavenworth, Kansas, Kinsey Institute.

79 Booklets, items 2011.50.4.225, CCIV-1, and 2011.50.4.226, CCIV-1, North America: United States, 20th Century, Prison Art: San Quentin, California, Box 4, Kinsey Institute.

80 Unknown Artist, pamphlet, 1962, item 2010.4.508, XLIX-1, North America: United States, 20th century, Prison Art: Baltimore, Maryland, Kinsey Institute.

81 "I Was a White Slave for Mexico," n.d., Box 1, Series II, Prisoner Erotica—Diaries. Fiction,

Autobiographical Sketches—Male, B, Chino, Kinsey Institute.

82 Drawings, items 2010.4.1–2010.4.117, received 1958–62, North America: United States, 20th century, Prison Art: Baltimore, Maryland, Kinsey Institute.

83 "Hiden Madness," item 2010.4.1.6, received 1958–62, North America: United States, 20th century, Prison Art: Baltimore, Maryland, Kinsey Institute.

84 "8 Cell Series of Two Couples Performing Intercourse," item 2010.4.1.23, North America: United States, 20th century, Prison Art: Baltimore, Maryland, received 1958–62, Kinsey Institute.

85 Drawing of a gun, item 2010.4.1.22A, North America: United States, 20th century, Prison Art: Baltimore, Maryland, received 1958–62, Kinsey Institute.

86 B., "All for Love (A Study in Psychiatry)," A11434, Box 1, Series II, Prisoner Erotica— Diaries. Fiction, Autobiographical Sketches— Male, B, Chino, Prison Archives, Kinsey Institute.

87 Prisoners have been foundational to the development of sexual theories. Criminalization of a wide variety of sexual desires, including same-sex desires and fetishism, meant people who had non-conforming desires feared being pushed into the criminal classes or classified as mentally ill. Richard von Krafft-Ebing, the author of *Psychopathia Sexualis* (1886), used case studies based upon the "medico-forensic" model to develop his theories of sexual identity, while early criminologists like Cesare Lombroso studied the criminal masses, including prostitutes, to develop theories of criminality. See Harry Oosterhuis, *Stepchildren of Nature: Krafft-Ebing, Psychiatry, and the Making of Sexual Identity* (Chicago, IL, 2000); Cesare Lombroso's *La donna delinquente* (1893) was translated as *The Female Offender* in 1895.

88 "Psychiatric Interview S. Q. From Our Side," 1949, Prison Art: San Quentin, California, Kinsey Institute.

89 See Kenneth R. Stevens, "United States v. 31 Photographs: Dr. Alfred C. Kinsey and Obscenity Law," *Indiana Magazine of History*, LXXI/4 (December 1975), pp. 299–316; Jones, *Alfred C. Kinsey*, pp. 669–70.

90 The sorts of materials that had been seized by Customs included thirty-one photographs, a book entitled *The Memoirs of Dolly Morton*, an album of six paintings from China that claimed to have been made in 1750, a small bronze plaque, a small wooden plaque, a folder of twelve lithographs entitled "Charges of Descharges Diaboliques," a book entitled *Trois filles de leur mer* (1897) with sixteen color drawings, a book entitled *Trois filles de leur me* (1897) with twelve color drawings, and so on. "Also seized were six sheets of plain white paper with obscene drawings and writing thereon." "USA vs 31 Photographs," exhibit 1, p. 1.

91 Judith A. Allen et al., *The Kinsey Institute: The First Seventy Years* (Bloomington, IN, 2017), p. 78.

92 H. O. Teets, State of California, Department of Corrections, California State Prison, San Quentin, to Mr. Paul H. Gebhard, Executive Director, Institute for Sex Research, Indiana University, Bloomington, IN [1957?], Correspondence, Kinsey Institute.

93 H. O. Teets, Affidavit, in "USA vs 31 Photographs."

94 James V. Bennett to Mr. Paul H. Gebhard, Executive Director, Institute for Sex Research, Indiana University, Bloomington, IN, May 20, 1957, Correspondence, Kinsey Institute.

95 Paul H. Gebhard to Mr. Bert O Webb, Warden, California State Prison at Soledad, April 11, 1958, Correspondence, Kinsey Institute.

96 Kinsey wrote: "Just a word to thank you again for your thought and cooperation when I was at San Quentin last week. It was very good of you to remember the material from the HOT ROOM." Alfred Kinsey to Mr. Teets, San Quentin Prison, San Quentin, CA, July 12, 1950, Correspondence, Kinsey Institute.

97 Paul Gebhard to Warden Douglass C. Rigg, Minnesota State Prison, Stillwater, MN, April 11, 1958, Correspondence, Kinsey Institute.

98 Alfred Kinsey to Mr. Harley Teets, San Quentin
    Prison, San Quentin, CA, September 22, 1950,
    Correspondence, Kinsey Institute.
99 Paul Gebhard to Mr. E. J. Oberhauser,
    California Institute for Men, Chino, CA,
    April 11, 1958, Correspondence, Kinsey Institute.
100 Richard Meyer, *Outlaw Representation:
    Censorship and Homosexuality in Twentieth-
    century Art* (Boston, MA, 2002).

4   The Postwar World and the Making of a
    People's Pornography, 1940s–1970s

1   See Elaine Tyler May, *Homeward Bound:
    American Families in the Cold War Era* (New
    York, 1988); Allan Bérubé, *Coming Out Under
    Fire: The History of Gay Men and Women
    in World War II* (New York, 1990); Mary
    Louise Roberts, *What Soldiers Do: Sex
    and the American GI in World War II France*
    (Chicago, IL, 2014).
2   Nicholas J. Saunders, "Bodies of Metal, Shells
    of Memory: Trench Art and the Great War
    Re-cycled," *Journal of Material Culture*, V/1
    (March 2000), pp. 43–67.
3   Nicholas J. Saunders, "Trench Art," *History
    Today*, LIII/11 (November 2003), pp. 32–7.
4   All of these objects were for sale on eBay and
    Etsy on November 20, 2015. The prices ranged
    from $20 to $340. I have found no repositories
    for erotic trench art or academic papers that deal
    with the subset of the genre. This is unsurprising.
    Trench art has only recently been recognized
    as a rich category, one mostly considered by
    archeologists from their excavations of wartime
    landscapes and structure.
5   Robert B. Westbrook, "'I Want a Girl, Just Like
    the Girl that Married Harry James': American
    Women and the Problem of Political Obligation
    in the Second World War," *American Quarterly*,
    XLII/4 (December 1990), pp. 587–614.
6   For a discussion of the "Petty Girl," see Kenon
    Breazeale, "In Spite of Women: 'Esquire'
    Magazine and the Construction of the Male

Consumer," *Signs*, XX/1 (Fall 1994), pp. 1–22;
    for a comparison of the pin-up and the
    burlesque, see Kathleen Spies and Reginald
    Marsh, "'Girls and Gags': Sexual Display and
    Humor in Reginald Marsh's Burlesque Images,"
    American Art, XVIII/2 (Summer 2004),
    pp. 32–57: p. 36.
7   Marilyn E. Hegarty, *Victory Girls, Khaki-
    Wackies, and Patriotes: The Regulation of
    Female Sexuality During the Second World War*
    (New York, 2008), p. 114.
8   Unknown artists, U.S., [194?], A630R A869A–F,
    U.S., Kinsey Institute (formerly Institute for Sex
    Research), Bloomington, Indiana.
9   Westbrook, "'I Want a Girl'," p. 611.
10 See for example Jay A. Gertzman, *Bookleggers and
    Smuthounds: The Trade in Erotica, 1920–1940*
    (Philadelphia, PA, 1999), p. 279; Jill Lepore,
    The Secret History of Wonder Woman (New
    York, 2015), Chapter 29; David K. Johnson, *The
    Lavender Scare: The Cold War Persecution of
    Gays and Lesbians in the Federal Government*
    (Chicago, IL, 2004).
11 Rick Klaw, "The Notorious Irving Klaw,"
    Austin Chronicle, March 10, 2006,
    www.austinchronicle.com.
12 Lepore, *Secret History of Wonder Woman*.
    Lepore documents the personal history of
    William Marston, who created Wonder Woman,
    but she skirts some of the implications for the
    history of sexuality; see pp. 118–19 in particular.
13 Ibid., p. 267.
14 Senate Committee on the Judiciary, *Juvenile
    Delinquency (Obscene and Pornographic
    Magazines), Hearings before the Subcommittee
    to Investigate Juvenile Delinquency*
    (Washington, DC, 1955).
15 Ibid., p. 61.
16 "Blondie" and "Dick Tracy," items 2010.4.308
    and 2010.4.368, North America: United States,
    20th century, Prison Art, Maryland-Baltimore,
    Kinsey Institute.
17 Unknown artists [U.S.], 20th century, Box
    28, United States, 630R A 789 A–G, Kinsey
    Institute.

18 Senate Committee on the Judiciary, *Juvenile Delinquency*, p. 78.

19 Frank Maresca and Roger Ricco, *American Vernacular: New Discoveries in Folk, Self-taught, and Outsider Art* (Boston, MA, 2002), pp. 160–61.

20 Anonymous, "Jerkie Boy," Kinsey Institute, n.d. A photograph of this figure is reproduced in Blaise Cronin, Garry Milius, and Betsy Stirratt, *Private Eyes: Amateur Art from the Kinsey Institute Collection*, exh. cat., Kinsey Institute (Bloomington, IN, 2010), p. 22.

21 Nature boy, Realia, [196?], ISR 1366, Kinsey Institute.

22 There is a large literature on the transformation of Santa Claus throughout history. See for example Karak Ann Marling, *Merry Christmas! Celebrating America's Greatest Holiday* (Cambridge, MA, 2000); Gerry Bowler, *Santa Claus: A Biography* (Toronto, 2007).

23 Masturbating Santa Claus, Realia, [195?], ISR 595, Kinsey Institute.

24 Penis warmer, Realia [194?], ISR 239, Kinsey Institute.

25 Shorts, Realia, [195?], ISR 471, Kinsey Institute.

26 Pot holders, Realia, 1955, ISR 373, Kinsey Institute.

27 Phallic cookie, Realia, 1952, ISR 342, Kinsey Institute.

28 Whitney Strub, *Perversion for Profit: The Politics of Pornography and the Rise of the New Right* (New York, 2011), p. 12.

29 Ibid., pp. 11–12.

30 Brian Hoffman, *Naked: A Cultural History of American Nudism* (New York, 2015), Chapter Five.

31 John D'Emilio and Estelle B. Freedman, *Intimate Matters: A History of Sexuality in America* (Chicago, IL, 1988), p. 284.

32 James M. Jones, *Alfred C. Kinsey: A Public/Private Life* (New York, 1997), p. 602; D'Emilio and Freeman, following the rhetorical construction of Kinsey's persona, characterize him as "an unlikely candidate to instigate" the assault on reticence. D'Emilio and Freedman, *Intimate Matters*, p. 285.

33 Brian Hoffman, *Naked: A Cultural History of American Nudism* (New York, 2015), p. 132.

34 See D'Emilio and Freedman, *Intimate Matters*, pp. 275–6.

35 Bérubé, *Coming Out Under Fire*.

36 Thomas Waugh, *Out/Lines: Underground Gay Graphics from Before Stonewall* (Vancouver, 2002), p. 11; Bérubé, *Coming Out Under Fire*.

37 See Richard Ekins and Dave King, eds, "Virginia Prince: Transgender Pioneer," in *Virginia Prince: Pioneer of Transgendering* (Binghamton, NY, 2005); Robert S. Hill, "'As a Man I Exist; As a Woman I Live': Heterosexual Transvestism and the Contours of Gender and Sexuality in Postwar America," PhD dissertation, University of Michigan, 2007.

38 Susan Stryker calls Lawrence the "crucial interface between medical researchers and transgender social networks." Susan Stryker, *Transgender History* (Berkeley, CA, 2008), p. 44.

39 Janet Thompson [Louise Lawrence], "Transvestism: An Empirical Study," *International Journal of Sexology*, IV/4 (May 1951), pp. 216–19: p. 216.

40 Louise Lawrence, San Francisco, to Alfred Kinsey, November 23, 1950, Correspondence, Louise Lawrence Collection, Kinsey Institute; Book Title/Authors with Male Transvestite Subject Matter, Louise Lawrence Papers, Series II, Folder 46, Kinsey Institute.

41 William Edward Beck, *Happenings: The Story of Bessie*, ed. Peter Farrer (Liverpool, 2012), p. 9.

42 There is a large and well-developed historiography of the gay rights movement but as Thomas Waugh notes, few scholars engage with the erotic. See John D'Emilio, *Sexual Politics, Sexual Communities: Of a Homosexual Minority in the United States, 1940–1970* (Chicago, IL, 1983); Martin Meeker, "Behind the Mask of Respectability: Reconsidering the Mattachine Society and Male Homophile Practice, 1950s and 1960s," *Journal of the History of Sexuality*, X/1 (2001), pp. 78–116; Simon Hall, "The American Gay Rights Movement

and Patriotic Protest," *Journal of the History of Sexuality*, XIX/3 (2010), pp. 536–62.

43 Alta-Glamour has a wide variety of gay typescripts for sale, including "Bob Meets the Sailors," "Bushleager," and "A Day at the Beach." These are unpublished and undated. They are priced at between $35 and $350.

44 Thomas Waugh, *Hard to Imagine: Gay Male Eroticism in Photography and Film from Their Beginnings to Stonewall* (New York, 1996), p. 6; Waugh, *Out/Lines*, p. 11.

45 "Down on the Farm," in "A Collection of Gay Typescripts and Illustrations," item 76645, n.p., n.d, p. 7, courtesy of Alta-Glamour.com. A snippet of the original can be seen at www.alta-glamour.com, accessed September 4, 2019.

46 "College Daze," in "A Collection of Gay Typescripts and Illustrations," item 76645, n.p., n.d.

47 "A Collection of Gay Typescripts and Illustrations," item 76645, www.alta-glamour.com.

48 See Maria Reidelbach, *Completely Mad: A History of the Comic Book and Magazine* (Boston, MA, 1991), Chapter One; Lepore, *Secret History of Wonder Woman*, p. 178.

49 G. Scts, [crayon drawings], [*c.* 1962], item 630R S4357.1, Art Collection, Kinsey Institute.

50 Etienne, artwork, 2002.25.1-181, Art Collection, Kinsey Institute.

51 Reidelbach, *Completely Mad*, pp. 14, 21, 32.

52 Girls! Girls! [19??], CA630R_A765, Kinsey Institute.

53 Charles Clay Doyle, "Rhyming Sobriquets: 'Tricky Dick' and Richard the 'Trichard,'" *Western Folklore*, XXXII/4 (October 1973), pp. 280–81.

54 "Tricky Dicky's Dick," Realia, Indianapolis, 1971, ISR 1324, Kinsey Institute.

55 Anonymous [Collection of 112 Drawings], 1956–65, 2012.26.1-112, Kinsey Institute.

56 Fantastic art [1962], 630R A008.1, Kinsey Institute.

57 Consago, sketch [1960], 630.c7551, Kinsey Institute.

58 Jim Linderman, email correspondence with the author, March 19, 2019. Contains blogpost "The Eccentric, Eerie, Erotic Outsider Art of D. H."

59 See John M. MacGregor, *The Discovery of the Art of the Insane* (Princeton, NJ, 1989), pp. 292–308.

60 Everett Edwards, totem pole, *c.* 1960s, author's collection.

61 John MacGregor, *Dwight Mackintosh: The Boy Who Time Forgot* (Oakland, CA, 1992), p. 24.

62 See "Steve Ashby", Smithsonian American Art Museum, www.americanart.si.edu/art/artists, accessed September 4, 2019; Phyllis Kind, "Steve Ashby," in *Souls Grown Deep: African American Vernacular Art*, vol. I, ed. Paul Arnett and William S. Arnett (Atlanta, GA, 2000), pp. 224–5.

63 See Lee Kogan, "Mose Tolliver," in *Souls Grown Deep*, vol. I, ed. Arnett and Arnett, pp. 330–55. For those images, see pp. 346–7.

64 Regenia Perry, "Sam Doyle: St. Helena Island's Native Son," *Raw Vision* (1998), pp. 27–35.

65 See Milton Simpson, *Folk Erotica: Celebrating Centuries of Erotic Americana* (New York, 1994), p. 108; Kristin G. Congdon and Kara Kelley Hallmark, *American Folk Art: A Regional Reference*, vol. II (Santa Barbara, CA, 2012), pp. 1, 171–4, 172.

66 Simon J. Bronner, "Secret Erections and Sexual Fabrications: Old Men Crafting Manliness," in *Manly Traditions: The Folk Roots of American Masculinities*, ed. Simon J. Bronner (Bloomington, IN, 2005), p. 276.

67 For example, the American Folk Art Museum opened in 1961 and started the *Clarion: The Folk Art Newsletter* in 1971.

68 William Accorsi, "Saturday Night," "Office Party," and "Centaur and Friend," in *Hardcore Crafts*, ed. Nancy Bruning Levine (New York, 1976). n.p.

69 For a discussion of William Accorsi's erotic works, see Steve Desroches, "Inside Out: The Playful Eroticism of Outsider Artist William Accorsi," *Inside Out: Provincetown Magazine* (September 19, 2018), online at http://pmag.provincetownmagazine.com.

70 "Orange Artist Exhibits," *Evening News, NY*, September 14, 1977, p. 10.

71 Obituary: "Louis Mendez," *New York Times*, August 5, 2012, p. 20.

72 "Louis Mendez," in Levine, ed., *Hardcore Crafts*, n.p.

73 "Textile Artists' Show Opens at a J. Cusano," *The Hour* (Norwalk, CT), December 31, 1985, p. 8.

74 See for example Rhett Delford Brown, "Very Busy Bunnies," in *Hardcore Crafts*, ed. Levine (New York, 1976), n.p., and Allan Tannenbaum, "An Erotic Tapestry by Rhett Delford Brown on the Underground Tonight Show" (UGTS_Rhett_Brown_Tapestry.jpg), www.sohoblues.com, accessed September 8, 2019.

75 Angela C. Fina, quoted in *Hardcore Crafts*, ed. Levine, n.p.

5 Marketing Authenticity, 1970s Onward

1 Grayson Perry, "Provincial Punk," Turner Contemporary, Summer 2015, at www.youtube.com, May 23, 2015.

2 Adam Cohen, "Guest Commentary: He Doesn't Need Acclaim, Just Paint and Plywood," *New York Times*, March 28, 2003, www.nytimes.com.

3 Michael Ettema makes this point in reference to the larger problem of material culture and museum display. Michael J. Ettema, "History, Nostalgia, and American Furniture," *Winterthur Portfolio*, XVII/2–3 (Summer–Fall 1982), pp. 135–44: p. 136. For a discussion of how materials move from "old stuff" into "antiques," see Peter Bleed, "Purveying the Past: Structure and Strategy in the American Antiques Trade," *Plains Anthropologist*, XLV/172 (May 2000), pp. 179–88. For a philosophy of antiques, see Leon Rosenstein, "The Aesthetic of the Antique," *Journal of Aesthetics and Art Criticism*, XLV/4 (Summer 1987), pp. 393–402. Rosenstein posits that 1830 might be a cutoff for antiques because it stands as the beginning of the age of mechanization, a point that echoes the sentiments of Charles Messer Snow, "Antiques: A Concrete Form of History," *New York History*, XXVIII/2 (April 1947), pp. 200–207: p. 201.

4 Linda Nochlin, *Women, Art, and Power and Other Essays* (New York, 1988), p. 17.

5 David Brody, "The Building of a Label: The New American Folk Art Museum," *American Quarterly*, LV/2 (June 2003), pp. 257–76: p. 260.

6 This point was raised by Mark Rotenberg, who discussed how objects come to him anonymously on eBay. Mark Rotenberg, interview with the author, Milford, NJ, July 13, 2015.

7 Cynde Moya, email correspondence with the author, July 10, 2012.

8 Steve Bornfield, "Sexpot of Gold," *Las Vegas Review*, 21 July, 2011, p. E1.

9 Dennis, "Obscenity Regulation, New York City, and the Creation of American Erotica, 1820–1880," PhD dissertation, Princeton University, New Jersey (2005), p. 175.

10 Julia M. Klein, "Art That Defies Categories," *Chronicle of Higher Education*, XLVIII/37 (May 24, 2002), p. B14.

11 Joan M. Benedetti, "Words, Words, Words: Folk Art Terminology—Why It (Still) Matters," *Art Documentation: Journal of the Art Libraries Society of North America*, XIX/1 (Spring 2000), pp. 14–21.

12 John Michael Vlach, "American Folk Art: Questions and Quandaries," *Winterthur Portfolio*, XV/4 (Winter 1980), pp. 345–55: p. 346.

13 Brody, "The Building of a Label," pp. 257–8.

14 Robert Darnton, "Peasants Tell Tales: The Meaning of Mother Goose," in Robert Darnton, *The Great Cat Massacre and Other Episodes of French Cultural History* (New York, 1984), p. 16.

15 See for example Marianne Brocker, "Folk Dance Revival in Germany," *World of Music*, XXXVIII/3 (1996), pp. 21–36, for a discussion of folk dancing; see also Zuzana Stefanikova, "Slovak National Costume and Its Role in

the Ethno-identification Process," *Civilizations*, 2 (1993), pp. 229–34.

16 The relationship between fascism, modernism, and the folk has benefited from careful scholarship. See for example Mark Antliff, "Fascism, Modernism, and Modernity," *Art Bulletin*, LXXXVIV/1 (March 2002), pp. 148–69; Stephanie Barron, ed., *"Degenerate Art": The Fate of the Avant-garde in Nazi Germany* (New York, 1991).

17 Peter Adam, *Art of the Third Reich* (New York, 1992), Chapter Eight.

18 Lyle Rexer, *How to Look at Outsider Art* (New York, 2005), Chapter One.

19 Kenneth L. Ames, "American Decorative Arts/Household Furnishings," *American Quarterly*, XXXV/3 (1983), pp. 280–303.

20 Elizabeth Manley Delacruz, "Outside In: Deliberations on American Contemporary Folk Art," *Journal of Aesthetic Education*, XXXIV/1 (Spring 2000), pp. 77–86: p. 78. See also Jack T. Ericson, "Introduction," in *Folk Art in America*, ed. Jack T. Ericson (New York, 1979), pp. 7–8.

21 Delacruz, "Outside In," p. 80.

22 Diana Loercher, "Whitney Museum Assembles Exhibition of American Folk Art," *Independent Journal*, February 15, 1974, p. 25.

23 John L. Baur, part of "What Is American Folk Art: A Symposium," in *Folk Art in America*, ed. Ericson, p. 14.

24 Delacruz, "Outside In," p. 82.

25 Paul Arnett and William S. Arnett, eds, *Souls Grown Deep: African American Vernacular Art*, (Atlanta, GA, 2000).

26 Carl Hammer, interview with the author, Carl Hammer Gallery, Chicago, IL, March 25, 2014.

27 Lyle Rexer, *How to Look at Outsider Art* (New York, 2005), p. 29.

28 Vivien Raynor, "Art: Naiveté for Its Own Sake," *New York Times*, 28 August, 1988, p. A24.

29 Elaine Louie, "Where Art's Outsiders Are Totally In," *New York Times*, February 1, 1996, p. C6.

30 Ibid.

31 Holland Cotter, "When Outsiders Make it Inside," *New York Times*, April 10, 1998, p. E35.

32 Sylvia Rubin, "Artist Doesn't Know He's Famous," *San Francisco Chronicle*, April 13, 1992, p. D3.

33 Mary Daniels, "A Who's Who List on Outsider Artists of Stature," *Chicago Tribune*, October 10, 1993, p. 9.

34 Nathaniel Rich, "A Training Ground for Untrained Artists," *New York Times*, Magazine Section, December 16, 2015, www.nytimes.com.

35 Cohen, "Guest Commentary: He Doesn't Need Acclaim, Just Paint and Plywood."

36 Leah Eskin, "Henry Darger Moves Out," *Chicago Tribune*, December 17, 2000, www.chicagotribune.com.

37 The valuation of folk and outsider art nonetheless appears blunted when compared with other sorts of collections. Despite the growing popularity of folk and outsider art and the surge in value of work by folk and outsider artists, those realms lagged behind other more prestigious sorts of art. The American Folk Art Museum, which had opened a new building in 2001, had by 2011 defaulted on its bond and moved into a smaller space. The architect who designed the new building said in a 2011 *New York Times* article that "The big money collectors do not sit on that board . . . Being on that board doesn't inch you up two more rings on the social ladder." Robin Pogrebin, "Options Dim for Museum of Folk Art," *New York Times*, August 25, 2011, p. C1. The building was sold to the Museum of Modern Art, which planned to demolish it in favor of a soaring 76-story tower, and the collection was moved to a smaller space near Lincoln Center. Whereas MOMA received pledges of $40 million from a single donor, the Folk Art Museum celebrated when its gala raised a mere $1 million. Randy Kennedy, "Museum of Modern Art Gets $40 Million Gift," *New York Times*, December 23, 2015, p. C6; Rebecca Bratburd, "Heard and Scene: Different Strokes at the Folk Art Gala," *Wall Street Journal*, October 27, 2014, p. A27.

38 Eskin, "Henry Darger Moves Out."

39 Robin Pogrebin, "'Boxer' Is Sold for $785,000," *New York Times*, January 25, 2016, p. C3.

40 Carl Hammer, interview with the author, March 25, 2014.
41 Ibid.
42 Charles Edgley and Kenneth Kiser, "Polaroid Sex: Deviant Possibilities in a Technological Age," *Journal of American Culture*, v/1 (March 1, 1982), pp. 59–64: p. 59.
43 *Health and Efficiency*, for example, the long-running naturist magazine that served both the UK and U.S. markets, advertised in its small advertisement section: "Developing, Printing, and Enlarging: with prompt confidential services, through a number of small firms." *Health and Efficiency* (February 1936), p. 72; see Jonathan Coopersmith, "Pornography, Technology, Progress," *Icon: The Journal of the International Committee for the History of Technology*, IV (1998), pp. 94–125: p. 106.
44 Emanuel Cooper, *Fully Exposed: The Male Nude in Photography* (London and New York, 1990), p. 130.
45 Thomas Waugh, *Hard to Imagine: Gay Male Eroticism and Film from their Beginnings to Stonewall* (New York, 1996), p. 348; See also Justin Spring, *Secret Historian: The Life and Times of Samuel Steward, Professor, Tattoo Artist, and Sexual Renegade* (New York, 2010).
46 Waugh, *Hard to Imagine*, p. 348.
47 For considerations of the history of Polaroids, see Peter Buse, "Polaroid into Digital: Technology, Cultural Form, and the Social Practices of Snapshot Photography," *Continuum: Journal of Media and Cultural Studies*, XXIV/2 (April 2010), pp. 215–30; Peter Buse, "Photography Degree Zero: Cultural History of the Polaroid Image," *New Formations*, LXII (November 1, 2007), pp. 29–44.
48 Coopersmith, "Pornography, Technology, Progress," p. 107.
49 Cooper, *Fully Exposed*, p. 132; Edgley and Kiser, "Polaroid Sex," p. 59.
50 Edgley and Kiser, "Polaroid Sex," pp. 61, 62.
51 Jim Ross, "Personal Photos Face Obscenity Test," *St. Petersburg Times*, May 9, 1993.
52 Edgley and Kiser, "Polaroid Sex," pp. 61, 62.
53 Thomas Waugh notes films made by Otis Wade, a skilled filmmaker with a friend at a processing lab. These films document gay male sex from the mid-1930s until the mid-1950s. Waugh, *Hard to Imagine*, pp. 353–9.
54 Chuck Kleinhans, "The Change from Film to Video Pornography: Implications for Analysis," in *Pornography: Film and Culture*, ed. Peter Lehman (New Brunswick, NJ, 2006), pp. 154–67: p. 156.
55 Peter Alilunas, "Smutty Little Movies: The Creation and Regulation of Adult Video, 1976–1986," PhD dissertation, University of Michigan (2013); Michael Z. Newman, *Video Revolutions: On the History of a Medium* (New York, 2014), p. 29.
56 Kleinhans, "The Change from Film to Video Pornography," p. 157.
57 Newman, *Video Revolutions*, p. 38.
58 As Jonathan Coopersmith notes in his analysis of DIY pornography, "Polaroid still photography and camcorders eliminated the distinction between producers and consumers as well as the need for distribution channels. In a sense, these technologies can be seen as liberating and empowering, allowing individuals to create, not just passively consume, their own pornography." Coopersmith, "Pornography, Technology, Progress," p. 106.
59 For instance, in discussing the video revolution, Lawrence O'Toole moves from teenagers taking photos of themselves kissing in photobooths to them using a camcorder to document their sex lives to selling the tapes as amateur pornography within a single sentence, despite very limited substantiation. Laurence O'Toole, *Pornocopia: Porn, Sex, Technology and Desire* (London, 1998), p. 180.
60 Coopersmith, "Pornography, Technology, Progress," p. 107.
61 Niels van Doorn, "Keeping it Real: User-Generated Pornography, Gender Reification, and Visual Pleasure," *Convergence: The International Journal of Research into New Media Technologies*, XVI/4 (2010), pp. 411–30: p. 414.

62 Coopersmith, "Pornography, Technology, Progress," p. 107.

63 O'Toole, *Pornocopia*, p. 181.

64 Guy Williams, "Dirty Business: Despite a Tough New Law, Pornography Proves the Price of Vice Still Pays Huge Profits," *Business, North Carolina*, VII/4 (April 1987), Section 1.

65 Jim Schachter, "Woman Worked in San Clemente, Laguna Niguel Offices DMV Official Arrested in Obscene Film Case," *Los Angeles Times*, May 10, 1987, p. 7.

66 Minette Hillyer, "Sex in the Suburban: Porn, Home Movies and the Live Action Performance of Love in 'Pam and Tommy Lee: Hardcore and Uncensored,'" in *Porn Studies*, ed. Linda Williams (Durham, NC, 2004), pp. 50–76.

67 Ibid., p. 50.

68 Van Doorn, "Keeping it Real," p. 411.

69 Kleinhans, "The Change from Film to Video Pornography," p. 159.

70 For a fascinating ethnography of professional cameramen for the franchise, see Vicki Mayer, "'Guys Gone Wild'? Soft-core Video Professionalism and New Realities in Television Production," *Cinema Journal*, XLVII/2 (Winter 2008), pp. 97–116.

71 Ivan Stormgart, interview with author, March 24, 2016, Seattle, WA.

Bibliography

Primary Sources

ARCHIVAL AND MUSEUM COLLECTIONS

Intuit: The Center for Intuitive and Outsider Art,
    Chicago, Illinois
    General Collection
    Henry Darger Collection
Kinsey Institute, Bloomington, Indiana
    Altered Photographs
    Art Collection
    Artist's Books Collection
    BEM Erotic Manuscript Collection
    Correspondence (Alfred Kinsey Era; Paul
    Gebhard Era)
    Library
    Louise Lawrence Collection
    Novelties
    Prison Art Collections
    Prison Collections
    Realia
    Sexual Offenders Collection
    Vertical Files
Museum of Sex, New York
    General Collection
Mystic Seaport Museum and Library, Mystic,
    Connecticut
    General Collection

MANUSCRIPT AND PRINT SOURCES

Anonymous, *The Pearl* [1879]
    (New York, 1968)
Anonymous, "A Pretty Girl's Companion
    and Guide to Loves [*sic*] Sweetest
    Delights" (n.p, n.d [1900–1910?])

Beck, William Edward, *Happenings: The Story
    of Bessie*, ed. Peter Farrer (Liverpool, 2012)
Bureau of Criminal Statistics, Department of Justice,
    "California Prisoners 1956 and 1957: Summary
    Statistics of Prisoners and Parolees" (Sacramento,
    CA, 1958)
Bureau of Criminal Statistics, Prepared for the
    Department of Corrections, "California
    Prisoners 1954: Summary Statistics of Prisoners
    and Parolees" (Sacramento, CA, 1955)
"A Collection of Gay Typescripts and Illustrations,"
    item 76645 (n.p., n.d.), courtesy of Alta-
    Glamour.com
—, "The Story of the Vivian Girls, in What is
    Known as the Realms of the Unreal, of the
    Glandeco-Angelinian War Storm, Caused by the
    Child Slave Rebellion," typed copy, transferred to
    computer file. Owned by author.
"Dr. Kahn's Museum of Anatomy, Science and Art:
    294 Broadway, above Houston Street, New York
    City: Gotham's greatest attraction, open day and
    evening from 9 A.M. . . . only to men" (New York:
    n.d. [1880])
Fishman, Joseph F., *Sex in Prison: Revealing Sex
    Conditions in American Prisons* (New York, 1934)
Gagnon, John H., "Some Aspects of Sexual Behavior
    in Adult Male Prisons," unpublished paper
    (1964)
Gebhard, Paul, John Gagnon, Wardell Pomeroy, and
    Cornelia Christenson, *Sex Offenders: An Analysis
    of Types* (New York, 1965)
Jacobs, James B., and Eric H. Stelle, "Sexual
    Deprivation and Penal Policy," *Cornell Law
    Review*, LXII/2 (January 1977), pp. 289–312

Johnson, Charles S., *The Negro in Chicago: A Study of Race Relations and a Race Riot in 1919* [1922] (New York, 1968)

Karpman, Benjamin, "Sex Life in Prison," *Journal of Criminal Law and Criminology*, XXXVIII/5 (1948), pp. 475–86

Krafft-Ebing, Richard von, *Psychopathia Sexualis: A Medico-Forensic Study* (New York, 1964)

New York Department of Mental Hygiene, "Report on Study of 102 Sex Offenders at Sing Sing Prison" (Albany, NY, 1950)

Pomeroy, Wardell, *Dr. Kinsey and the Institute for Sex Research* (New Haven, CT, 1972)

"Prison Mail Censorship and the First Amendment," *Yale Law Journal*, LXXXI/1 (November 1971), pp. 87–111

Reynolds, James Bronson, "International Agreements in Relation to the Suppression of Vice," *Social Hygiene*, II/1 (January 1916)

Senate Committee on the Judiciary, *Juvenile Delinquency Obscene and Pornographic Magazines: Hearings before the Subcommittee to Investigate Juvenile Delinquency* (Washington, DC, 1955)

Thompson, Janet [Louise Lawrence], "Transvestism: An Empirical Study," *International Journal of Sexology*, IV/3 (May 1951), pp. 216–19

"USA vs 31 Photographs," case file compiled by Greenbaum, Wolff & Ernst, June 16, 1959, United States District Court, Southern District of New York, United States of America

MULTIMEDIA PROJECTS

"Dr. Kahn's Anatomical Museum," Lower East Side History Project, April 16, 2011, http://leshp.org, accessed April 9, 2016

Coleen Fitzgibbon, "Henry Darger's room, 1973," uploaded on September 9, 2013, https://archive.org, accessed April 9, 2016

Galleries, Alta-Glamour, www.alta-glamour.com

NEWSPAPERS AND MAGAZINES

American Libraries Magazine
Austin Chronicle
Business-North Carolina
Chicago Magazine
Chicago Tribune
Child Life: The Children's Own Magazine
Chronicle of Higher Education
Evening News
Forbes
Frolic: The Magazine of Entertainment
Health and Efficiency
The Hour
Independent Journal
Inside Out: Provincetown Magazine
Las Vegas Review
Los Angeles Times
National Post
New York Times
Physique Pictorial
St. Petersburg Times
San Francisco Chronicle
Slate
Smithsonian Magazine
Variety
Wall Street Journal
Washington City Paper

Secondary Sources

Adam, Peter, *Art of the Third Reich* (New York, 1992)

Alilunas, Peter, "Smutty Little Movies: The Creation and Regulation of Adult Video, 1976–1986," PhD dissertation, University of Michigan (2013)

Allen, Judith A., et al., *The Kinsey Institute: The First Seventy Years* (Bloomington, IN, 2017)

Ames, Kenneth L., "American Decorative Arts/Household Furnishings," *American Quarterly*, XXXV/3 (1983), pp. 280–303

Antliff, Mark, "Fascism, Modernism, and Modernity," *Art Bulletin*, LXXXIV/1 (March 2002), pp. 148–69

Arnberg, Klara, "Under the Counter, Under the Radar? The Business and Regulation of the Pornographic Press in Sweden, 1950–1971," *Enterprise and Society*, XIII/2 (June 2012), pp. 350–77

Arnett, Paul, and William S. Arnett, eds., *Souls Grown Deep: African American Vernacular Art*, (Atlanta, GA, 2000)

Barron, Stephanie, ed., *"Degenerate Art": The Fate of the Avant-garde in Nazi Germany* (New York, 1991)

Bates, A. W., "Dr. Kahn's Museum: Obscene Anatomy in Victorian London," *Journal of the Royal Society of Medicine*, XCIX (December 2006), pp. 618–24

—, "'Indecent and Demoralising Representations': Public Anatomy Museums in mid-Victorian England," *Medical History*, LII/1 (2008), pp. 1–22

Battan, Jesse F., "The Word Made Flesh: Language, Authority, and Sexual Desire in Nineteenth Century America," *Journal of the History of Sexuality*, III (1992), pp. 223–44

Baudrillard, Jean, *Simulacra and Simulation*, trans. Sheila Faria Glaser (Ann Arbor, MI, 1994)

Baur, John L., et al., "What is American Folk Art: A Symposium," in *Folk Art in America*, ed. Jack T. Ericson (New York, 1979), pp. 14–21

Beisel, Nicola, *Imperiled Innocents: Anthony Comstock and Family Reproduction in Victorian America* (Princeton, NJ, 1997)

Benedetti, Joan M., "Words, Words, Words: Folk Art Terminology—Why It Still Matters," *Art Documentation: Journal of the Art Libraries Society of North America*, XIX/1 (Spring 2000), pp. 14–21

Bérubé, Allan, *Coming Out Under Fire: The History of Gay Men and Women in World War II* (New York, 1990)

Biesenbach, Klaus, *Henry Darger* (Munich, 2009)

—, *Henry Darger: Disasters of War* (Munich, 2009)

Bleed, Peter, "Purveying the Past: Structure and Strategy in the American Antiques Trade," *Plains Anthropologist*, XLV/172 (May 2000), pp. 179–88

Bonesteel, Michael, *Henry Darger: Art and Selected Writings* (New York, 2000)

Bowler, Gerry, *Santa Claus: A Biography* (Toronto, 2007)

Boyer, Paul S., *Purity in Print: Book Censorship in America* (New York, 1968)

Breazeale, Kenon, "In Spite of Women: 'Esquire' Magazine and the Construction of the Male Consumer," *Signs*, XX/1 (Fall 1994), pp. 1–22

Brocker, Marianne, "Folk Dance Revival in Germany," *World of Music*, XXVIII/3 (1996), pp. 21–36.

Brody, David, "The Building of a Label: The New American Folk Art Museum," *American Quarterly*, LV/2 (June 2003), pp. 257–76

Bronner, Simon J., ed., *Manly Traditions: The Folk Roots of American Masculinities* (Bloomington, IN, 2005)

Burnett, Andrew, *Coins* (Berkeley, CA, 1991)

Buse, Peter, "Photography Degree Zero: Cultural History of the Polaroid Image," *New Formations*, LXII (November 1, 2007), pp. 29–44

—, "Polaroid into Digital: Technology, Cultural Form, and the Social Practices of Snapshot Photography," *Continuum: Journal of Media and Cultural Studies*, XXIV/1 (April 2010), pp. 215–30

Cahill, Spencer E., "The Boundaries of Professionalization: The Case of North American Funeral Direction," *Symbolic Interaction*, XXII/2 (1999), pp. 105–19

Charles, Douglas M., *The FBI's Obscene File: J. Edgar Hoover and the Bureau's Crusade Against Smut* (Lawrence, KS, 2012)

Cohen, Patricia Cline, Timothy Gilfoyle, and Helen Lefkowitz Horowitz, *The Flash Press: Sporting Male Weeklies in 1840s New York* (Chicago, IL, 2008)

Colligan, Colette, "Anti-Abolition Writes Obscenity: The English Vice, Transatlantic Slavery, and England's Obscene Print Culture," in *International Exposure*, ed. Lisa Sigel (New Brunswick, NJ, 2005), pp. 67–99

—, *A Publisher's Paradise: Expatriate Literary Culture in Paris, 1890–1960* (Amherst, NY, 2014)

Congdon, Kristin G., and Kara Kelley Hallmark, *American Folk Art: A Regional Reference* (Santa Barbara, CA, 2012)

Cooper, Emmanuel, *Fully Exposed: The Male Nude in Photography* (London and New York, 1990)

Coopersmith, Jonathan, "Do-it-yourself Pornography: The Democratization of Pornography," in *PrOnnovation? Pornography and Technological Innovation*, ed. Johannes Grenzfurthner, Gunther Friesinger, and Daniel Fabry (Vienna, 2009), pp. 48–55

—, "Pornography, Technology, Progress," *Icon: The Journal of the International Committee for the History of Technology*, IV (1998), pp. 94–125

Couvares, Francis G, "Hollywood, Censorship, and American Culture," *American Quarterly* (December 1992), pp. 509–24

Cronin, Blaise, Garry Milius, and Betsy Stirratt, *Private Eyes: Amateur Art from the Kinsey Institute Collection*, exh. cat., Kinsey Institute (Bloomington, IN, 2010)

Cross, Gary, and Gregory Smits. "Japan, the U.S. and the Globalization of Children's Consumer Culture," *Journal of Social History*, XXXVIII/4 (Summer 2005), pp. 873–90

Cross, Paul James, "The Private Case: A History," in *The Library of the British Museum*, ed. P. R. Harris (London, 1991), pp. 201–40

Darnton, Robert, *The Forbidden Best-sellers of Pre-Revolutionary France* (New York, 1995)

—, *The Literary Underground of the Old Regime* (Cambridge, MA, 1982)

—, "Peasants Tell Tales: The Meaning of Mother Goose," in Robert Darnton, *The Great Cat Massacre and Other Episodes of French Cultural History* (New York, 1984), pp. 9–72

Delacruz, Elizabeth Manley, "Outside In: Deliberations on American Contemporary Folk Art," *Journal of Aesthetic Education*, XXXIV/1 (Spring 2000), pp. 77–86

D'Emilio, John, *Sexual Politics, Sexual Communities: Of a Homosexual Minority in the United States, 1940–1970* (Chicago, IL, 1983)

—, and Estelle B. Freedman, *Intimate Matters: A History of Sexuality in America* (Chicago, IL, 1988)

Dennis, Donna, *Licentious Gotham: Erotic Publishing and its Prosecution in Nineteenth-century New York* (Cambridge, MA, 2009)

—, "Obscenity Regulation, New York City, and the Creation of American Erotica, 1820–1880," PhD dissertation, Princeton University, New Jersey (2005)

Devereux, Cecily, "'The Maiden Tribute' and the Rise of the White Slave in the Nineteenth Century: The Making of an Imperial Construct," *Victorian Review*, XXVI/2 (2000), pp. 1–23

Dietrich, R. V., "Peach Pit Carving," http://stoneplus.cst.cmich.edu, accessed October 2, 2019

Dines, Gail, *Pornland: How Porn Has Hijacked Our Sexuality* (Boston, MA, 2010)

Donovan, Brian, *White Slave Crusades: Race, Gender, and Anti-vice Activism, 1887–1917* (Champaign, IL, 2006)

Doorn, Niels van, "Keeping It Real: User-generated Pornography, Gender Reification, and Visual Pleasure," *Convergence: The International Journal of Research into New Media Technologies*, XVI/4 (2010), pp. 411–30

Doyle, Charles Clay, "Rhyming Sobriquets: 'Tricky Dick' and Richard the 'Trichard,'" *Western Folklore*, XXXII/4 (October 1973), pp. 280–81

Eberstadt, Mary, "Is Pornography the New Tobacco?" *Policy Review*, CLIV (April 1, 2009), www.hoover.org/publications/policy-review

Edgley, Charles, and Kenneth Kiser. "Polaroid Sex: Deviant Possibilities in a Technological Age," *Journal of American Culture*, V/1 (March 1, 1982), pp. 59–64

Ehrenreich, Barbara, *The Hearts of Men: American Dreams and the Flight from Commitment* (Garden City, NJ, 1983)

Ekins, Richard, and Dave King, eds, "Virginia Prince: Transgender Pioneer," in *Virginia Prince: Pioneer of Transgendering* (Binghamton, NY, 2005)

Elledge, Jim, *Henry Darger, Throwaway Boy: The Tragic Life of an Outsider Artist* (New York, 2013)

Emery, Michael, and Edwin Emery, *The Press and America*, 6th edn (Needham Heights, MA, 1996)

Ericson, Jack T., ed., *Folk Art in America* (New York, 1979)

Ettema, Michael J., "History, Nostalgia, and American Furniture," *Winterthur Portfolio*, XVII/2–3 (Summer–Fall 1982), pp. 135–44

Farber, Naomi, "Charles S. Johnson's 'The Negro in Chicago,'" *American Sociologist*, XXVI/3 (Fall 1995), pp. 78–88

Findlay, Heather, "Freud's 'Fetishism' and the Lesbian Dildo Debates," *Feminist Studies*, XVIII/3 (1992), pp. 563–79

Fisher, Will, "Queer Money," ELH: *English Literary History*, LXVI/1 (1999), pp. 1–23

Fraterrigo, Elizabeth, *Playboy and the Making of the Good Life in Modern America* (Oxford, 2009)

Garrett, Jane, "*Bizarre* Exchange: Postwar Fetish Art and Publishing in Japan and the United States," unpublished paper, 2019

Garson, Robert, "Counting Money: The U.S. Dollar and American Nationhood, 1781–1820," *Journal of American Studies*, XXXV/1 (April 2001), pp. 21–46

Gertzman, Jay A., *Bookleggers and Smuthounds: The Trade in Erotica, 1920–1940* (Philadelphia, PA, 1999)

Giesberg, Judith, *Sex and the Civil War: Soldiers, Pornography, and the Making of American Morality* (Chapel Hill, NC, 2017)

Gilfoyle, Timothy, *City of Eros: New York City, Prostitution, and the Commercialization of Sex, 1790–1920* (New York, 1992)

Gussak, David E., and Evelyn Ploumis-Devick, "Creating Wellness in Correctional Populations through the Arts: An Interdisciplinary Model," *Visual Arts Research*, XXX/1 (2004), pp. 35–43

Halavais, Alexander C., "Small Pornographies," *ACM SIGGROUP Bulletin*, special issue on virtual communities, XXV/2 (February 2005), pp. 19–22

Hall, Simon, "The American Gay Rights Movement and Patriotic Protest," *Journal of the History of Sexuality*, XIX/3 (2010), pp. 536–62

Halttunen, Karen, "Humanitarianism and the Pornography of Pain in Anglo-American Culture," *American Historical Review*, C/2 (April 1995), pp. 303–34

Hatch, Kristen, "Discipline and Pleasure: Shirley Temple and the Spectacle of Child Loving," *Camera Obscura*, XXVII/79 (January 2012), pp. 127–55

Hau, Michael, *The Cult of Health and Beauty in Germany: A Social History, 1890–1930* (Chicago, IL, 2003)

Hawley, Elizabeth Haven, "American Publishers of Indecent Books, 1840–1890," PhD dissertation, Georgia Institute of Technology (2005)

Hegerty, Marilyn E., *Victory Girls, Khaki-Wackies, and Patriotutes: The Regulation of Female Sexuality During World War II* (New York, 2008)

Hensly, Christopher, Cindy Struckman-Johnson, and Helen M. Eigenberg, "Introduction: The History of Prison Sex Research," *Prison Journal*, LXXX/4 (December 2000), pp. 360–67

Herring, Scott, "Collyer Curiosa: A Brief History of Hoarding," *Criticism*, LIII/2 (Spring 2011), pp. 159–88

Hill, Robert S., "'As a man I exist; as a woman I live': Heterosexual Transvestism and the Contours of Gender and Sexuality in Postwar America", PhD dissertation, University of Michigan, 2007

Hillel, Margot, "'She Makes Them Tingle All Over': Eroticising the Child in Twentieth-century Australian Picture Books," *History of Education and Children's Literature*, VI/1 (2011), pp. 199–214

Hillyer, Minette, "Sex in the Suburban: Porn, Home Movies and the Live Action Performance of Love in 'Pam and Tommy Lee: Hardcore and Uncensored'," in *Porn Studies*, ed. Linda Williams (Durham, NC, 2004), pp. 50–76

Hoffman, Brian, *Naked: A Cultural History of American Nudism* (New York, 2015)

Horowitz, Helen Lefkowitz, *Rereading Sex: Battles over Sexual Knowledge and Suppression in Nineteenth-century America* (New York, 2003)

Howell, William Hunting, "A More Perfect Copy: David Rittenhouse and Reproduction of Virtue," *William and Mary Quarterly*, 3rd ser., LXIV/4 (2007), pp. 757–90

Hunt, Lynn, ed., *Eroticism and the Body Politic* (Baltimore, MD, 1991)

—, "Hercules and the Radical Image in the French Revolution," *Representations*, 2 (Spring 1983), pp. 95–117

—, ed., *The Invention of Pornography* (New York, 1993)

Irvin, Benjamin H., "Benjamin Franklin's 'Enriching Virtues,'" *Common-Place*, VI/3 (April 2006), www.common-place.org

Johns, Catherine, *Sex or Symbol? Erotic Images of Greece and Rome* (New York, 1982)

Johnson, David K., *The Lavender Scare: The Cold War Persecution of Gays and Lesbians in the Federal Government* (Chicago, IL, 2004)

Johnson, Lee Michael, "Jail Wall Drawings and Jail Art Programs: Invaluable Tools for Corrections," *International Journal of Criminal Justice Sciences*, II/2 (2007), pp. 66–84

Jones, James M., *Alfred C. Kinsey: A Public/Private Life* (New York, 1997)

Karak, Ann Marling, *Merry Christmas! Celebrating America's Greatest Holiday* (Cambridge, MA, 2000)

Karlins, N. F., "The Past, the Ironic Present, or Passion?" *Art Journal*, LVI/4, Performance Art: Some Theory and Selected Practice at the End of This Century (Winter 1997), pp. 93–7

Kearney, Patrick, *The Private Case: An Annotated Bibliography of the Private Case Erotica Collection in the British Museum Library* (London, 1981)

Kellner, Douglas, "Jean Baudrillard," *The Stanford Encyclopedia of Philosophy*, ed. Edward N. Zalta, summer 2015 edition, http://plato.stanford.edu

Kelly, Edward, "A New Image for the Naughty Dildo?" *Journal of Popular Culture*, VII/4 (1974), pp. 804–9

Kendrick, Walter, *The Secret Museum: Pornography in Modern Culture* (Berkeley, CA, 1996)

Kimmel, Michael, *Guyland* (New York, 2008)

Kind, Phyllis, "Steve Ashby," in *Souls Grown Deep: African American Vernacular Art*, vol. I, ed. Paul Arnett and William S. Arnett (Atlanta, GA, 2000), pp. 224–5

Kipnis, Laura, *Bound and Gagged: Pornography and the Politics of Fantasy in America* (New York, 1996)

Kleinhans, Chuck, "The Change from Film to Video Pornography: Implications for Analysis," in *Pornography: Film and Culture*, ed. Peter Lehman (New Brunswick, NJ, 2006), pp. 154–67

Klotman, Phyllis R., "Dick-and-Jane and the Shirley Temple Sensibility in *The Bluest Eye*," *Black American Literature Forum*, XIII/4 (Winter 1979), pp. 123–5

Kogan, Lee, "Mose Tolliver," in *Souls Grown Deep: African American Vernacular Art*, vol. I, ed. Paul Arnett and William S. Arnett (Atlanta, GA, 2000), pp. 330–55

Kornfeld, Phyllis, *Cellblock Visions: Prison Art in America* (Princeton, NJ, 1997)

Kunzel, Regina, *Criminal Intimacy: Prison and the Uneven History of Modern American Sexuality* (Chicago, IL, 2008)

Laqueur, Thomas, *Solitary Sex: A Cultural History of Masturbation* (New York, 2003)

Lepore, Jill, *The Secret History of Wonder Woman* (New York, 2015)

Lepselter, Susan, "Disorder of Things: Hoarding Narratives in Popular Media," *Anthropology Quarterly*, LXXXIV/4 (2011), pp. 919–47

Levine, Nancy Bruning, ed., *Hardcore Crafts* (New York, 1976)

Lindgren, James M., "'Let Us Idealize Old Types of Manhood': The New Bedford Whaling Museum, 1903–1941," *New England Quarterly*, LXXII/2 (1999), pp. 163–206

Lindsey, Shelley Stamp, "'Oil upon the Flames of Vice': The Battle over White Slave Films in New York City," *Film History*, IX/4 (1997), pp. 351–64

Lu, Mary Ting Yi, "Saving Young Girls from Chinatown: White Slavery and Woman Suffrage, 1910–1920," *Journal of the History of Sexuality*, XVIII/3 (September 2009), pp. 393–417

McCalman, Iain, *Radical Underworld: Prophets, Revolutionaries and Pornographers in London, 1795–1840* (Cambridge, 1988)

MacCannell, Dean, "Marilyn Monroe Was Not a Man," *Diacritics*, XVII/2 (1987), pp. 114–27

McDowell, Kathleen, "Toward a History of Children as Readers, 1890–1930," *Book History*, XII (2009), pp. 240–65

MacGregor, John M., *The Discovery of the Art of the Insane* (Princeton, NJ, 1989)

—, *Dwight Mackintosh: The Boy Who Time Forgot* (Oakland, CA, 1992)

—, *Henry Darger: In the Realms of the Unreal* (New York, 2002)

Maizels, John, ed., *Raw Creation: Outsider Art and Beyond* (London, 1996)

Malley, Richard C., "Graven by the Fishermen Themselves: Scrimshaw in Mystic Seaport Museum," *Log of the Mystic Seaport*, XXXV/1 (1983), pp. 16–21

Marcum, Catherine D., and Tammy L. Castle, eds, *Sex in Prison: Myths and Realities* (Boulder, CO, and London, 2014)

Maresca, Frank, and Roger Ricco, *American Vernacular: New Discoveries in Folk, Self-taught, and Outsider Art* (Boston, MA, 2002)

May, Elaine Tyler, *Homeward Bound: American Families in the Cold War Era* (New York, 1988)

Mayer, Vicki, "'Guys Gone Wild'? Soft-core Video Professionalism and New Realities in Television Production," *Cinema Journal*, XLVII/2 (Winter 2008), pp. 97–116

Meeker, Martin, "Behind the Mask of Respectability: Reconsidering the Mattachine Society and Male Homophile Practice, 1950s and 1960s," *Journal of the History of Sexuality*, X/1 (2001), pp. 78–116

Mendes, Peter, *Clandestine Erotic Fiction in English, 1800–1930* (Aldershot, 1993)

Meyer, Richard, *Outlaw Representation: Censorship and Homosexuality in Twentieth-century Art* (Boston, MA, 2002)

Meyerowitz, Joanne, "Women, Cheesecake, and Borderline Materials: Responses to Girlie Pictures in the Mid-twentieth Century," *Journal of Women's History*, VIII/3 (Fall 1996), pp. 9–35

Monter, William, "Gendered Sovereignty: Numismatics and Female Monarchs in Europe, 1300–1800," *Journal of Interdisciplinary History*, XLI/4 (Spring 2011), pp. 533–64

Morris, Adelaide, "Dick, Jane, and American Literature: Fight with Canons," *College English*, XLVII/5 (September 1985), pp. 467–81

Mullen, R. D., "From Standard Magazines to Pulps and Big Slicks: A Note on the History of U.S. General and Fiction Magazines," *Science Fiction Studies*, XXII/1 (March 1995), pp. 144–56

Newman, Michael Z., *Video Revolutions: On the History of a Medium* (New York, 2014)

Nochlin, Linda, *Women, Art, and Power and Other Essays* (New York, 1988)

Oosterhuis, Harry, *Stepchildren of Nature: Krafft-Ebing, Psychiatry, and the Making of Sexual Identity* (Chicago, IL, 2000)

O'Toole, Laurence, *Pornocopia: Porn, Sex, Technology and Desire* (London, 1998)

Paasonen, Susanna, "Labors of Love: Netporn, Web 2.0 and the Meanings of Amateurism," *New Media and Society*, XII/8 (2010), pp. 1297–312

Palfreyman, Harriet, "Visualising Venereal Disease in London," PhD dissertation, University of Warwick (2012)

Park, Edwards, "The Object at Hand," *Smithsonian* (October 1995), www.smithsonianmag.com

Patterson, Zabet, "Going On-line: Consuming Pornography in the Digital Age," in *Porn Studies*, ed. Linda Williams (Durham, NC, 2004), pp. 104–23

Paul, Pamela, *Pornified: How Pornography Is Transforming Our Lives, Our Relationships, and Our Families* (New York, 2005)

Peacey, Jason, "The Print Culture of Parliament, 1600–1800," *Parliamentary History*, XXVI, part 1 (2007), pp. 1–16

Peakman, Julie, *Mighty Lewd Books: The Development of Pornography in Eighteenth-century England* (Basingstoke, 2003)

Pearson, Ralph L., "Charles S. Johnson and the Chicago Commission on Race Relations," *Illinois Historical Journal*, LXXI/3 (Fall 1988), pp. 211–20

Perry, Grayson, "Provincial Punk," Turner Contemporary, summer 2015, uploaded to www.youtube.com, May 23, 2015

Perry, Regenia, "Sam Doyle: St. Helena Island's Native Son," *Raw Vision* (1998), pp. 27–35

Person, Ethel Spector, ed., *On Freud's "A Child is Being Beaten"* (New Haven, CT, 1997)

Piepmeier, Alison, "Why Zines Matter: Materiality and the Creation of Embodied Community," *American Periodicals: A Journal of History, Criticism, and Bibliography*, XVIII/2 (2008), pp. 213–38

Pine, Julia, "In *Bizarre* Fashion: The Double-voiced Discourse of John Willie's Fetish Fantasia," *Journal of the History of Sexuality*, XXII/1 (2013), pp. 1–33

Reidelbach, Maria, *Completely Mad: A History of the Comic Book and Magazine* (Boston, MA, 1991)

Reumann, Miriam G., *American Sexual Character* (Berkeley, CA, 2005)

Rexer, Lyle, *How to Look at Outsider Art* (New York, 2005)

Richard, Emmanuelle, "The Perils of Covering Porn: Rash of Recent Dotcom-angle Stories Perpetuate Myths about the Industry," USC Annenberg *Online Journal Review*, www.ojr.org, April 3, 2002

Roberts, Mary Louise, *What Soldiers Do: Sex and the American GI in World War II France* (Chicago, IL, 2014)

Roediger, David, "Race, Ethnicity and White Identity," *Encyclopedia of Chicago*, 2005, www.encyclopedia.chicagohistory.org

Rosenstein, Leon, "The Aesthetic of the Antique," *Journal of Aesthetics and Art Criticism*, XLV/4 (Summer 1987), pp. 393–402

—, *Antiques: The History of an Idea* (Ithaca, NY, 2009)

Ross, Chad, *Naked Germany: Health, Race and the Nation* (Oxford, 2005)

Rundblad, Georganne, "Exhuming Women's Premarket Duties in the Care of the Dead," *Gender and Society*, IX/2 (1995), pp. 173–92.

Rundquist, Leisa, "Pyre: A Poetics of Fire and Childhood in the Art of Henry Darger," PhD dissertation, University of North Carolina at Chapel Hill (2007)

Sarracino, Carmine, and Kevin M. Scott, *The Porning of America: The Rise of Porn Culture, What It Means and Where We Go from Here* (Boston, MA, 2008)

Saunders, Nicholas J., "Bodies of Metal, Shells of Memory: Trench Art and the Great War Re-cycled," *Journal of Material Culture*, V/1 (March 2000), pp. 43–67

—, "Trench Art," *History Today*, LIII/11 (November 2003), pp. 32–7

Schrift, Melissa, "Angola Prison Art: Captivity, Creativity, and Consumerism," *Journal of*

American Folklore, CXIX/473 (Summer 2006), pp. 257–74

Sigel, Lisa Z., "Flagrant Delights," *Antiques* (July–August 2014), pp. 104–11

—, *Governing Pleasures: Pornography and Social Change in England, 1815–1914* (New Brunswick, NJ, 2002)

—, *Making Modern Love: Sexual Narratives and Identities in Interwar Britain* (Philadelphia, PA, 2012)

Simons, Patricia, *The Sex of Men in Premodern Europe: A Cultural History* (Cambridge, 2011)

Simpson, Milton, *Folk Erotica: Celebrating Centuries of Erotic Americana* (New York, 1994)

Slade, Joseph, "Eroticism and Technological Regression: The Stag Film," *History and Technology*, XXII/1 (March 2006), pp. 27–52

—, *Pornography and Representation: A Reference Guide* (Westport, CT, 2001)

—, "Pornography in the Late Nineties," *Wide Angle*, XIX/3 (July 1997), pp. 1–12

Slauter, Eric, "Reading and Radicalization: Print, Politics, and the American Revolution," *Early American Studies: An Interdisciplinary Journal*, VIII/1 (Winter 2010), pp. 5–40

Smith, Clarissa, *One for the Girls! The Pleasures and Practices of Reading Women's Porn* (Bristol, 2007)

Smith, David C., "Wood Pulp and Newspapers, 1867–1900," *Business History Review*, XXXVIII/3 (Fall 1964), pp. 328–45

Smith, Erin A., "How the Other Half Read: Advertising, Working-class Readers, and Pulp Magazines," *Book History*, III (2000), pp. 204–30

Spies, Kathleen, and Reginald Marsh, "'Girls and Gags': Sexual Display and Humor in Reginald Marsh's Burlesque Images," *American Art*, XVIII/2 (Summer 2004), pp. 32–57

Spring, Justin, *Secret Historian: The Life and Times of Samuel Steward, Professor, Tattoo Artist, and Sexual Renegade* (New York, 2010)

Srebnick, Amy Gilman, *The Mysterious Death of Mary Rogers: Sex and Culture in Nineteenth-century New York* (New York, 1995)

Stefanikova, Zuzana, "Slovak National Costume and Its Role in the Ethno-identification Process," *Civilizations*, 2 (1993), pp. 229–34

Stengers, Jean, and Ann van Neck, *Masturbation: The History of the Great Terror* (New York, 2001)

Stevens, Kenneth R., "United States v. 31 Photographs: Dr. Alfred C. Kinsey and Obscenity Law," *Indiana Magazine of History*, LXXI/4 (December 1975), pp. 299–316

Stow, Charles Messer, "Antiques: A Concrete Form of History," *New York History*, XXVIII/2 (April 1947), pp. 200–207

Strange, Carolyn, and Michael Kempa, "Shades of Dark Tourism: Alcatraz and Robben Island," *Annals of Tourism Research*, XXX/2 (2003), pp. 386–405

Strub, Whitney, "Black and White and Banned All Over: Race, Censorship and Obscenity in Postwar Memphis," *Journal of Social History*, XL/3 (2007), pp. 685–715

—, "The Clearly Obscene and the Queerly Obscene: Heteronormativity and Obscenity in Cold War Los Angeles," *American Quarterly*, LX/2 (June 2008), pp. 373–98

—, *Perversion for Profit: The Politics of Pornography and the Rise of the New Right* (New York, 2011)

—, "Challenging the Anti-Pleasure League: *Physique Pictorial* and the Cultivation of Gay Politics," in *Modern Print Activism in the United States*, ed. Rachel Schreiber (Burlington, VT, 2013), pp. 161–74

Stryker, Susan, *Transgender History* (Berkeley, CA, 2008)

Swanson, Dwight, "Home Viewing: Pornography and Amateur Film Collections, A Case Study," *The Moving Image: The Journal of the Association of Moving Image Archivists*, V/2 (Fall 2005), pp. 136–40

Toepfer, Karl, *Empire of Ecstasy: Nudity and Movement in German Body Culture, 1910–1935* (Berkeley, CA, 1997)

Trent, Mary, "Henry Darger's Reworking of American Visual Culture," *American Art*, XXVI/1 (Spring 2012), pp. 74–101

Vlach, John Michael, "American Folk Art: Questions and Quandaries," *Winterthur Portfolio*, XV/4 (Winter 1980), pp. 345–55

Vose, Margaret Lentz, "Identification of the Origins and Sources of Selected Scrimshaw Motifs in 18th and 19th Century Contemporary Culture," PhD dissertation, New York University (1992)

Waugh, Thomas, *Hard to Imagine: Gay Male Eroticism in Photography and Film from their Beginnings to Stonewall* (New York, 1996)

—, *Out/Lines: Underground Gay Graphics from Before Stonewall* (Vancouver, 2002)

Werrlein, Debra, "Not so Fast, Dick and Jane: Reimagining Childhood and Nation in *The Bluest Eye*," *MELUS*, XXX/4 (Winter 2005), pp. 53–72

West, Janet, "Scrimshaw and the Identification of Sea Mammal Products," *Journal of Museum Ethnography*, 2 (March 1991), pp. 39–79

Westbrook, Robert B., "'I Want a Girl, Just Like the Girl that Married Harry James': American Women and the Problem of Political Obligation in World War II," *American Quarterly*, XLII/4 (December 1990), pp. 587–614

Wilkinson, Doris Yvonne, "Racial Socialization through Children's Toys: A Sociohistorical Examination," *Journal of Black Studies*, V/1 (September 1974), pp. 96–109

Williams, Linda, "Porn Studies: Proliferating Pornographies On/Scene: An Introduction," in *Porn Studies*, ed. Linda Williams (Durham, NC, 2004), pp. 1–23

Wilson, Charles R., "The Southern Funeral Director: Managing Death in the New South," *Georgia Historical Quarterly*, LXVII/1 (1983), pp. 49–69

Winter, Timothy Stewart, "Queer Law and Order: Sex, Criminality, and Policing in the Late Twentieth-century United States," *Journal of American History*, CII (June 2015), pp. 61–72

Yu, Jessica, *In the Realms of the Unreal: The Mystery of Henry Darger* (New York: Wellspring Media, 2004), DVD

Zimmerman, Patricia R., *Reel Families: A Social History of Amateur Film* (Bloomington, IN, 1995)

Acknowledgments

For thirty years, I have been working on the history of pornography and it hasn't gotten any easier. I started at the heyday of anti-pornography feminism and I continue through an anti-pornography feminist revival. If anything unites disparate groups, it's a mutual disgust over pornography. Decades ago, James Joyce argued that he ought to be given the Nobel Prize for Peace for uniting Puritans, English Imperialists, Irish Republicans, and Catholics against *Ulysses*. Today, feminists, Republicans, parents, community activists, religious conservatives, and virtually all of the public unite against pornography.

Because I work on the history of pornography, I have been turned down for residential fellowships, grants, and talks. In one case, after having been turned down for a fellowship, I was asked to talk about the horrors of pornography and what life will be like in a post-pornography world. (Well, for one thing, there goes my field of study.) I have been turned down for jobs. I have been turned down for jobs with the sympathetic, double-grasp hand-pat used only at funerals. People have refused to include images and artifacts in this book. According to them, the works shouldn't be included because the works are beautiful and pornography isn't. I have been asked whether, in fact, war is pornography and I have been told that pornography is rape, misogyny, hatred. My natal family was embarrassed to see a show that I advised at a major museum. My children had to be photographed outside of the building because it was against the law for them to enter.

It's not just me. Few scholars who work on the topic can get jobs. There is no money to work on pornography or erotica. If one condemns pornography, one can get funding. But there are no big grants or prizes for the study of pornography. Foundations, ever since the year of the Mapplethorpe (1990), do not fund general scholarship on pornography or erotica and most institutions will be penalized with cuts in federal funding if they inadvertently discuss erotic objects. We know very little about the history of pornography because no one can afford to do the research.

What is wrong with this world?

Pornography is a culturally shaped product. If we are ashamed of pornography, we should double down to understand why pornography is the way it is. We should find out when it became that way. We should consider who wants it that way. We should understand what they see when they look at it. Instead, we cover our eyes and look away. Even worse, we condemn those who are willing to think long and hard about pornography as a category. It is easier to make specious claims than to justify research. Most people would rather take the easy way out.

After thirty years, I should be used to it. But I am not.

I am tired of anti-pornography activism precluding historical scholarship. I am tired of there being no grants, no fellowships, no scholarships. I am tired of telling junior scholars that they might have an easier time with an alternate topic. I am tired of truisms standing in for knowledge. I am tired of there being endless books defining "pornography," but virtually none historicizing it.

Despite all that my work has cost me both financially and culturally, if I had to start over, I would do it again. I have interesting things to think about and have met good minds along the way. I have found other scholars who are willing to follow their intellect wherever it leads, who try to understand the world in all of its oddity, who are willing to work on topics that don't bring money, glory, or respect. Every day, there is something new to learn.

It is in that spirit that I would like to thank the people and institutions that have given me assistance. Hopefully, you will not find yourself embarrassed to be listed in this book. But if you are embarrassed, you will find yourself in good company (see above) and should find some solace in that.

I would like to thank the anonymous reviewers and Annette F. Timm, the editor of the *Journal of the History of Sexuality*, for their thoughtful feedback on an article based upon Chapter One.

It takes many people's efforts to publish a book and everyone quite rightly feels a sense of ownership. These acknowledgments are but a small nod to a great effort. Vivian Constantinopoulos commissioned this book. Her work to integrate the many images with the text let it be greater than the sum of its parts. Special thanks go to Phoebe Colley, a fantastic editor, whose accuracy is surpassed only by her tact and kindness. Reaktion Books recognized the potential in this project and I appreciate their faith.

This project has been strengthened by early readings by Kathleen Lubey, Valentina Tikoff, Julia Woesthoff, Tom Foster, Robin Mitchell, Colleen Doody, and Sara Kimble, as well as the participants of "A Hands-on Approach: Do-it-yourself Culture and Economy in the Twentieth Century," a workshop at the German Historical Institute, April 2014, particularly Reinhild Kreis and David Farber. A symposium put on by Bowdoin on the centennial anniversary of Kinsey's graduation provided an opportunity to talk with students and scholars including Annette Timm, Donna Drucker, Liana Zhou, Dagmar Herzog, Robert Tobin, Whitney Strub, Michael Pettit, David Hecht, Marilyn

Reizbaum, Jill Smith, and Harrison King McCann about Kinsey and his legacy. Discussions with Jane Garrett, Colette Colligan, and Justin O'Hearn have deepened my understanding of the most recent research on pornography.

I would like to thank members of my department for their support and DePaul University for its commitment to academic freedom. I would like to thank the University Research Council of DePaul University and the Liberal Arts and Social Science Faculty Research Grant for support with this project.

I would like to thank Mystic Seaport and Intuit: The Center for Self-Taught and Outsider Art. I would also like to thank the Kinsey Institute and everyone who works there. The Kinsey has been fighting the good fight for decades, even as its budget has been slashed and its institutional support eroded. I only hope that some great foundation finally funds the Kinsey again so that it can return to glory and scholars can do the kind of work that should have been getting done all along.

I would like to thank the many collectors who have generously talked to me about their art and educated me about the process of collecting itself. Most collectors are savvy and smart about what it all means. Collectors have shared their knowledge and their erudition. I have had long conversations that have taught me about ethics and materials, collecting and collections, galleries and dealers, selling and buying. They shared their collections with me for no reason other than the love of art. In doing so, they have shown a great deal of bravery and faith in human nature. They also took photographs so that I could include images of their objects in my book, for which I thank them. In particular, I would like to thank Robert A. Roth, who has been gracious, thoughtful, and generous to a fault. He has a stunning collection that proves how valuable a good eye for art can be. He has been a guiding force in Chicago for the appreciation of self-taught and outsider art. His support has made our town culturally richer as a result. Carol Cone bravely let me use the image "Very Busy Bunnies," made by her mother. She wants her mother's legacy as an artist to be remembered, as well it should. Her mother's work is charming and funny and erotic. If we think of sex that way, we will all be richer for it.

I would also like to thank Jim Linderman, who spent many hours talking with me about art and antiques. He offered an insider's perspective on both buying and selling and provided a smart and thoughtful analysis of the economics of the art and antiquities world. Kirk Landauer responded to a letter out of the blue about his artifacts and has given his time and energy to this project. Louis Picek also responded to such a missive and very kindly brought my attention to some beautiful artifacts that I would not have known about. His "Adam and Eve" cane is heartbreakingly lovely and I appreciate his willingness to include it in this volume. Justin Engers has exquisite pieces, some of which are featured in this book. He kindly took the time to contact me and respond to queries. Barry M. Cohen has been the soul of generosity. He has been willing to share images and information despite a busy schedule and tight time line. Michael and Elaine Bennett very generously provided examples of their collections and their art.

I would also like to thank the many gallery owners, antiques dealers, used books, and erotica dealers who have helped me. For an early article that informed this book, I interviewed antiques dealers including Carl Hammer, Steve Powers, Patrick Bell, and Arthur Liverant.

Carl Hammer gave me a crash course in art brut, outsider art, self-taught art, and folk art. Steve Powers is the consummate professional who combines depth of knowledge with depth of organization. Mark Rotenberg has been a delight. He not only spent a good bit of time showing me his collection but was also willing to work with me to provide very fine photographs of some of his favorite artifacts. He is endlessly knowledgeable about erotic and pornographic images and has a memory that just won't quit. If he retires as he threatens, the world will be a poorer place because no one will be able to replicate the lifetime he has spent accruing information. Ivan Stormgart works in the areas of ephemera and antique books. He spoke with me about his collection, his work, and his

experience as an antique book dealer. He illustrates what is best in the trade; he is knowledgeable, erudite, thoughtful, and witty. He has been generous in his expertise and his collection.

Michael Embree, a good friend and colleague, helped solve seemingly intractable research problems. He has proven just what a great librarian can do. Michael Riordan has given his time and expertise to photograph my artifacts. His help has been greatly appreciated.

My daughters and spouse have lived with this project for many years with good humor. While my kids kept quiet about my area of scholarship for years, I hope that they see their mom as a radical now that they are reaching adulthood. My spouse, Ljubomir Perkovic, has been my biggest support. He has seen me through draft after draft, reading one version after another as the book took shape. He watched the kids while I went on research trips, kept me company while I talked my way through the book, and worked as my tech aid when dragged into it against his will. I dedicate this book, an oddity, to him.

Photo Acknowledgments

The author and publishers wish to express their thanks to the below sources of illustrative material and/or permission to reproduce it. Every effort has been made to contact copyright holders; should there be any we have been unable to reach or to whom inaccurate acknowledgments have been made please contact the publishers, and full adjustments will be made to any subsequent printings.

Alta-Glamour: 47, 48, 79, 80; collection of American Folk Art Museum, New York—Gift of Kiyoko Lerner: 51; collection of the author: 19, 27, 69, 70, 71, 72, 74, 75, 77, 78, 84 (all photos Michael Riordan); collection of the artist (Elaine Bennett): 97; collection of the artist (Michael Bennett): 95; by permission of Carol Cone: 96; collection of Brian Emrich: 37, 38; collection of Justin Enger: 7, 8, 23; collection of Intuit: The Center for Intuitive and Outsider Art, Chicago, IL: 89; Kinsey Institute, Bloomington, IN: 3, 5, 6, 11, 12, 16, 33, 34, 35, 36, 39, 40, 41, 54, 55, 56, 57, 58, 59, 60, 61, 62, 63, 64, 65, 66, 67, 68, 73, 81, 82, 92; collection of Kirk Landauer: 21; © 2019 Kiyoko Lerner/Artists Rights Society (ARS), New York: 49, 50 (Gift of the artist's estate in honor of Klaus Biesenbach—Museum of Modern Art, New York), 51 (Collection of American Folk Art Museum, New York—Gift of Kiyoko Lerner), 52 (Collection of Robert A. Roth—photo John Faier), 53 (Collection of Robert A. Roth—photo John Faier); collection of Jim Linderman: 20, 22, 42, 43, 44, 45, 46, 83; Mystic Seaport Museum, Mystic, CT: 1, 2, 9, 10; private collection, Pennsylvania: 4, 13 (photos Gavin Ashworth); collection of Louis Picek: 14, 15; courtesy of Steve Powers: 76; collection of Mark Rotenberg: 17, 18, 24, 25, 26, 28, 29, 30, 31, 22, 91, 93, 94; collection of Robert A. Roth: 52, 53, 85, 86, 87, 88, 90 (all photos John Faier).

Index

Illustration numbers are indicated by *italics*